RELIGION AROUND EMILY DICKINSON

Religion Around VOL. 2

PETER IVER KAUFMAN, *General Editor*

Books in the Religion Around series examine the religious forces surrounding cultural icons. By bringing religious background into the foreground, these studies give readers a greater understanding of and appreciation for individual figures, their work, and their lasting influence.

RELIGION AROUND
EMILY DICKINSON

W. CLARK GILPIN

THE PENNSYLVANIA STATE UNIVERSITY PRESS
UNIVERSITY PARK, PENNSYLVANIA

Library of Congress Cataloging-in-
Publication Data
Gilpin, W. Clark, author.
Religion around Emily Dickinson /
W. Clark Gilpin.
        pages   cm—(Religion around)
Summary: "Examines how the religious
environment around Emily Dickinson,
specifically New England Protestantism,
helps in understanding her poetry,
and conversely how her poetry brings
attention to religious aspects of her
culture and surroundings"—Provided by
publisher.
ISBN 978-0-271-06476-5 (cloth : alk.
paper)
1. Dickinson, Emily, 1830–1886—
Criticism and interpretation.
2. Dickinson, Emily,
1830–1886—Religion.
3. Religious poetry, American—History
and criticism.
4. Religion and poetry—United States—
History—19th century.
5. Protestantism—New England—
History—19th century.
6. Protestantism and literature.
I. Title.
II. Series: Religion around.
PS1541.Z5G55 2014
811'.4—dc23
2014020325

The Pennsylvania State University
Press is a member of the Association of
American University Presses.

It is the policy of The Pennsylvania
State University Press to use acid-free
paper. Publications on uncoated stock
satisfy the minimum requirements
of American National Standard for
Information Sciences—Permanence
of Paper for Printed Library Material,
ANSI Z39.48–1992.

This book is printed on paper that
contains 30% post-consumer waste.

for NANCY

CONTENTS

ACKNOWLEDGMENTS

Peter Kaufman, my friend and colleague since graduate school at the University of Chicago, invited me to contribute to this series of books exploring *religion around* major cultural figures of the modern era. Emily Dickinson has appeared, episodically, in my writing and teaching for twenty years, and I am grateful for the opportunity to spend some time thinking more systematically about Dickinson and the light her poetry casts on religion, especially Protestant Christianity, in nineteenth-century America. Careful commentary on the manuscript by Peter Kaufman, Richard Rosengarten, Catherine Brekus, and two readers for Penn State University Press benefitted both my overall interpretation of Christianity in nineteenth-century America and my specific readings of Dickinson.

With respect to teaching about Dickinson and the relation between religion and literature in the nineteenth century, I am especially grateful for ideas that percolated during team-taught seminars at the University of Chicago with Janice Knight, Martin Marty, and David Tracy.

My thinking about the introductory chapter benefitted from participation in a conference in October 2012 at the Center for Advanced Study, University of Illinois, Urbana-Champaign, entitled "American Literatures/American Religions." I thank the planners of that conference, Jonathan Ebel and Justine Murison, for an intellectually stimulating event.

Portions of chapters 2, 4, and 5 recast ideas presented in three articles published in the *Journal of Religion* and *Spiritus: A Journal of Christian Spirituality*: "'Inward, Sweet Delight in God': Solitude in the Career of Jonathan Edwards," *Journal of Religion* 82 (2002): 523–38; "Writing Transcendence: When Words Exceed Themselves in Nineteenth-Century America," *Journal of Religion* 92 (2012): 469–81, © 2002 and

RESHAPING A RELIGIOUS
REPERTOIRE

The title of this book, *Religion Around Emily Dickinson*, raises a preliminary question. What do I mean when I refer to religion that is *around* any individual person? In this case, the person—Emily Dickinson (1830–1886)—was a reclusive, unmarried woman who lived out life in her family home in Amherst, Massachusetts. By the time she was thirty, Dickinson had fully committed herself to poetry and was producing what would become an extraordinary corpus of nearly eighteen hundred poems. However, fewer than a dozen appeared in print during her lifetime, and these publications occurred primarily through the insistence and mediation of friends. Instead, the letter became Dickinson's preferred medium for circulating her work; across three decades she enclosed several hundred poems in letters to more than forty friends and family members. After Dickinson's death, her younger sister, Lavinia, discovered a mass of poems in manuscript, many carefully copied and stitched together into handmade booklets. Despite family feuds and editorial worries about Dickinson's unconventional meters and rhymes, an initial group of these poems was published in 1890. The volume received notable acclaim, prompting two additional series of poems, in 1891 and 1896, and an edition of letters in 1894.[1] Especially since the 1950s, recognition of Dickinson's stature as a poet has steadily increased, and—along with Walt Whitman—she is now generally regarded as one of the two greatest American poets of the nineteenth century, read and pondered not only by American literary historians but also by a devoted public following.

Throughout Emily Dickinson's posthumous rise to fame, her biography has presented readers with a seeming paradox. Both her poems and her letters were suffused with explicitly religious themes and concepts: the soul, heaven, redemptive suffering. Yet, despite the omnipresence of Christian symbolism in her writing, Dickinson resisted joining Amherst's First Congregational Church and as an adult rarely attended its services, preferring from time to time to sit on her lawn on a Sunday morning and "listen to the anthems."[2] Dickinson's "overhearing" of religion strongly marked her writing, and her ambivalent obsession propels the following narrative. From one perspective, how does the religion around Emily Dickinson help us to understand and appreciate her poetry? From another perspective, how does Dickinson's poetry illuminate religious dimensions of the surrounding culture that might otherwise escape our attention? In order to address these intertwined questions, *Religion Around Emily Dickinson* explores three different connotations of the phrase *religion around*.

First, perhaps most straightforwardly, the religion around Emily Dickinson consisted of the religious practices, literature, architecture, and ideas that were inescapable features of everyday life in Amherst and the Dickinson family routine: attending worship services at the Congregational church, listening to sermons delivered from its pulpit, singing hymns, reading regularly from the Christian Bible in the Authorized (King James) Version of 1611, and attending family prayers led by her father, Edward Dickinson. These practices incorporated the Dickinson family into patterns of religious tradition and religious change that were shaping regional, national, and transatlantic Protestant culture. Emily Dickinson's familiarity with Protestant hymnody, for instance, linked her to a wider nineteenth-century context of both devotion and writing. When she quoted hymns in her letters, Dickinson could assume that her correspondent understood the reference, and, when writing her older brother, Austin, she could recast the lyrics into a family joke, fully confident that Austin would recognize the source of her phrasing. Asahel Nettleton, a Connecticut minister and family friend who had been instrumental in the conversion of Dickinson's aunt, Lavinia Norcross, compiled one of the favorite antebellum hymnals, *Village Hymns* (1824), one of many printed in the nineteenth century to transmit the piety of transatlantic evangelical missions and of individual Protestant denominations.[3]

Women writers seized on this expanding market for religious music, and composing hymns became one avenue for their entrance into print. Susan Warner, an American novelist best known for *The Wide, Wide World* (1851), collaborated with her sister, Anna Warner Bartlett, to publish *Hymns of the Church Militant* in 1858. Another pair of songwriting sisters, Phoebe and Alice Cary, composed evangelical hymns of consolation in the love of Jesus, "No Trouble Too Great But I Bring It to Jesus," or "To Suffer for Jesus Is My Greatest Joy." And devotion to Jesus took a decidedly militant turn in Julia Ward Howe's "Battle Hymn of the Republic," first published in the *Atlantic Monthly* in February 1862.[4] Dickinson, too, turned to Protestant hymnody in her writing, not because she wrote hymns but because the metrical structure of hymns became a paradigm for her verse. Helen Vendler, among our most incisive contemporary interpreters of Dickinson's poems, comments that the poetry was, "in the past, sometimes considered amateurish because it is for the most part constructed within a single frame, the 'childish' four-line stanza of hymn-meter: 4 beats, 3 beats, 4 beats, 3 beats, with a single rhyme-sound linking lines 2 and 4." Barton Levi St. Armand, author of *Emily Dickinson and Her Culture*, has likened the metrical form of her poems to self-conscious innovation based on folk art, since the consistency of the form "allowed Dickinson to condense and abstract complex motifs as she fitted them to the purposely limited requirements of her art, as rigid as the geometric patterns dictated for patchwork quilts." *Poem* and *song* were interchangeable terms in the middle decades of the nineteenth century, and Dickinson has been described as "a poet of sounds" because the rhythms of hymns and ballads were "in her ears" as she wrote.[5]

Like hymns and hymn writers, sermons and preachers were also around Emily Dickinson. As a young adult, Dickinson was an attentive student of sermons, and her letters regularly commented on preachers she heard at Amherst or at South Hadley during her year as a student at Mary Lyon's Mount Holyoke Female Seminary. Sermons, not only on Sunday mornings but also on public occasions such as thanksgiving days and election days, influenced regional identity and standards of oratory throughout New England. The sermons of notable preachers increasingly circulated in print as individual pamphlets, in sermon collections, and in magazines devoted to the profession such as the *National Preacher*, which had begun publication in New York in 1826. In the course of the century, in both the United States and England, ministers expanded their writing into other genres: poetry, literary reviews, occasional essays, and novels. So much was this the case that William R. McKelvy has argued for the importance of a Victorian social persona, "the clerical author," who engaged in both literary and religious pursuits "at a time when the practical, institutional, and professional links between the religious and the literary were manifold."[6] When Emily Dickinson listened to an individual sermon in Amherst, it thus reflected a much wider context of religious, literary, and oratorical sensibilities. Furthermore, after Dickinson had developed her own poetic talents, she sought out ministers—most notably the social crusader, Civil War officer, and expansive essayist Thomas Wentworth Higginson—who might become her "preceptors" as she honed her craft. These relationships have attracted great attention from Dickinson's biographers, and I shall return to them in a later chapter.

Emily Dickinson's father, Edward Dickinson, was a lawyer who was active in Whig politics and elected to Congress in 1852. The family exemplified what the historian Daniel Walker Howe has termed "Whig culture." That is, the men of the family were engaged in business and the professions, favored government-aided economic development, and, in New England, frequently came from families active in Congregationalist, Unitarian, and Presbyterian congregations. The Second Great Awakening—an umbrella term for antebellum evangelical revivals, benevolent societies, and home missions—deeply imprinted Whig social theory, which stressed the organic unity of society and the signal importance of Protestant religious guidance in addressing the era's dramatic social changes and conflicts. Howe proposes that the missionary spirit of the Awakening instilled an "aggressive didacticism" in the Whig cultural program of education and moral self-discipline. The Whigs, Howe remarks, wanted to teach people that "liberty has no real value without responsibility and order."[7] Whig culture, including its religious aspect, emphatically marked Emily Dickinson's views, even when she resisted its didactic insistence on order.

Through many such connections, the religion around Emily Dickinson was New England Protestant culture, in both its specific practices and its transatlantic conversation with the English-speaking religious and literary world. But religion was also around Emily Dickinson at a second, more general level. Religion exerted a shaping influence of considerable consequence on deeper habits of thought, styles of expression, and daily routines, influences that often extended beyond what Dickinson and her contemporaries explicitly perceived. At this level, religious presuppositions affected the normative patterns of social organization, including gender roles, hierarchies of status, and the aims of education. Religious narratives vividly represented the arc of time across which not only individual lives but also nations and empires ran their course. These social patterns and archetypal narratives constituted the organizing assumptions of what the pragmatist philosopher William James once called "the background of possibilities" that are *around*—that encircle or encompass—individual lives.[8] In the summer of 1856, for instance, Dickinson wrote playfully to her longtime friend and correspondent Elizabeth Holland, "don't tell, dear Mrs. Holland, but wicked as I am, I read my Bible sometimes, and in it as I read today, I found a verse like this, where friends should 'go no more out'; and there were 'no tears,' and I wished as I sat down to-night that we were *there*—not *here*—and that wonderful world had commenced, which makes such promises, and rather than to write you, I were by your side."[9] I return to this letter later in the book, but I cite it now to call attention to the way in which Dickinson's regular practice of reading the Bible provided her with a style and vocabulary (in this case, borrowed from Revelation 3:12 and 21:4) for depicting the "heavenly" joys of correspondence and companionship with an intimate friend. Habitual practices such as reading the Bible, pursued across generations, incorporate members of a culture in patterns of speech, common narratives, and shared symbols that—as in Emily Dickinson's letter to Elizabeth Holland—situate daily activities such as writing a letter within a cosmic frame of reference. These culturally influential religious practices persist across long periods of history, and Robert Alter has deftly argued that the King James Bible had a "powerful afterlife" in the prose style of American writing and rhetoric from the nineteenth century to the twenty-first. "Style," Alter proposes, "is not merely a constellation of aesthetic properties but is the vehicle of a particular vision of reality" or a "way of imagining the world."[10] In short, when religiously inflected patterns of nineteenth-century culture were so thoroughly taken for granted, their invisibility may well have made them more powerful, not less so.

This second level of the religion around Emily Dickinson—the broad cultural presuppositions that created a "background of possibilities"—instilled assumptions about the very nature of religion and what "counted" as being religious. In the tradition that developed from seventeenth-century Puritanism to the evangelical Protestantism of the eighteenth and nineteenth centuries, religion, whatever else it may have included, centered on a personal relationship with God. As chapters 2 and 3 discuss in more detail, this focus on personal devotion shaped expectations about individual religious experience and prompted the development of aids to devotion (private prayer, diary keeping, and meditative reading practices) that cultivated a sense of religious interiority. To cite Williams James once more, his famous book *The Varieties of Religious Experience* (1902) epitomized these cultural assumptions about the core of religion in James's definition of the term: "religion, therefore, as I now ask you arbitrarily to take it, shall mean for us *the feelings, acts, and experiences of individual men in their solitude, so far as they apprehend themselves to stand in relation to whatever they may consider the divine.*"[11] In his emphasis on individual experience, on solitude, and on the indeterminate object of this solitary experience—"*whatever they may consider the divine*"—James identified crucial features of the religion around Emily Dickinson.

To the extent that contemporaries did become self-consciously aware of these taken-for-granted, widely shared practices and symbols, it was in no small measure because historical forces had begun to exert disruptive pressure on them. These disruptive pressures came from diverse directions: new immigration, the transatlantic circulation of scientific and religious ideas, a wider encounter with non-Christian religions, and the transition from a largely agricultural economy to a commercial and industrial one. In this context of social and intellectual change, religion became an arena of conflict over ideas and patterns of conduct about which members of the society fundamentally disagreed. In most cases these were disagreements of long standing that had reached a point of urgent social decision by the middle of the nineteenth century. Most obviously, many decades of debate about enslavement and racial theories culminated in irresolvable political conflict over the continuance and expansion of slavery in the United States and its territories, a conflict in which antagonists used Christian theology to buttress directly contradictory positions.[12] At the same time, rapidly expanding scientific investigation of the earth's geological history and the place of the human species in that history fueled long—and continuing—debates over scriptural accounts of creation and the human engagement with nature as a source of religious insight. Wide-ranging cultural debate became most intense when it directly impinged on questions of human nature, personal meaning, and identity. The nineteenth-century "age of the first person singular" thus also became an age of tremendous anxiety over the immortality of the soul and a search for evidence of the soul's endurance beyond death.[13] Sixty years ago, the literary historian R. W. B. Lewis made the important point that a culture produces, and is produced by, the debates that "preoccupy" it over long periods of time. I share Lewis's view that "a culture achieves identity not so much through the ascendancy of one particular set of convictions as through the emergence of its peculiar and distinctive dialogue."[14]

We might, therefore, think of the religion around Emily Dickinson as a rich, although by no means unlimited, repertoire of cultural forms and images. The forms had been created at many different times and, by the middle of the nineteenth century, had served many different purposes. Religious traditions such as Christianity that develop across extended periods and in diverse cultural contexts gradually accumulate multiple layers of practice and reflection. In these shifting historical contexts, Christian communities have marshaled their symbolic resources to address a host of different problems or questions. Ideas and practices prominent—even central—in one epoch recede to the margins in another. Often, they have combined with political and economic power, but sometimes they have emboldened rebellion against such combinations. The variety is sufficiently great that it implicitly invites arrangement in new patterns. Recognizing this, the historian of religion Catherine Albanese has invented the word "combinativeness" to describe the eclectic shaping and reshaping of religions in American history.[15] At any given moment of cultural history or in the life experience of any individual, certain elements of the religious repertoire may be selected, accentuated, paired, mixed, contrasted, or called into question in ways that effectively reshape the whole.

To a considerable degree, the kaleidoscopic power of imaginatively rearranging inherited patterns is a capacity of both art and religion. Creativity, whether in art or in religion, is culturally embedded without being culturally determined. This suggests a third sense in which we may think of religion *around* Emily Dickinson. This third connotation sets Dickinson at the center of an imaginatively reconfigured world, proposing through her poetry, as she famously put it, to "tell all the truth, but tell it slant" (F1263).[16] In Denis Donoghue's pithy summary, Dickinson "took her Christianity not as she found it but as she altered it. She read her Bible as a rhetorical manual."[17] Culturally available religious symbols commanded her sustained reflection not because they provided authoritative answers from Bible or creed but because they evoked an interconnected set of questions about desire and sorrow, the self and human fulfillment, which she pursued through her poetic and epistolary art.

The four main chapters of *Religion Around Emily Dickinson* investigate both the nineteenth-century repertoire of religious practice and religious ideas and Dickinson's imaginative reshaping of them. Chapters 2 and 3 explore her reconfiguration of a classic religious practice: solitude. Disciplines of solitary reading, meditation, and writing had been prominent ingredients of Christian devotion in New England since first colonization. In Dickinson's own time, American Romantic writers, preeminently Ralph Waldo Emerson and Henry David

Thoreau, refocused these traditions on solitude in nature as the site of encounter with the Absolute and the sustenance of artistic imagination. Emily Dickinson took these disciplines of meditative and artistic solitude "not as she found them but as she altered them," and her purpose in altering them was to develop and clarify her vocation as a poet. Chapters 4 and 5 turn attention from religious practices to the reconfiguration of religious ideas. These two chapters examine how classic ideas of heaven, immortality, and eternity enabled Dickinson to interpret experiential problems of mourning, desire, and the transience of all things human. Taken as a whole, the book attempts to understand Dickinson's "slant," in order to arrive at a better appreciation of the workings of the creative religious imagination and a clearer historical sense of the cultural work performed by religious thought and practice in nineteenth-century America. To the extent that the book succeeds in this effort at understanding, it will have accomplished my purpose in writing it.

INTERSECTIONS BETWEEN AMERICAN RELIGIOUS AND LITERARY HISTORY

What do we see when we look for the religion around Emily Dickinson? In no small measure, the answer depends on ideas about the nature of religion and its relations to literature, politics, and civil society that are current in the time in which we live. Interpretations of Emily Dickinson—or any historical figure—shift as changes in the interpreter's own culture elicit new questions. Scholarship on Emily Dickinson came of age in the mid-twentieth century, especially with the critical editions of her poems and letters by Thomas H. Johnson in 1955 and 1958. At that time, scholarship on the literary history and the religious history of the United States intersected at the juncture of Protestantism and American national identity. Today, dialogue between the two academic disciplines continues, but the points of intersection have expanded markedly to investigate new categories of analysis, including gender, race, material culture, and the diversity of religions in America. For the purpose of exploring the religion around Emily Dickinson, both eras of scholarship have indispensable contributions to make, but it is important to know the differences between them and the difference that those differences make.

During the middle decades of the twentieth century, when the academic study of both American literature and American religion achieved firm institutional form, the foundational scholarship established not only a series of canonical texts but also a canonical narrative. In both literary studies and religious studies, this narrative began with the New England Puritans and culminated in the years prior to the Civil War, when the religious and political vision of the Puritans was intellectually revised by writers such as Emerson, Hawthorne, and Melville and institutionally reshaped by religiously motivated social reforms, ranging from temperance and the abolition of slavery to utopian communities. At its core, this canonical narrative unfolded a reciprocal relationship between personal identity and national identity, the American self and the American nation, and it situated both within a comprehensive order of existence as a whole. Provocatively summarized by the literary historian Sacvan Bercovitch in *The Puritan Origins of the American Self* (1975), the myth of America amounted to a national autobiography: "the celebration of the representative self as America, and of the American self as the embodiment of a prophetic universal design."[18]

Influential texts in literary studies by Perry Miller, Alan Heimert, R. W. B. Lewis, and Bercovitch paralleled scholarship on religions, especially Protestantism, by Sidney Mead, Robert Handy, Martin Marty, and Sydney Ahlstrom.[19] In his magisterial *Religious History of the American People* (1972), Ahlstrom portrayed Puritanism culminating in the eighteenth-century New England theologian Jonathan Edwards and traced the permutations of this legacy in Protestant leaders of the mid-nineteenth century, including the Transcendentalist Theodore Parker and the Congregationalist theologian Horace Bushnell. Ahlstrom concluded that it was not until the 1920s that "the Puritan heritage lost its hold on the leaders of public life."[20] Earlier, Perry Miller had reified this tacit teleology in the title of his seminal essay "From Edwards to Emerson," and numerous variations on this phrase would appear in the subtitles of subsequent articles and monographs.[21] Throughout, these scholars sought a critical appraisal of the historical process that reciprocally shaped Protestantism and American national identity around the cultural ideal that Martin Marty epitomized in 1970 as "righteous empire." The erudition, rhetorical skill, and close textual analysis that characterized the work of these scholars and their midcentury contemporaries continue to stimulate and inform. Nonetheless, both religious studies and literary studies have undergone a dramatic expansion and revision of methods, issues, and perspectives over the past twenty-five years.

As my earlier quotation of Sacvan Bercovitch indicates, the canonical narrative of American literary and religious history enunciated at midcentury acknowledged an explicitly theological dimension of the national myth. The narrative, that is to say, described how successive generations of Americans had situated their understandings of social order and the conduct of personal life within an evolving interpretation of what Jonathan Edwards had once termed "the universal system of existence."[22] It is therefore not surprising that mainstream Protestant theologians, teaching at university-related divinity schools and graduate theological seminaries, actively participated in the academic conversation that fabricated this narrative. At a session of the American Studies section of the American Historical Association, meeting in Chicago in 1953, the Yale theologian H. Richard Niebuhr (1894–1962) propounded a general hypothesis regarding what he called a close correspondence "among ideas men hold about themselves, their societies, and the world." It reads: "There is at all times a close correspondence and a dialectical relationship among general ideas men hold about their own constitution, that of the societies and of the world in which they live; their efforts at self-control (ethics), at social construction (politics), and their attitudes toward their ultimate environment (religion) are in consequence influenced by similar ideas."[23]

Across times and cultures, Niebuhr thought, several conceptual patterns of self, society, and "ultimate environment" had emerged and exerted their influence in ethics, politics, and religion. But, aligning his argument with the narrative emerging in the mid-twentieth-century scholarly conversation, Niebuhr chose to illustrate this general hypothesis by means of a conceptual pattern specific to the religious thought of the Puritans. The Puritans had employed the concept of *covenant*, Niebuhr argued, to describe the structure of the self, the order of society, and the divine promise that guided the universe toward its fulfillment. The image of the covenant embedded human destiny—both personal and social—in the wholeness of all that is.

Niebuhr aligned his essay with the canonical narrative of American religious and literary history in a second way, by titling it "The Idea of Covenant and American Democracy." In colonial America the notion of the covenant had provided what Niebuhr called a *"fundamental pattern"* that displaced earlier organic and hierarchical patterns and thereby became the ethical and intellectual underpinning of democratic national identity. Like his scholarly contemporaries, Niebuhr called attention to the Puritan convictions that "what is possible and required in the political realm" presupposed "a world that has the moral structure of a covenant," and that the ethical measure of persons and nations was their fidelity as covenanters in this "universal community."[24]

Niebuhr's hypothesis presumed that a coherent culture arose when a governing concept established "a close correspondence among ideas" about self, society, and ultimate environment. The canonical narrative of American literatures and American religions thus became the history of the successive governing concepts that ordered these three conceptual domains. Niebuhr's rhetorical choice of the term *ultimate environment* for the most comprehensive of these conceptual domains (rather than, say, God) underscored his recognition that the representation of each of these domains was shaped by the governing concept that established reciprocal relations among them.

During the past twenty-five years, scholars have thoroughly disrupted the canonical narrative that had prevailed at midcentury, dramatically expanding and diversifying the individuals, social groups, and archival materials investigated by American religious and literary historians. Recent scholarship has challenged the earlier emphasis on Puritan origins, underscored the eclectic religious sensibilities of the nineteenth century, and accentuated the transatlantic circulation of social movements, texts, and ideas.[25] In particular, study of Emily Dickinson today benefits from a full generation of extensive research on the women writers and social activists who were her contemporaries, on the cultural expectations placed on women during the nineteenth century, and on the responsibilities of religious leadership that women assumed during the century. More recent scholarship has, in short, attended to those features of nineteenth-century religious and literary history that most contribute to understanding Dickinson in context.

The expanded scope of scholarly inquiry has contributed to the interpretation of Emily Dickinson in another, somewhat indirect way. It has decentered the earlier focus on national identity as the axial issue of religious and literary studies. As Thomas Bender has argued, recent "strategies of narrative synthesis" have challenged the tacit national boundaries of narrative, by focusing on "subnational and transnational solidarities" that accentuate difference, empowerment, and contestation and are, he hopes, consequently "less susceptible to teleology."[26] Here, again, the consequences for contextual interpretation of Emily Dickinson cannot be underestimated. When nationhood controls the narrative, cultural history tends to be read in terms of the contribution of religion, poetry, or art to national identity and political history. To take only one example, when Thomas Johnson and Theodora Ward published their critical edition of Dickinson's letters in 1958, Johnson commented that Dickinson's maturity as a poet coincided with the years of the Civil War. But Dickinson, unlike Walt Whitman or Herman Melville, seldom made the war an overt subject of her writing, and, Johnson concluded, "the fact is that she did not live in history and held no view of it, past or current."[27] Was this the case, or had the mid-twentieth-century focus on national identity misled Johnson into looking in the wrong places for Dickinson's response to the war? Chapter 4, "An Intimate Absence," proposes that more recent scholarship on women, religion, and the Civil War demonstrates significant intersections between the war and Dickinson's years of greatest poetic productivity.[28]

Given the disruption of the canonical narrative, what are the consequences of this disruption for the "correspondence of ideas" that Niebuhr had posited as the underlying structure of that narrative? Has Niebuhr's hypothetical structure of corresponding ideas about self, society, and cosmos undergone a similar disruption? If so, what new interpretive possibilities does that disruption open for the investigation of both the religion around Emily Dickinson and Emily Dickinson's use of religious symbols, practices, and ideas?

A response to these questions requires, first, more specific terminology than Niebuhr's rather imprecise references to "similar ideas" and a "*fundamental* pattern." In his example, the Puritan concept of the covenant functions as a metaphor, that is, a figure of speech that identifies a point of similarity between two dissimilar things while continuing to presume their general dissimilarity. The covenantal metaphor unfolded from the domain of law, first becoming a metaphor or metonymy for the ordering of social relations, then for the moral ordering of the self, and finally for the moral order of the universe. But general metaphorical patterns can proceed from various points of beginning—personal or cosmic, as well as social—as when we speak of "the body politic" or refer to the human as "microcosm." Furthermore, when a tangible object—a house—becomes a metaphor for the "exterior" and "interior" of a human self or a metaphor for the "architecture" of the universe, these metaphorical usages rebound back onto the physical house, attributing to it, for example, the power to link generations, hold secrets, or present a misleading façade to the world. Finally, when the same metaphor is deployed across markedly different cultural domains, its use in one cultural domain has both similarity and dissimilarity to its use in another domain. When performing these imaginative mediations across the three domains of self, society, and cosmos, the metaphors themselves are related metaphorically. Metaphorical systems of this sort are, I assume, what Niebuhr gestured toward in his references to fundamental patterns. The creation and maintenance of such systems is one of the classic cultural functions of religion.[29]

In the process of composing a world, such metaphorical systems not only orient thought and behavior in time and space but also shape and delimit what members of a given society see—or fail to see.[30] In a metaphorically constituted world, what lies beyond the line of the horizon or lives within the locked room? When the covenant lays down its boundaries, what persons or what part of all persons does it thereby drive into exile? In part, then, metaphorical systems engage in their cultural work through a constellation of ideas and practices that shape attentiveness to the world, inclining members to notice and link together certain features of the surrounding environment while allowing other features to recede in significance, even to become invisible, or to float as fragments cut off from the metaphorically constituted web of meaning.

Second, Niebuhr and his contemporaries, partly because of their focus on national identity, tended to emphasize that these governing metaphorical patterns lent distinctive coherence or cohesion to American life. "Similar ideas," to invoke Niebuhr's phrase, conveyed a coherent world picture of self and society within a normative cosmic environment. And it certainly seems the case that metaphorical systems have historically functioned in this way. In *Making the American Self* (1997), Daniel Walker Howe identifies a sustained analogy employed in the early American Republic, in which the mind resembled a well-ordered commonwealth and "the institutions of government were analogous to the individual's faculties of mind."[31] Likewise, Christopher Looby has pointed out that "in the thought of the cultural leaders of the early national period, there is a kind of automatic metaphorical exchange between images of natural order and ideas of social and political order." But, as I have indicated, both the greater diversity of contemporary American society and scholars' greater awareness of that diversity have challenged the assumption of a governing metaphorical system and, instead, prompted interpretations that portray Americans living within a collage of partially overlapping patterns. Thus, after Christopher Looby reviewed the commonplace idea of the late eighteenth century that a singleness of purpose evident in the natural order provided the foundation for social order and personal self-discipline, he responded that "there is very little in our everyday experience, I would say, to suggest that nature in all its parts is involved in a single task, that it is moving as a whole toward some goal; there is, on the contrary, everything to suggest otherwise."[32] As Looby's remark implies, scholarly sensibilities attuned to contemporary social diversity have recognized the presence of diversity in early American society, and, in the process, they have called into question the eighteenth- and nineteenth-century metaphorical systems that promoted the idea that human conduct cohered within a natural order of things.

Third, when nineteenth-century writers or communities employed metaphors to articulate relationships within a cultural system, it is of the utmost importance that we interpreters notice their point of beginning. Did their metaphorical system take its departure from the nature of the self, the society, the universe? Did they give equal weight to each domain of this triad? How did they represent the three domains interpenetrating and influencing one another? The beginning points for metaphorical systems, whether self, society, or cosmos, reflect the needs and interests of their proponents. With respect to the relationship of self to society, several influential nineteenth-century thinkers and social movements began from a concept of society and argued that self-conscious individuality arose from the prior reality of the community that incorporated the individual. Isaac Hecker, for example, was persuaded by Transcendentalism to join the communitarian experiment at Brook Farm and afterward converted to Catholicism and founded the Paulist Fathers. Hecker admired the widespread contemporary "desire, after a more spiritual life" and considered it "one of the chief characteristics of the American people," but he concluded that "the Catholic Church alone is able to give unity to a people composed of such conflicting elements as ours, and to form them into a great nation."[33] The Methodist Phoebe Palmer established her Tuesday afternoon prayer meetings in New York City, so that, through a social piety built around mutual testimony, corporate singing, and common prayer, members of this interdenominational gathering might experience "entire sanctification." Further west, the Kentucky revivalist Richard McNemar pursued a spiritual journey that led him from the Presbyterians, to the newly founded Christian movement, and finally to the minutely organized communal life of the Shakers. The Connecticut theologian Horace Bushnell mistrusted what he saw as the individualistic tendencies at work in American Protestantism, and he summarily asserted his alternative perspective by declaring that "all society is organic,—the church, the state, the school, the family—and there is a spirit in each of these organisms, peculiar to itself. . . . A pure, separate, individual man, living *wholly* within, and from himself, is a mere fiction."[34]

Of course, the "pure, separate, individual man" also had his nineteenth-century advocates, and Ralph Waldo Emerson magnetized the cultural history of the nineteenth century precisely by announcing as possibility what Bushnell dismissed as "mere fiction." Emerson's aim was to carve out a space for artistic creativity and social criticism in a society he found beset by conformity to convention. Emerson imagined an intellectual vocation that derived both energy and authority from intuitive immersion in the natural environment as a counterauthority to that vested in social institutions. Both Bushnell and Emerson—each in his own way—had broken from the assumption that individual, society, and cosmos could be represented through the replication of similar ideas in a mutually reinforcing metaphorical system. Instead, each man aligned two of these domains and identified the connection between the two with "spirit" or "soul," in order to challenge regnant presuppositions about the third domain.

Precisely this challenge made the writings of Bushnell and Emerson simultaneously popular and controversial among their contemporaries. Their ideas were controversial because they had implications for the way in which individuals placed themselves (or were placed) in relation to society and cosmos. From one perspective, their challenges to the metaphorical system spilled over in implications for practical conduct in religion, education, and personal ethics. Chapters 2 and 3 follow this metaphorical placement of the self through Emily Dickinson's decision for solitude as the enactment of her vocation as a poet. From another perspective, debates about the relationship of individual and collective human life to its "ultimate environment" also prompted a series of fundamental questions about a metaphorical system as a system of thought, and Emily Dickinson's experimental poetics are an especially illuminating instance of the nineteenth-century debate over the nature of theological language, which is the subject of chapters 4 and 5. In light of these considerations about religious practice and religious thought, *Religion Around Emily Dickinson* employs Niebuhr's analytical device to call attention to critical debates of the nineteenth century, around the relation of the artist or intellectual to society, the nature and destiny of the self, and the cultural work performed by the religious imagination. My objective, therefore, is not biographical. Instead, I focus on the ways in which Emily Dickinson appropriated and reconstrued what I earlier called the repertoire of religious practices and ideas at work in her culture.

DIVERSIFICATION IN NINETEENTH-CENTURY CHRISTIANITY

As the examples of Emerson, Bushnell, McNemar, Palmer, and Hecker indicate, the religion around Emily Dickinson was neither static nor homogeneous. The title of this book is misleading to the extent that it implies a stable religious environment that one can simply describe before turning attention to Dickinson's poetry. To the contrary, the historian William Hutchison has evocatively portrayed the years after 1820 as "the great diversification." Hutchison focused particularly on the religious diversity brought to the United States by new immigrants, a demographic change that greatly reduced the "numerical dominance in the American population" of English-speaking Protestants. The three million immigrants who arrived in the decade from the mid-1840s to the mid-1850s and "who added themselves to a population of only twenty million, represented by far the largest proportional increase experienced in any period of American history." The great diversification, Hutchison wrote, made it an era of "upheaval" in religion.[35] But, in addition to the important changes brought about by immigration, Hutchison's evocative phrase calls attention to a whole range of diversifications that were reshaping the religion around Emily Dickinson. When church establishments ended and longer-term trends toward voluntary religious participation prevailed, the change prompted new forms of religious affiliation and organized older communities in new ways. With no particular Christian group enjoying a formally privileged connection to the government, each of the various denominations prospered according to its own powers of persuasion, and individuals like McNemar, Hecker, or Emerson freely joined and moved between denominations, created new religious movements, or departed institutions entirely to pursue their singular quests. American spiritual travelogues abounded, as individuals converted from one religion to another or appropriated ideas from the religions of India and Asia.

"The great diversification," thus broadly conceived, prompted many responses by New England Protestants, but for understanding the religion around Emily Dickinson two were most important: the pressure for cultural continuity and the exercise of critical distance. First, diversification, and the experimentation with ideas and forms of community that attended diversification, led many New England religious leaders to underscore the importance of transmitting a cohesive religious culture. As Robert Handy has argued, ending the patterns of colonial religious establishment "did not at all mean that the Christian hope for the triumph of Christian civilization was being given up, but that voluntary ways of working towards it were being extended." The voluntary system of church membership provoked mighty efforts to create schools, colleges, interdenominational reform societies, and agencies of mission and evangelism that would bring about Protestantism's "righteous empire." It produced equally mighty efforts to mark boundaries and push some groups and individuals beyond the pale.[36]

An 1850 Election Day sermon by Edward Hitchcock, entitled *The Inseparable Trio*, exemplified this concern for the cohesive transmission of New England culture. Well known to Emily Dickinson and her family, Hitchcock was the president of Amherst College, a Congregationalist minister, and one of the nation's most eminent geologists. In his sermon, Hitchcock was at pains to emphasize that a healthy social system took form around mutually supportive relations among religion, education, and freedom. To communicate his social theory, Hitchcock elaborated an extended analogy between human physiology and the structure of society: "true Religion, an enlightened system of Education, and genuine Freedom, form the three great vital centres of the Social System; just as the Brain, the Heart, and the Lungs, are the centres of life in the Animal System. Nor can you separate these centres from one another in one case, any more than in the other, without destroying them all." Religion, Hitchcock maintained, stood foremost among the influences that "determine a nation's character," in the same way that the brain was preeminent in a human body. In the body's interdependent system, "the influence that emanates" from the brain "causes the heart to beat and the lungs to heave," even though "disordered action" in heart or lungs will impair the brain. In the same way, religion was "at the head" of all the influences by which national character and destiny were shaped: "moral obligation is the only power that can give genuine life and regulated action to a nation's energies: and if that do not send its galvanic shocks into the whole system, not only will education and freedom fail of vitalization, but paralysis will seize upon the whole body politic."[37]

For the steady stream of Congregationalists and Presbyterians from New England, New York, and Pennsylvania who migrated west seeking opportunities in Ohio, Indiana, Michigan, and Illinois, Hitchcock's emphasis on the inseparable link between religion and education became a regularly reiterated ideal for the transmission of culture and the "regulated action" of both personal and national energies. In 1847 Horace Bushnell articulated his fear to the American Home Missionary Society that any new settlement "involves a tendency to social decline," indeed, "a relapse toward barbarism." Only when religion and education blend "their healthful power" would this danger be averted, and he urged the missionary society not to cease in its labors until "the bands of a complete christian commonwealth are seen to span the continent."[38] The Philadelphia Presbyterian Albert Barnes similarly prophesied that "the power which is to determine the question, whether this land is to enjoy the blessings of liberty, civilization, and Christianity" was "indubitably now developing" in the western territories. "The designs of God" and the efforts of the American Home Missionary Society, Barnes declared, would combine to defeat the dangers of "barbarism, infidelity, Romanism" by planting "evangelical religion," schools, public libraries, and temperance societies throughout the region.[39] In 1833, as part of this evangelical transit of civilization, Emily Dickinson's grandfather, Samuel Fowler Dickinson, had joined the administration of Lane Theological Seminary in Cincinnati, Ohio, where one of the patriarchs of Connecticut Congregationalism, Lyman Beecher, had assumed the presidency in the previous year.

Although her grandfather had directly involved himself in fulfilling the ideal of what Bushnell called "a complete christian commonwealth" and her father was a prominent Whig politician, Emily Dickinson typically held herself at ironic distance from the politics of cultural cohesion. In so doing, she exemplified a second range of responses to "the great diversification." Youthful examples of Dickinson's stance took the form of comedic banter in her letters from Mount Holyoke to her brother, Austin. In October 1847, for instance, she asked Austin, "has the Mexican war terminated yet & how? Are we beat? Do you know of any nation about to besiege South Hadley?"[40] But, as I indicate in the following chapters, Dickinson's distancing or detachment became a more sustained reflective enterprise as she matured. She was not alone. As Amanda Anderson has demonstrated, a host of Victorian writers and intellectuals similarly experimented with "the powers of distance," variously understood as detachment, objectivity, or dislocation, because they understood detachment to have "an intimate and profound bearing on moral character"—sometimes for good and sometimes for ill.[41] Carlo Ginzburg has traced a longer history back to Marcus Aurelius and the Roman Stoics, for whom the philosophical way of life required the disciplined repudiation of seemingly obvious postulates or habitual perceptions of the world. "In order to *see* things," as Ginzburg summarized this stance, "we must first of all look at them as if they had no meaning, as if they were a riddle." This philosophical effort to alter perception subsequently took literary form in the persona of the savage, the hermit, or the animal who offered "a viewpoint from which it is possible to turn upon society a distanced, estranged, and critical gaze." By the eighteenth century, Voltaire was using "defamiliarization as a delegitimating device at every level—political, social, religious."[42] By the nineteenth century, societal awareness of the diversity of religions in American culture and in world cultures further increased the opportunities for individuals to distance themselves from the choice for any one form of religion.

In her assessment of Victorian writers, Anderson interpreted these distanced viewpoints, which defamiliarized the ordinary and cast doubt on presupposed cultural norms, by consolidating them around the idea of cosmopolitanism. But, although Emily Dickinson developed sophisticated strategies of distance, cosmopolitanism does not seem quite the word to capture her method. Instead, I would say that Dickinson cultivated a self-aware provincialism as the vantage point from which to turn upon New England society "a distanced, estranged, and critical gaze." She fully displayed this self-aware provincialism in a poem that began "The Robin's my Criterion for Tune – / Because I grow – where Robins do." It was "the ode familiar" that governed local taste in music, and, because of provincial upbringing, the poet favored her native flowers, buttercups and daisies; "But, were I Britain born, / I'd Daisies spurn." As the poem proceeded, Dickinson portrayed the subtle influence on her perception wrought by each season in New England:

> Without the Snow's Tableau
> Winter, were lie – to me –
> Because I see – New Englandly –
> The Queen, discerns like me –
> Provincially –
>
> (F256)

Awareness of the limited perspective from which she viewed the world brought with it the awareness that each perspective was relative to its time and place. Helen Vendler thus remarks of this poem that, "although Dickinson does not widen her remarks beyond preferences in nature, her subversive perception—that in every nation the inhabitants see provincially—can equally apply to food, religion, or politics."[43]

In the middle decades of the nineteenth century, Dickinson's self-aware provincialism exemplified a broader movement of thought that stressed the ways in which religion was relative to the epoch, region, and culture in which it was articulated. "The great diversification" of the nineteenth century pressed Americans to recognize and ponder the implications of diversity itself, and the century from the 1780s to the 1880s witnessed a proliferation of books that sought to describe the religions of the world for popular audiences. While seldom entirely successful in their efforts to present a detached interpretation, such books significantly enlarged that portion of the population who, instead of simply dividing religion between "true" and "false," began to think of religions as distinctive components of world cultures. The abolitionist and novelist Lydia Maria Child (1802–1880) nicely articulated her purposes in the introduction to her three-volume treatment *The Progress of Religious Ideas, Through Successive Ages* (1855). "I recollect wishing, long ago," Child began, "that I could become acquainted with some good, intelligent Bramin, or Mohammedan, that I might learn, in some degree, how their religions appeared to *them*. This feeling expanded within me, until it took form in this book." She aimed for a detached but not unsympathetic representation of the religions, neither exaggerating merits nor concealing defects, and declaring theological systems neither true nor false. Although "many good and conscientious people will consider it a great risk to treat religious history in this manner," Child declared her "firm faith that plain statements of truth can never eventually prove injurious, on *any* subject."[44] In this way, the category *religion* was gradually entering the popular vocabulary as a term that encompassed all the specific religions and thereby altered perception of each of them. The social historian E. J. Hobsbawm has employed an arresting simile to suggest how, in the transatlantic region transformed by the American and French Revolutions, the experience of diversification introduced to popular culture this new way of thinking about religion. In this era, Hobsbawm proposed, religion ceased to be "something like the sky," which inescapably encompassed and contained the earth and all that was above. It became, instead, "something like a bank of clouds, a large but limited and changing feature of the human firmament." Of all the ideological changes of the early nineteenth century, Hobsbawm considered this "by far the most profound, though its practical consequence were more ambiguous and underdetermined than was then supposed."[45]

The religion around Emily Dickinson thus offered two distinct responses to "the great diversification," each with a different implication for the relation between self and society. The first underscored the importance of self-disciplined moral activism that incorporated the person into the prevailing ideas and institutions of the surrounding society. The second deployed the diversities within the culture—its various provincialisms—in order to open a social space for creative independence. In the relatively conservative society of Connecticut River valley Congregationalism, the inherent tensions between these alternative conceptions of the relation between self and society converged on the religious process of "conversion" into full church membership.

Chapter 2 discusses at more length changing notions of conversion and religious experience from the Puritans to the nineteenth century, but one preliminary point is important here. Since the seventeenth century, conversion had emphasized a process of interior transformation. This change of heart entailed both incorporation in a "godly" community and alienation from what was regarded as the religious complacency of the surrounding society. In the course of the eighteenth and nineteenth centuries, New England Congregationalism had stressed incorporation. It situated personal religious experience within a gathered congregation that represented the spiritual compass of the town, instilling moral and spiritual values that resonated through home, college, and the institutions of civil society.[46] This broadly Puritan legacy became ritualized in periodic revivals in congregations and at colleges, incorporating successive cohorts of townspeople and students into the life of the church through personal experiences of "conviction" of sin and commitment to Christ and his cause in this world. I would infer that when Emily Dickinson's father testified to his faith and joined Amherst's First Church in 1850, his affirmation did not arise from inner spiritual ecstasy but rather from his sincere fidelity to these interlocking moral purposes of church, college, and town.

Such a response on the part of Edward Dickinson is strongly suggested by recollections of the 1850 revival from Aaron Colton, minister of First Church, Amherst, from 1840 to 1852. Colton remembered the revival as "a work of marked depth and power," during which prayer meetings were "notably fuller and more solemn" than was usually the case. But despite this sincerity of purpose, there was also a notable absence of conversions. Colton and the congregation's deacons met to discuss this lack and concluded that the principal impediment to revival could be traced to "the rum places in the village, with fires of hell in full blast." At a town meeting, Amherst College president Edward Hitchcock stood to proclaim "'it were better the college should go down, than that young men should come here to be ruined by drink.'" The selectmen, with only one dissenting vote, determined to close the "rum resorts," and shortly thereafter "the heavens gave rain—blessed showers—and there was a great refreshing" of spiritual experience, with more than 150 conversions during a revival that continued through the summer.[47]

Conversion through the instrumentality of revivals thus primarily took the form of social pressure to appropriate a role, and this role included gendered expectations that were fully at work in the Dickinson household. Nevertheless, the concept of conversion retained, as a minor motif, its second connotation: resistance against conformity to the predominant religious practice. The tension between these alternative connotations is aptly illustrated by an oft-repeated story about Emily Dickinson's days as a student at Mount Holyoke, during the presidency of the noted educator and ardent evangelical Mary Lyon (1797–1849). Located a scant nine miles from Amherst, Mount Holyoke stirred with the spiritual impulses of a revival, and many students, including Dickinson's closest friends, underwent conversions. Emily Dickinson, however, resisted, and her resistance continued into maturity. She came to doubt the religious commonplaces of the surrounding religious culture, without ceasing thereby to harbor profound religious sensibilities.

The importance of this vignette from Dickinson's year of study at Mount Holyoke becomes more apparent when it is set within a slightly longer narrative. In the winter and early spring of 1846, shortly after her fifteenth birthday, Dickinson engaged in an earnest exchange of letters with her intimate friend Abiah Root that revolved around the subject of "becoming a Christian." In these pious deliberations, the young women were pursuing a nineteenth-century version of the interrogation of personal religious experience that had deep roots in New England's Puritan past. When Dickinson wrote Abiah Root in late January 1846, she explained that she had delayed responding to Root's earlier letter because Dickinson feared that "in the unsettled state of your mind" regarding the "choice" for Christ, Dickinson might inadvertently say something that would "turn your attention from so all important a subject." For a short time, Dickinson explained, she herself was "almost persuaded to be a christian," and in that brief span "in which I felt I had found my savior," she had experienced "perfect peace and happiness." But, soon afterward, Dickinson found herself setting aside such disciplines as morning prayer, and "one by one my old habits returned and I cared less for religion than ever." Lapse included loss, and Dickinson confessed to "an aching void in my heart which I am convinced the world can never fill." Although she was "continually putting off becoming a christian," she could also "continually hear Christ saying to me Daughter give me thine heart."[48]

Two months later, another letter to Abiah Root continued these ruminations on salvation, with the request not to let anyone "see this letter." In the interim, Root had "found a Saviour," while Dickinson sat "alone before my little writing desk," wishing that she "had found the peace which has been given to you." Dickinson reiterated her narrative of a mistaken sense of redemption followed by lapse into worldly concerns. It had been "my greatest pleasure to commune alone with the great God & to feel that he would listen to my prayers," but she had let her guard down, "the world allured me," and gradually "I seemed to lose my interest in heavenly things," including participation in the "small circle" of friends who regularly met together for prayer. "I feel," Dickinson continued, "that I am sailing upon the brink of an awful precipice, from which I cannot escape & over which I fear my tiny boat will soon glide if I do not receive help from above." Self-interrogation continued into the autumn, when Dickinson wrote to Abiah Root that she had "not yet made my peace with God" and found herself a stranger to "the delightful emotions which fill your heart." Despite "perfect confidence in God & his promises," Dickinson continued to "feel that the world holds a predominant place in my affections."[49]

This epistolary dialogue about personal religious experience contained at least three features that connected Dickinson's youthful turmoil to wider patterns of nineteenth-century evangelical piety. First, the letters followed upon a revival in the First Congregational Church of Amherst led by Reverend Colton, meetings during which even "those who sneered loudest at serious things" were soon "brought to see their power, and to make Christ their portion." As the story of the Mount Holyoke revival has indicated, both congregations and colleges actively participated in evangelization. During Amherst's revival, "many hearts have given way to the claims of God," and at Mount Holyoke revival brought many students "flocking to the ark of safety." As to herself, Dickinson assured Abiah Root that she was "not entirely thoughtless" on this all-important subject but had "not yet given up to the claims of Christ." She characterized the interior spiritual struggle as one set of ingrained habits against another: "my old habits returned," she lamented. Amid these revivals, friends and family gradually made their commitments, first Abiah Root and Sarah Tracy, then Abby Wood, and, on August 11, 1850, her father, Edward Dickinson.[50] Throughout the dialogue between Dickinson and Abiah Root, the older Puritan ideal of conversion, as God's claim upon the soul that drew it apart from the claims of the world, commingled with the routinized recruitment of the next generation and its incorporation into respectable society. In a striking way, the "claims" of the world more thoroughly roused Dickinson to introspection than did the conventional interiority of revival. She was not alone in her resistance. The co-optation of conversion by convention regularly provoked challenges from nineteenth-century New England intellectuals. Some, such as Noah Porter, president of Yale from 1871 to 1886, looked back with distaste on the college revivals of their youth because they remembered these efforts at spiritual awakening as external impositions on their studies rather than as arising from intrinsic connections to philosophy, literature, and science.[51] Others, such as Ralph Waldo Emerson, transmuted conversion's ideal of interior transformation into a departure from social convention in the pursuit of creative individuality. Collectively, the vigorous, frequently acrimonious debates surrounding revivalism stimulated the search, throughout Emily Dickinson's lifetime, for a vocabulary of interiority, a way to describe what William James would later term "*the feelings, acts, and experiences of individual men in their solitude.*"

Second, when Dickinson chose language to describe the process of religious assessment that she and her friends were undergoing, she disclosed the influences of a long debate over the relative weight of human initiative and the divine in the process of conversion. As cited above, her letters frequently spoke of *choice* and *decision*. At the same time, the letters also described skeptics who, attending a revival, were "melted" by religion's power. In Dickinson's telling, spirit sometimes seemed to have seized the initiative: "it was really wonderful to see how near heaven came to sinful mortals." But whether human decision or God's determination propelled conversion, emotional attachment was paramount: "I feel that I shall never be happy without I love Christ." Dickinson also recognized that, in her case at least, such emotional responses to the appeals of revival were not without their hazards, and she confided to Root that she had attended "none of the meetings" during the Amherst revival of 1845. Assessing herself, Dickinson had come to the conclusion that "I was so easily excited that I might again be deceived and I dared not trust myself."[52] This early awareness of emotions and their distinctive embodiments matured in her writing not only as a discipline of her own emotions but as the astute analysis of varied forms and expressions of emotion. More strongly put, writing became for Emily Dickinson what Pierre Hadot has called "a therapeutic of the passions," a spiritual exercise that aimed to form her representation of the world, regulate her "inner climate," and shape a way of life.[53]

Third, since the question of conversion was at root a question about the ultimate fate of the soul, Dickinson couched it in broader ruminations about death and eternity. She announced to Abiah Root, "I almost wish there was no Eternity." Although humans dreaded death "because it launches us upon an unknown world," would this not be preferable to "so endless a state of existence" as eternity? The entire question piqued Dickinson's curiosity: "I dont know why it is but it does not seem to me that I shall ever cease to live on earth—I cannot imagine with the farthest stretch of my imagination my own death scene— It does not seem to me that I shall ever close my eyes in death." Much more concretely, Dickinson's letters discussing her spiritual estate also commented directly on the individual deaths of townspeople and friends. During her epistolary exchange with Root, Dickinson delivered a poignant commentary on the death in April 1844 of her friend Sophia Holland. Dickinson's persistent desire to see her dying friend had finally led the doctor and her parents to relent: "I took off my shoes and stole softly to the sick room. There she lay mild & beautiful as in health & her pale features lit up with an unearthly—smile. I looked as long as friends would permit & when they told me I must look no longer I let them lead me away." After Sophia was "laid in her coffin" and Dickinson realized "I could not call her back," she "gave way to a fixed melancholy." Her family sent her to Boston to live with Aunt Lavinia Norcross for a month "until my health improved so my spirits were better." Dickinson concluded confidently to Abiah Root, "I trust she is now in heaven & though I shall never forget her, yet I shall meet her in heaven."[54] As chapters 4 and 5 discuss at length, Dickinson puzzled across long periods of her life over these problems of time, death, and eternity, returning to them in different ways throughout her letters and poems. Although she had declared to Abiah Root that "I cannot imagine with the farthest stretch of my imagination my own death scene," precisely the act of imagining the moment of death would propel several of her most powerful and creative poems.

SOCIETY AND SOLITUDE

In an epoch notable for religious activism and institutional innova-
tion, Emily Dickinson elected seclusion. In an epoch when women
were entering popular print as historians, poets, and novelists, she
claimed her vocation as a poet but avoided publication. Dickinson's
withdrawal from society was gradual; in the late 1850s she was still
attending church (irregularly) and calling on neighbors. But during
the early 1860s, her most stunningly productive years as a poet, Dick-
inson's retreat from society became more complete. It had its practical
side, care for an ailing mother, and its self-dramatizing features, inter-
viewing visitors from behind closed doors or wearing white clothing
(a practice that seems to have become habitual after her father's death
in 1874). But, in addition to its gradualness and occasional theatricality,
her seclusion was also purposeful. For this reason, Mabel Loomis Todd,
the first editor of Emily Dickinson's poetry, dismissed Amherst leg-
ends of Dickinson as a "white-draped" eccentric and instead observed
that Dickinson's solitude expressed the underlying "trend of her inner
movement" since the time of her studies at Mount Holyoke.[1]

Several adjectives appropriately capture features of Dickinson's seclusion: reclusive, withdrawn, lonely, reticent, private. Some of these adjectives connote a personal disposition, and the literary critic Denis Donoghue once remarked that "some requirement of her sensibility was fulfilled by seclusion which could not have been fulfilled by company."[2] Others, such as *private*, call attention to the boundary that Dickinson set between herself and the institutions of civil society. But beyond these psychological and sociological aspects, Dickinson's withdrawal interacted with—even enacted—her vocational decision to become a poet. Richard Sewall has proposed that Dickinson's decision for seclusion gave her life actions a "metaphoric purport" that paralleled the carefully crafted metaphors of her writing, and Judith Farr has employed the motif of "renunciation" to explore how Dickinson's "acculturation through schooling and reading caused her to lead her life in art as a contemplative."[3]

From among the descriptive terms for Dickinson's seclusion, both this chapter and the following one emphasize *solitude*, in order to accentuate the religious aspect of her self-understanding as a poet. I have chosen solitude not to exclude such terms as *privacy* and *withdrawal*; they will have their roles to play in this cultural portrait. Rather, solitude situates Emily Dickinson in a long, variegated tradition of Christian spirituality that had achieved a distinctive distillation in the spiritual disciplines of New England Puritanism and that funded, in her own time, Romantic images of solitude as the condition for artistic creativity. In its various modern forms, solitude was a social practice. The aim of this social practice was twofold. Solitude both resisted conventional thinking, in order to pursue an alternative, "higher" goal, and solitude established a meditative retreat from quotidian routine, in order to appraise the purposes and patterns of personal life. It was both departure and quest.[4]

As a departure from the everyday converse of social life, solitude seldom if ever took the form of an utter withdrawal from all things human. Instead, solitude's resistance was selective, its objections focused. It protested some certain feature of the social order that it deemed false to the aim of human life. Since the sixteenth century, writers had explored many facets of the departure into solitude: as a setting aside that left a space to be filled by something else; as embarking on a journey; as detachment that prized independence; as seclusion that waited alone for the companion; as flight from danger; as purification that purged some deeply residing ill; as renunciation that turned its back on former attractions. The famous opening scene of John Bunyan's *Pilgrim's Progress* (1678) captured many of these motifs when it depicted Christian leaving behind wife and children, their appeals unheard above Christian's own cry of "Life, Life, Eternal Life," as he set out on his long journey toward the heavenly city.[5]

In all of these connotations, to many of which I shall return, solitude carried the shadow, the memory, and the weight of what it had left behind. Thus the objectionable feature of society that first impelled the departure into solitude remained present as an absence that was integral to the meaning of solitude and its protest. Norms of social conformity had inadvertently created the spaces from which the solitary critic might launch a religious and literary opposition. Thought of in another way, departure, by the very act of leaving something behind, created a space for artistic innovation and communication. The journey into solitude was an act not simply of resistance but also of prophecy. Fresh possibility was present in solitude, at least as anticipation or hope, and the sense of possibility suffused the actual place of retreat with the imaginative and symbolic. Among Dickinson's contemporaries, Henry David Thoreau capitalized on the symbolic possibilities of solitude, reporting that his hut at Walden Pond was as distant from Concord "as many a region viewed nightly by astronomers. We are wont to imagine rare and delectable places in some remote and more celestial corner of the system, behind the constellation of Cassiopeia's Chair, far from noise and disturbance. I discovered that my house actually had its site in such a withdrawn, but forever new and unprofaned, part of the universe."[6]

As the examples of Bunyan and Thoreau suggest, solitude placed the writer, the religious seeker, or the intellectual on a margin of society. Sometimes the marginalization was compulsory; Bunyan wrote *The Pilgrim's Progress* while in prison. Sometimes the writer chose his margin, as when Thoreau built his cabin by the pond. But in either circumstance, the writer understood solitude to provide an imaginative location from which to look back toward society in criticism and look into the self for its constitutive, enduring feature. Emily Dickinson's withdrawal into solitude presupposed this complex tradition in which meditative self-appraisal was the precondition for spiritual or artistic maturation. She drew on both traditional Protestant spiritual practices of solitude and Romantic representations of the solitary intellectual in order to fashion her vocation as a poet. In addition, she was attracted to images of solitary reverie, secluded retreats, and imaginative flights of fancy that frequently appeared in popular novels, essays, and poetry of the nineteenth century. Her solitude, in short, did not abstract Dickinson from the cultural currents of the age; it *was* one of the cultural currents of the age.

Two strands of the practice of solitude strongly influenced Emily Dickinson's understanding of her poetic vocation, and this chapter begins with an analysis of solitude in the careers of two New Englanders who exemplify those strands. The first is Jonathan Edwards (1703–1758), minister in Northampton, Massachusetts, and the most intellectually powerful preacher of the eighteenth century. As I discuss in the first section of the chapter, Edwards drew on disciplines of solitude developed by the Puritan movement of the sixteenth and seventeenth centuries, which had understood solitary meditation, prayer, and writing as therapy for the soul in quest of God. Edwards shared the Puritan emphasis on solitude as spiritual self-interrogation, but he revised these disciplines, in a way that would have major consequences for later forms of American spirituality, by accentuating the importance of solitude in nature.[7] My second exemplary figure is the most famous American essayist of the nineteenth century, a luminous orator in an age of oratory, Ralph Waldo Emerson (1803–1882). Like Edwards, Emerson sought direct encounter with the Absolute through solitude in nature, but unlike Edwards he emphasized the purpose of solitude as resistance against social convention on behalf of intellectual independence and artistic creativity. Further, although solitude had taken shape for both men as a culturally formed attentiveness that anticipated the possibility of divine presence in nature, they understood this experience quite differently, with different consequences for the effects of solitude on the formation of the self.

Thus, despite the fact that *nature* and *solitude* became critical terms in the nineteenth-century lexicon of American religion and literature, the terms confronted writers and intellectuals such as Emily Dickinson with many choices regarding their meaning and relationship to each other. Solitude in nature was a contested space. And the space was an ellipse with two foci: encounter with the divine and the vocation of the self. In order to situate the distinctive form in which Dickinson pursued her vocation as a poet, the chapter therefore concludes by considering the range of meanings that nineteenth-century intellectuals attached to nature and solitude. To illustrate the nineteenth-century contest over nature, I have placed Dickinson in an imaginary conversation with two of her contemporaries, all three responding to Emerson and, behind Emerson, to Edwards. The writers—perhaps best thought of for my purposes as imaginary "dinner companions"—are the abolitionist, feminist, and political correspondent Margaret Fuller (1810–1850), and the abolitionist and advocate of women's rights Frederick Douglass (1818–1895). The texts that focus their discussion are Fuller's *Summer on the Lakes, in 1843; Narrative of the Life of Frederick Douglass, an American Slave*; and a poem by Emily Dickinson, "There's a certain Slant of light." To suggest the meanings of solitude that I consider most important for interpreting the relation of Emily Dickinson to the surrounding religious culture, I then look at two poems that family members, Susan Gilbert Dickinson and Martha Dickinson Bianchi, considered appropriate summations of the poet's life. Building on these considerations in the present chapter, chapter 3 then investigates in more detail Emily Dickinson's poetic vocation as it took shape in solitude and attentiveness to nature on the grounds of her father's house, the Homestead.

JONATHAN EDWARDS AND THE PURITAN LEGACY OF SELF-REFLECTION

From its beginnings in Elizabethan England during the 1560s, the Puritan movement had protested that the Church of England needed a thorough reformation: erroneous human opinions had accumulated over time to corrupt the church's worship, doctrines, and moral standards. With increasingly militant zeal during the early seventeenth century, the Puritans preached, debated, and organized in order to purify these errors according to standards they found revealed in scripture. They considered themselves the faithful church within an errant church and aimed to leaven the whole loaf.

Although factional disagreements over specific liturgical and political reforms would fragment the Puritan movement, the various parties remained convinced that the motivating energy for reformation in church and society arose from personal spiritual transformation—conversion. Hence, even worse than the corrupt practices of the established church, the Puritans declared, was the church's complacent acceptance of merely nominal conformity on the part of its members, when what God actually required was a change of heart. Their zeal for transformation was emboldened by their confidence that divine providence was effecting its purposes in history for society and individual alike. The proper conduct of life therefore required careful attention to the evidence of history, including the internal history of the soul. The power of God was welling up and expressing itself through human devotion to the divine cause, they asserted, and this required a scrupulous examination of personal religious motives.

This emphasis on self-examination meant that the core spiritual disciplines of the Puritans were retrospective. Their ministers preached sermons and published devotional manuals that urged the faithful to search their lives for evidence of God's presence, in both mercy and judgment. Individuals acted on the ministers' advice, assiduously composing journals, diaries, and autobiographies that recorded life's passage in order to look back on the course traveled, trace its major contours, and thereby discern the providential hand of God. By means of this retrospective spirituality, the Puritans sought to discover and then cultivate the principle that unified a person's life and oriented it toward a single end, that is, to trace the nature and destiny of the soul. In their search for this unifying plot to life, they turned to the Christian Bible for both model narratives and evaluative norms. Hence, the Puritans' principal contribution to modern religious thought lay in conceiving theology as practical wisdom about the coherence of one's life over time.

The self fashioned in the Puritan tradition of "experimental divinity" achieved self-knowledge and responsibility by discerning the way a particular life distinctively expressed a general human pattern, revealed in scripture. The archetypal narrative assumed that the sinful self simultaneously grasped the world in pride, clung to it in desperation, but could not preserve itself from ultimate destruction without a conversion, effected by the infusion of a supernatural and saving grace. Further, it assumed the continuity of the self through the most dramatic reshaping.[8] The old self and the new self were the same self, a single self transformed and made new. The truth or authenticity of any individual Puritan's conversion rested on the recognizable enactment of this archetypal narrative of redemption in a form that, at the same time, displayed those singular features that served to make it one's personal narrative.

This conception of the self and the spiritual disciplines that supported it persisted into the eighteenth century among both ministers and the laity. Around the year 1740 the New England theologian Jonathan Edwards drew on these traditions to compose a brief "Personal Narrative" that recounted his religious development, beginning with his childhood and student days at Yale College. At the time he wrote the narrative, Edwards was in his late thirties and the minister of Northampton, the most prominent congregation in central Massachusetts. He had recently gained international repute through a published account of religious revival in the region, *A Faithful Narrative of the Surprising Work of God*, which had attracted attention in England from Isaac Watts and John Wesley. In 1740, the British itinerant preacher George Whitefield visited Northampton on one of his evangelistic tours that precipitated the colonial revivals known collectively as the Great Awakening. During those religious excitements, Edwards himself would preach the sermon for which he has been most widely remembered, "Sinners in the Hands of an Angry God." But the "Personal Narrative" almost entirely ignored external events such as these in order to take stock of the inner course of life. Edwards compiled his brief autobiography from a diary and theological notebooks in which he had recorded the waxing and waning of his spiritual state for nearly twenty years.

The pivot of the narrative was Edwards's account of the "inward, sweet delight in God" that enveloped him as he meditated over a passage of scripture, 1 Timothy 1:17: "now unto the King eternal, immortal, invisible, the only wise God, be honor and glory forever and ever, Amen." As he read these words, Edwards recalled, "there came into my soul, and was as it were diffused through it, a sense of the glory of the divine being; a new sense, quite different from anything I ever experienced before." In the immediate aftermath of this transformation, while contemplating Christ and the divine glory, he had experienced "a calm, sweet abstraction of soul from all the concerns o[f] this world; and a kind of vision, or fixed ideas and imaginations, of being alone in the mountains, or some solitary wilderness, far from all mankind, sweetly conversing with Christ, and wrapt and swallowed up in God."[9]

Edwards's rapturous vision of mountain solitude was not an isolated incident but, instead, a characteristic feature of a complex regimen of solitude. Immediately after conversing about his religious vision with his father, Timothy Edwards, for example, the young Edwards retreated to a "solitary place" in his father's pasture, "and as I was walking there, and looked up on the sky and clouds; there came into my mind, a sweet sense of the glorious majesty and grace of God, that I know not how to express. I seemed to see them both in a sweet conjunction: majesty and meekness joined together: it was a sweet and gentle, and holy majesty; and also a majestic meekness; an awful sweetness; a high, and great, and holy gentleness." Reading, meditation, writing, and "secret prayer" became regular features of every day for Edwards and quite frequently occurred out of doors: walking alone in the fields or along the banks of a river, meditating under an oak tree, riding alone in the woods. To miss no opportunity for this soul work, he urged himself to "remember as soon as I can, to get a piece of slate, or something, whereon I can make short memorandums while traveling."[10]

Scripture had wrought a new affective disposition toward God, and as part of this change Edwards found that he perceived the world differently from before. Events such as thunderstorms, which previously had frightened him, now became emblems of divine beauty.[11]

"The appearance of everything was altered," he wrote, and "there seemed to be, as it were, a calm, sweet cast, or appearance of divine glory, in almost every thing . . . in the sun, moon, and stars; in the clouds, and blue sky; in the grass, flowers, trees; in the water, and all nature." An emblematic depth to nature had captured his attention or, as Edwards put it, worked "greatly to fix my mind."[12] The grace-wrought "sense of the heart" had transmuted the terrible into the beautiful, and the appearance of nature was altered such that it exhibited the divine attributes of wisdom, purity, and love.

Furthermore, Edwards now sought out natural locales in which he anticipated experiencing a sense of divine presence. In writing his "Personal Narrative," Edwards imaginatively located encounters with God beyond house and church in a nature untouched by human fashioning. Nature augmented and extended his repertoire of solitary spiritual disciplines: "I often used to sit and view the moon, for a long time; and so in the daytime, spent much time in viewing the clouds and sky, to behold the sweet glory of God in these things."[13] Although, as a practitioner of solitude, Edwards was highly attentive to place and circumstance, he did not customarily designate specific solitary locales as distinctively sacred spaces, set aside for a special kind of religious attention.[14] Instead, they were spatial occasions for reverie, potentially available in any natural landscape, and Edwards therefore approached natural settings with a theologically freighted expectancy. In addition, the theological predisposition he had cultivated led him quite consistently to stress the symbolic rather than the empirical dimension of a natural locale. It was the capacity of nature to disclose, exhibit, or reveal its source in the divine fecundity that sustained his attention, and for this reason Edwards's images of nature had a generalized, abstract quality at the farthest remove from the detailed representations of specific natural scenes in the later prose of Thoreau.

For Edwards, the disciplines of solitude instilled a distinctive attentiveness to nature, which as the creation of God bore traces of the divine presence. Natural settings cultivated a moral aesthetic that situated the self in the order of eternity and overcame two great, interlocking threats to the self: first, that worldly concerns would divert his attention from life's true and single aim, the glory of God, and, second, that human pride and ambition would displace from his heart what the Puritans had consistently regarded as the "fundamental grace," humility before the absolute God.[15] Edwards dramatized the "new sense" through images of his transformed perception of sun, moon, and thunderstorms, and at the same time represented the religious affections themselves through emblems derived from nature. Christian holiness must center itself, Edwards wrote, on the virtue of humility, and he retrieved for his "Personal Narrative" an early entry from his theological notebooks: "The soul of a true Christian, as I then wrote my meditations, appeared like such a little white flower, as we see in the spring of the year; low and humble on the ground, opening its bosom, to receive the pleasant beams of the sun's glory; rejoicing as it were, in a calm rapture; diffusing around a sweet fragrancy; standing peacefully and lovingly, in the midst of other flowers round about; all in like manner opening their bosoms, to drink in the light of the sun."[16]

One cannot but be struck by the extent to which these various natural emblems of Christian piety rendered nature so thoroughly harmonious and benign. They seem immeasurably distant from the drawn bow of God's wrath and the fire-engulfed soul depicted in Edwards's sermon "Sinners in the Hands of an Angry God." Yet Edwards was naïve neither about the hazards of nature nor about the continuing darkness of the human soul. The contrasts of his imagery are better understood, I think, as Edwards's means of stressing the radical perceptual transformation brought about by the infusion of "the new sense." The ordering power of a sovereign God, Edwards suggested, may be experienced in two ways: as a harmonious extension of the life-giving light of charity, or as the restraining hand that draws the bowstring of wrath and holds the slender thread from which a soul dangles over the fires of hell.

The interpretive structure within which Edwards deployed these natural images was a providential theology of history in its entire sweep, and his "Personal Narrative" was a meditation on the way in which his life was incorporated within that larger providential movement. The transforming infusion of the new sense, his episodes of declension and of progress in holiness, and the far prospect of heaven alike presumed a narrative of redemptive change guided by, and toward, a single telos. Reviewing his diaries and reworking them into autobiographical form enabled Edwards to compare stages in his life and discern directions of change. Memory worked by retrospection and recapitulation, seeking the religious thread that laced together twenty-five years and interpreted experiences through their placement in temporal sequence: that "which I now felt" was "an exceeding different kind" from "when I was a boy." Meaning derived especially from the temporal connections made between specific memories: "my experience had not then taught me, as it has done since." Nonetheless, diaries, journals, and autobiographical narratives are written in the flow of life and cannot, in the nature of the case, benefit from knowing how things will "turn out." In order to engage in moral and spiritual self-appraisal, the "Personal Narrative" therefore employed an additional set of spiritual disciplines that imaginatively looked back on the hazards and sorrows of this world from a felicitous realm beyond it. That is, Edwards attempted to survey personal life in its completeness through mental representations of death and heaven.

To distance oneself from the immediacy of life, English devotional literature had long counseled that the physical action of lying in bed should take on the emblematic meaning of lying in the grave. At the brink of eternity, no truth could be hidden and rationalizations became pointless; to place oneself imaginatively at that moment of ultimate transition would, it was thought, induce serious self-searching. In the mid-seventeenth century, the English divine Jeremy Taylor had advised that a person should "frequently and seriously by imagination place himself upon his death-bed, and consider what great joys he shall have for the remembrance of every day well spent, and what then he would give that he had so spent all his days." Similarly, Jonathan Edwards regularly employed the spiritual discipline of lying in bed and imaginatively looking back from the moment of his death to the actions of his life: "resolved, I will act so as I think I shall judge would have been best, and most prudent, when I come into the future world."[17]

Edwards imaginatively entered "the future world" not only as a space of ethical self-appraisal but also as an idealization of human sociality. His representations of heaven gave significant place to intimate friendship and spiritual conversation. Throughout Edwards's diary he referred to the difficulty of "giving vent" to the full ardor of his piety. He recalled in the "Personal Narrative" that while studying at Yale it had appeared "a great part of the happiness of heaven, that there the saints could express their love to Christ. It appeared to me a great clog and hindrance and burden to me, that what I felt within, I could not express to God, and give vent to, as I desired. The inward ardor of my soul, seemed to be hindered and pent up, and could not freely flame out as it would."[18] Heaven was the place of friendship and "conversing with Christ," where the affective core of true piety could well up unimpeded: "Heaven is a world of love."

With these images of heavenly companionship in mind, it is not surprising to find that Edwards's depictions of solitude in nature were filled with voices. Some were the voices of his friends, in particular John Smith of New York, with whom Edwards had walked the banks of the Hudson discussing religious matters. After his melancholy parting from Smith and Smith's mother in 1723, Edwards recorded his contemplation on heaven, "where is the enjoyment of the persons loved, without ever parting; where these persons that appear so lovely in this world, will really be inexpressibly more lovely, and full of love to us. And how sweetly will the mutual lovers join together to sing the praises of God and the Lamb!"[19] But, equally, the voice in solitude was that of God, as when Edwards went out to see the approaching thunderstorm and "hear the majestic and awful voice of God's thunder." And, while he watched, he "used to spend my time, as it always seemed natural to me, to sing or chant forth my meditations; to speak my thoughts in soliloquies, and speak with a singing voice." The locales of solitude thereby became places where Edwards would "spend abundance of my time, in walking alone in the woods, and solitary places, for mediation, soliloquy and prayer, and converse with God."[20] Neither literally nor imaginatively did he construe solitude as individual isolation. Solitude gave the foretaste of heaven, not because Edwards was alone but because there he expressed his affections toward the other or the one, unimpeded.

Writing, as one of the central spiritual disciplines of evangelical Protestantism, continued unabated into the nineteenth century. In 1743, at about the same time that Edwards wrote his "Personal Narrative," the Rhode Island evangelical leader Sarah Osborn (1714–1796) composed a memoir to make sense of both her spiritual awakening during the revivals and the financial upheaval of her family's bank-ruptcy. Afterward, Osborn remained unflagging in her devotional writing. She maintained extensive diaries throughout her life and, sewn together in booklets, they seem to have circulated after her death as sources of spiritual insight for evangelical ministers and laity. In eighteenth-century religious society, Osborn was known publicly for holding weekly prayer meetings that brought hundreds of persons, including many slaves, to her Newport home, but the historian Cather-ine Brekus persuasively argues that, behind this evangelistic outreach, "she saw her life first and foremost as a *writing* life."[21] Among Emily Dickinson's nineteenth-century contemporaries, the Methodist evan-gelical Phoebe Palmer (1807–1874), like Osborn, conducted heavily attended weekly prayer meetings at her home in New York City and was also a devoted writer, maintaining her diaries and occasionally becoming overwhelmed by voluminous correspondence. From child-hood, Palmer likewise wrote poetry, for its value as a meditative prac-tice rather than for publication.[22] The examples of Sarah Osborn and Phoebe Palmer suggest the long influence, through changing social contexts, of the Puritan practice of solitary writing aimed at the disci-pline of an ever-rebellious human will and the discernment of a spir-itual vocation. A reverberation of these spiritual practices appeared in a letter that Emily Dickinson wrote to Thomas Wentworth Higginson in 1862. Whenever events "troubled my attention," Dickinson explained to Higginson, composing poems had the power to "relieve."[23] When her biographer Richard Sewall employed this passage to describe Dickin-son's "notion of the therapeutic value of writing," he implicitly placed her in an enduring tradition of meditative writing.[24]

RURAL UTOPIAS

These Puritan and evangelical traditions of meditative writing were not, however, Dickinson's sole source for her image of artistic seclu-sion. In America during the eighteenth and early nineteenth centuries, numerous poems, essays, and novels envisioned an escape from the clamor and constraints of public life into an idealized rural retreat. The sixteenth-century essayist Michel de Montaigne had articulated what might serve as the guiding dictum for this literature: "the aim of all solitude" was "to live more at leisure and at one's ease," in order to pursue reflection, scholarship, and companionable conversation.[25] In a typical instance of this idyllic solitude, a poem entitled *Philosophic Solitude* (1747), the youthful William Livingston (later a member of the Continental Congress and governor of New Jersey) extolled the placid contentment of a rural retreat, "From noise remote, and ignorant of strife."

> *Full in the center of some shady grove,*
> *By nature form'd for solitude and love;*
> *On banks array'd with ever-blooming flow'rs;*
> *Near beauteous landskips, and by rosiate bow'rs;*
> *My neat, but simple structure I would raise,*
> *Unlike the sumptuous domes of modern days;*
> *Devoid of pomp, with rural plainness form'd,*
> *With savage game, and glossy shells adorn'd.*[26]

Livingston's utopian landscape of "ever-blooming flow'rs" represented his departure from a public world marked by vanity, display, ornament, gossip, and political intrigue. The rural life, in contrast to these vices of "masquerade" and "vain formality," offered the simplicity of direct and honest companionship. Imagining his rural paradise, Livingston portrayed the joys of "social converse, o'er the sprightly bowl" with college friends (both those living and those now dead), listed the works of literature that would fill a well-appointed library, and speculated on the virtues that ought to be embodied in a prospective wife.[27] Building on the utopian dimensions of his retreat, Livingston proceeded from the lush beauty of his imagined surroundings to consider the ordered cycles of creation and demanded a response from any who might doubt a benign creator:

> *Say, railing Infidel! canst thou survey*
> *Yon globe of fire, that gives the golden day,*
> *Th' harmonious structure of this vast machine,*
> *And not confess its Architect divine?*[28]

Although adopting a tone far removed from that of Jonathan Edwards, Livingston nonetheless shared Edwards's notion that his solitary site of philosophical meditation invited ardent conversation with the spirits that populated it.

> *Oft' would I wander thro' the florid field,*
> *Where clust'ring roses balmy fragrance yield;*
> *Or in lone grotts, for contemplation made,*
> *Converse with Angels, and the mighty dead.*[29]

Livingston's *Philosophic Solitude* was a relatively early instance of literature that, by the two decades after the American Revolution, had grown into what literary historian Eric Slauter has called a "cultural preoccupation with solitude." Many of these fantasy narratives adopted a semiautobiographical pose, presenting the narrator as a scholar-poet, hermit, or philosopher-in-the-forest who had taken temporary refuge from civil society in order to restore his intellectual powers and then employ insights gained in rural retreat to promote the moral and social improvement of the nation. In *Revolutionary Writers*, Emory Elliott identifies these rural utopians as most commonly men reared in the Protestant churches and trained for the professions, who considered authorship a "sacred calling" and aspired to the role of "moral preceptor and public poet." Elliott cites a classic exposition of this relationship between solitude and society from Philip Freneau: "Every rational man, let his business or station in life be what it may, should, in my way of thinking, at least once a year withdraw himself from the numerous connections and allurements that are apt to give us too great a fondness for life; he should then take time to reflect, as a rational being ought to do, and consider well the end of his being."[30]

Yet another version of solitude appeared in this same era and was, perhaps, epitomized by a series of essays that Charles Brockden Brown (1771–1810) wrote for the *Columbian Magazine*. Under the title "The Rhapsodist," Brown adopted the idealized social persona of a writer who delivered "the sentiments suggested by the moment in artless and unpremeditated language." Possessed of "a quick but thoughtful mind" from which poured forth "effusions of a sprightly fancy," the rhapsodist was impatient with social pleasantries. It was "only when alone that he exerts his faculties with vigour, and exults in the consciousness of his own existence." He relished solitary time "in the deepest recesses of his garden, or retired to muse and meditate in his chamber." There, he could write freely to his reader, as in direct speech, and at the same time "converse with beings of his own creation," whom he "described with a pencil dipt in the colours of imagination." Although "at present little more than a Rhapsodist in theory," the narrator claimed to have returned recently from the wilderness along the Ohio River, where he had sought out "the most sequestered scenes, and in the depth of solitude and silence, audibly invoked the genius of the place to be present to my meditations."[31] According to Brown, the solitary writer developed an extravagant spontaneity and a detached candor about human foibles but displayed little of Livingston's sense of obligation to deliver to society the moral insights gleaned from rural retreat.

Motifs of rural retreat and literary fancy bearing a family resemblance to those employed by Livingston and Brown were combined in *Reveries of a Bachelor* (1850), by Donald Grant Mitchell, writing under the pseudonym Ik Marvel. *Reveries* delighted the young Emily Dickinson, and, imitating Ik Marvel, she named her dog Carlo. Like William Livingston, Ik Marvel depicted his rural retreat as a quiet and humble country farmhouse. But, in the hands of the whimsical Mitchell, this bachelor's paradise had little in the way of Livingston's "rosiate bow'rs" and instead was notable chiefly for Marvel's "comfort in treating it just as I choose. I manage to break some article of furniture, almost every time I pay it a visit; and if I cannot open the window readily of a morning to breathe the fresh air, I knock out a pane or two of glass with my boot." Throughout, in fact, the predominating feature of the bachelor's rural retreat was the freedom it afforded to pursue "floating visions" and "whimseys," which "a great many brother bachelors are apt to indulge in" but are "too prudent to lay before the world," as, for instance, in Marvel's extended ruminations on the similarities between love and the lighting of a cigar. Although with a decidedly irreverent flair, Mitchell—like William Livingston and even Jonathan Edwards—composed his idyllic scenes as places in which the honest affections of the heart could be truly disclosed. Brown had clearly written the Rhapsodist series with a print audience in mind, but his portrayal nonetheless accentuated the candor and affective spontaneity that were customarily attributed to private writing. Most significantly in relation to Emily Dickinson, Mitchell's Ik Marvel declared that letters were "the only true heart-talkers." Whereas public speech degenerated into "conventional" views that were "moulded" by the immediately surrounding circumstances, in the solitary composition of a letter, "your soul is measuring itself by itself, and saying its own sayings."[32]

By 1860, when Dickinson had fully immersed herself in writing poetry, these various interpretations of solitude—evangelical, philosophical, literary—were circulating widely, albeit confusedly, in American popular culture. In that year, for instance, J. A. Turner contributed to the popular magazine *Godey's Lady's Book* the poem "Solitude," which cobbled together most of the themes I have just reviewed. Contrasting the "harsh" voices of society with "nature's whispers," the poet appealed, "Let me, escaping life's turmoil / One moment go where peace abides."

> *With nature would I spend an hour,*
> *With towering hill and humble sod,*
> *With barren rock and gaudy flower—*
> *For all record the hand of God.*

An inner voice had called the poet into nature, and when nature responded with gentle sounds of its own, the refugee from society discovered that "nature's spirit blends" with the human spirit. Renewed, the poet returned to society prepared to do battle for honor, right, virtue, and justice.

> *Baptized in nature's holy fire,*
> *And armed to meet the storms of life,*
> *Go fling away the timid lyre,*
> *And strike the higher notes of strife.*

The tranquil order of nature had focused the poet on the necessity of virtuous social strife, and the poem concluded in pious assurances that even with the arrival of death's "oblivion," heaven would assure "Thy deeds of good shall never die."[33] In sentimental verse of this sort, nature became a sanctuary, where periodic escape supplied restorative power for the continuation of social life. Not only had this attenuated Jonathan Edwards's ceaseless discipline of self-interrogation, it had even deflected the force of Ik Marvel's rebellious boot through the windowpane. Convention had co-opted the resistance of solitude.

THE ARTISTIC PROTEST

Writing to Margaret Fuller in 1840, Ralph Waldo Emerson remarked on her extended stay, along with other friends of theirs, at his home in Concord. The stimulation of the visit had been engaging, he admitted, but he emphatically pronounced his preference for the solitude he now enjoyed. Both in this letter and in other writings of the period, Emerson made it clear that solitariness was neither simply a personal idiosyncrasy nor merely a practical requirement for preparing the public lectures that provided him income. Instead, solitude was the fulcrum for an entire life regimen and the central necessity for the intellectual life. The regimen of solitude cultivated the standpoint toward society, the attentiveness to experience, and the self-possession that made possible distinctive literary expression. Solitude was the setting for raising and resolving the vocational question of being a writer, an artist, and an intellectual. Further, even though Emerson and his wife, Lydian, had absented themselves from church membership, this life regimen had a decidedly religious cast. Solitude cleared the space within which a direct encounter with the Absolute might occur; it was a place where Emerson the writer might find himself, as he explained to Fuller, "alone with the Alone."[34] By this phrase, adapted from Plotinus, Emerson signaled that, like Jonathan Edwards, he aimed to make solitude the basis for organizing a way of life. Also like Edwards, the act of writing became the bridge between solitude in nature and Emerson's public role as a religious thinker, essayist, and orator. But beyond these formal similarities, important differences emerge in the way these two thinkers envisioned the individual person's placement in society and the natural environment, and these differences are instructive for understanding Emily Dickinson's solitude.

In January 1839, Emerson delivered a lecture entitled "The Protest." It was the sixth in a series entitled Human Life, first delivered at the Masonic Temple, Boston, and repeated the following spring in Concord. In composing "The Protest," Emerson drew heavily from his private journals for 1838, and the lecture's central themes anticipated two of his best-known essays of the 1840s, "Circles" and "The Transcendentalist." As its title implied, Emerson devoted the lecture to extolling the necessity of solitary protest against social customs and conventions. It displayed his characteristic tendency to draw a sharp contrast between solitude and society and to identify the divine presence with the former. "God the Soul says one thing," he declared, while "the whole world says or seems to say another." In his conclusion, he acknowledged the likely objection from his audience that "I go too much alone" but replied that protest was the indispensable first step before any artist, writer, or intellectual "begins to affirm." Emerson had advocated shunning society, he explained, only in the hope of finding society: "I quit a society which is no longer one. I repudiate the false out of love of the true. I go alone that I may meet my brother as I ought." Only through silent resistance would authentic speech arise, and when a true word was uttered in "the midst of society," its source would have been "nothing but austerest solitude and conversation with God, with love, with death."[35]

The imaginary protagonist of the lecture was "the young person" or "the heart of Youth," impatient with the constraints of social custom. This figure recalled for Emerson an observation by Samuel Johnson that "there were no men of entirely sane mind; that every man was tainted with some vein of extravagance which spoiled the harmony of his character." Here, Johnson had playfully invoked "the Enlightenment model of the balanced character, in which reason reigned supreme over the passions" in a well-formed self. Emerson, however, immediately turned the seeming flaw of extravagance into life's prime virtue, the distinctive trait that made "every man and every woman in the planet a new experiment, to be and exhibit the full and perfect soul, and so we may count near a thousand million contemporary experiments." But such experimentation was constantly thwarted, because there existed "an ill-concealed diversity of aim, of religion, of theory of life between every newly arrived soul and the existing population of the planet and it is always breaking out afresh." In his lecture, Emerson proposed to expose this generational "Dissension," by pressing one question to his audience: "Will you fulfil the demands of the soul or will you yield yourself to the conventions of the world?"[36]

Resistance against the authoritative strictures of tradition cleared space for artistic experimentation. Indeed, spatial metaphors and allusions were intrinsic to Emerson's intellectual project of locating the intellectual on the boundary of conventional society. He made the point for his own life and intellectual vocation in a journal entry for September 1840, which later found its way into the essay "Circles": "Let me remind the reader that I am only an experimenter. Do not set the least value on what I do, or the least credit on what I do not, as if I pretended to settle any thing as true or false. I unsettle all things. No facts are to me sacred; none are profane; I simply experiment, an endless seeker, with no Past at my back."[37] At the opening of *Walden*, Emerson's younger friend and sometime boarder, Henry David Thoreau, pressed intellectual resistance still further, renouncing not merely the misguided veneration of prior generations but the generations themselves.

> Practically, the old have no very important advice to give the young, their own experience has been so partial, and their lives have been such miserable failures, for private reasons as they must believe. . . . I have lived some thirty years on this planet, and I have yet to hear the first syllable of valuable or even earnest advice from my seniors. They have told me nothing, and probably cannot tell me anything to the purpose. Here is life, an experiment to a great extent untried by me; but it does not avail me that they have tried it.[38]

Like Emerson in "The Protest," Thoreau here recast resistance as an *experiment*, tried as if for the first time, by a thinker whose own life was the experiment. Intellectual resistance, which must precede becoming an artist, presumed that the form of the artistic life could not be known in advance and must be sought by daring to live experimentally toward it.

Jonathan Edwards had also regarded society as a threat to the self, but he had pictured this threat as the "soul wounding" diversion of attention, away from the glory of God and toward "temporal concerns." Emerson identified the threat to the self as the imposition of social conventions that obscured a person's elemental individuality, and this central theme from "The Protest" was prominent throughout his essays and lectures of the late 1830s and early 1840s. Using Emerson's early writings (with assistance from Thoreau), I want to focus on this metaphor of the self—my life is an experiment—and probe its metaphorical connections to society and cosmos. In Emerson's case, the life experiment of resistance against social convention took the specific form of resistance against his own continuance in the ministry, and he had concluded by 1832 that "the best part of a man" revolts against the ministerial vocation, because "his good revolts against official goodness."[39] By emphasizing individual experimentation, Emerson did not, however, recommend sheer eccentricity for its own sake. Instead, the self-disciplined cultivation of a distinctive perspective on human nature and democratic citizenship constituted precisely the thinker's contribution to the commonweal. The lived experiment, according to a typically grand Emersonian analogy, was like the wave that washed farther up the beach than any preceding and thereby prefigured the advance of the whole sea to that point and beyond. In this sense the intellectual life was lived prospectively, as an experiment on behalf of the society in which the American scholar participated, anticipating—even representing—the possibilities of democratic citizenship for the nation. To borrow a phrase from Thoreau's *Walden*, Emerson acted on the principle that "the philosopher is in advance of his age even in the outward form of his life."[40]

The guarantor that emboldened this representative individuality was Emerson's philosophy of the unity of nature. "Self-reliance" was, in fact, reliance on the currents of nature, "whose floods of life stream around and through us, and invite us by the powers they supply, to action proportioned to nature."[41] Solitude could place the individual in reciprocal relations with the inward vital force of the universe and, through this act of mediation, raise the possibility of transforming society. Emerson asked, "what is the passionate love of nature that distinguishes all men of a poetic and susceptible constitution but an accusation of Society?" And characteristically he answered his own question through an image of the self oriented in space: "In the garden the eye watches the flying cloud and the distant woods but turns from the village. . . . The truth in Nature is loved by what is best in us. It is loved as the city of God although or rather because there is no citizen. . . . Carlyle and others who complain of the sickly separation of the beauty of nature in this age from the thing to be done do not see that our hunting of the picturesque is inseparable from our protest against false society. Man is fallen but Nature is unfallen."[42]

Throughout his early lectures and essays, Emerson thus set H. Richard Niebuhr's three domains—self, society, and ultimate environment—in a specific relation to one another. The protest pursued by living life experimentally pitted two of these domains against the third, society. By drawing intellectual power from "action proportioned to nature," the writer and the artist established a critical distance on society, from which to appraise its moral or spiritual condition. Images of a spectator in natural space suffused Emerson's rhetoric, as when "the eye" followed "the flying cloud" and in so doing turned its gaze away from "the village." The immediate experience of generative "floods of life" obviated the need for accumulated social experience and enabled the experimenter to live "with no Past at my back."

Resistant intellectual consciousness sufficient to contend with the danger that you might "yield yourself to the conventions of the world" is hard won, and never won fully. In order that resistance might have space to mature into intellectual artistry, Emerson practiced a series of intellectual disciplines intended to create an imagined domain of critical independence. He thought of these as disciplines of solitude, especially solitude in nature. Among them, perhaps the most characteristic was what he called "my strong propensity for strolling. I deliberately shut up my books in a cloudy July noon, put on my old clothes and old hat and slink away to the whortleberry bushes and slip with the greatest satisfaction into a little cowpath where I am sure I can defy observation."[43] The purpose of his daily walks was, however, far less casual than the term "strolling" would suggest. Its aim was attentiveness to nature.

But this reciprocity of the self with nature was fragile and required that attentiveness be constant, in order to maintain a receptive mood in the observer of nature. Having attempted to shear away Puritanism's narrative of the self, which retrospectively discerned its contours through self-interrogation, Emerson's experiment left his sense of self dependent on the evocative power of immediate intuition. In Emerson's manuscript journals for August 1836, for example, he recorded an instance of this affective reciprocity with nature: "I went to Walden Pond this evening a little before sunset, and in the tranquil landscape I behold somewhat as beautiful as my own nature."[44] This experience of the self mirrored in the natural scene contrasted sharply with a journal entry from 1840, in which *lack* of such attentiveness to nature entailed a corresponding loss of the self.

> I went into the woods. I found myself not wholly present
> there. If I looked at a pine-tree or aster, *that* did not seem
> to be Nature. Nature was still elsewhere: this, or this was
> but outskirt and far-off reflection and echo of the triumph
> that had passed by and was now at its glancing splendor and
> heyday,—perchance in the neighboring fields, or, if I stood
> in the field, then in the adjacent woods. Always the pres-
> ent object gave me this sense of the stillness that follows a
> pageant that has just gone by.[45]

In such passages, Emerson made that which was most fleeting, ephemeral, and evanescent the emblem of the eternal, and his affirmations of the authority of the present moment were thus frequently laced with a rueful sense of loss.

As this suggests, Emerson recognized the profoundly unsettling implications of living "experimentally," with "no Past at my back." How does a person—repudiating the accumulated guidance of the past, mistrusting the mores of the present, and facing an indeterminate future—engage, with ethical and philosophical integrity, in what

Emerson called "the conduct of life"? Consider the opening paragraph of Emerson's essay "Experience," which he wrote some two years after the sudden and devastating death of his son, Waldo, from scarlet fever in January 1842.

> Where do we find ourselves? In a series of which we do not know the extremes, and believe that it has none. We wake and find ourselves on a stair; there are stairs below us, which we seem to have ascended; there are stairs above us, many a one, which go upward and out of sight. But the Genius which, according to the old belief, stands at the door by which we enter, and gives us the lethe to drink, that we may tell no tales, mixed the cup too strongly, and we cannot shake off the lethargy now at noonday. Sleep lingers all our lifetime about our eyes, as night hovers all day in the boughs of the fir-tree. All things swim and glitter. Our life is not so much threatened as our perception. Ghostlike we glide through nature, and should not know our place again.[46]

How does a person take up a stance or standpoint in this flux? This is a question not only of the form and meaning of the external world but also—and simultaneously—of the form and meaning of the self. The affectively charged perception of nature that Emerson considered the principal fruit of solitude became the starting point for vigorous nineteenth-century debates over the authorization of social criticism and the vocation of the intellectual.

NATURE AND SOLITUDE: A NINETEENTH-CENTURY DIALOGUE

Margaret Fuller, Frederick Douglass, and Emily Dickinson were three writers who agreed with Emerson that the intellectual vocation began with personal resistance—the protest—against constraining social norms. Also like Emerson, each represented the self as an astute observer of the natural scene. But, having appropriated the Emersonian repertoire of metaphors, each reassembled the repertoire in ways that made the experiment his or her own, partly by reconfiguring the motif of evanescence and loss that had accompanied Emerson's perception of the natural environment. In so doing, each of the three also delivered a significantly different challenge to the surrounding society. In something not unlike a spirited dinner conversation, Fuller, Douglass, and Dickinson may be seen—through Fuller's travel narrative, Douglass's autobiography, and Dickinson's poem—raising objections to specific phrases from the soliloquy on experimental lives that I have just strung together from Emerson's early lectures and essays.

The first rejoinder came from Margaret Fuller, when Emerson described himself as "an endless seeker, with no Past at my back." Fuller had spent three months traveling across the Great Lakes and central Illinois during the summer of 1843, with her friend the artist Sarah Clarke and Sarah's brother, James Freeman Clarke, later well known for his two-volume comparative study *Ten Great Religions* (1871, 1883). Encouraged by Emerson, Fuller wrote a narrative of her journey. Although *Summer on the Lakes* described the course of her travels—touring Niagara Falls, the boat ride to Chicago, following the Rock River into Illinois—Fuller focused primarily on the self-reflective experiences prompted by traversing the land. In the process of this meditative travelogue, she interjected tales and incidents that blurred the boundaries between journalistic account, fiction, and self-reflective meditation.

When (in my imaginary conversation) Emerson described himself as "an endless seeker, with no Past at my back," Fuller agreed with his affirmation of boundless possibility. "What is limitless is alone divine," she declared; "there was neither wall nor road in Eden." The Illinois prairie provided her many analogies to this Edenic limitless vista, but, in several telling passages, Fuller went on to compare the prairie to the carefully composed parks and lawns of an English estate. The prairie, in Fuller's imaginative redescription, bore "the character of country which has been inhabited by a nation skilled like the English in all the ornamental arts of life, especially in landscape gardening. That the villas and castles seem to have been burnt, the enclosures taken down, but the velvet lawns, the flower gardens, the stately parks, scattered at graceful intervals by the decorous hand of art, the frequent deer, and the peaceful herd of cattle make the pleasure of the plain, all suggest more the masterly mind of man, than the prodigal, but careless, motherly love of nature."[47]

In composing this fantasy narrative of the artfully composed land-scape that a vanished civilization had left behind, Fuller was fully aware that white settlers now occupied lands that had formerly belonged to the native peoples of the region, and *Summer on the Lakes* devoted considerable space to reflection on her encounters with native peoples and time spent in "Indian encampment." In these several accounts, Fuller developed recurrent images of the native culture embedded in the natural landscape itself. As she crossed Illinois, Fuller observed that "the ground above and below, is full of their traces," and "you have only to turn up the sod to find arrowheads and Indian pottery"; the timber still showed "the marks of their tomahawks." Later, in Wisconsin, she listened to the aversion that settlers expressed toward the Indians, and she imagined "an Indian gazing" toward the "fair hill, which contained for the exile the bones of his dead, the ashes of his hopes." In these sentimentalized vignettes (Fuller remarked that "the Indian cannot be looked at truly except by a poetic eye"), *Summer on the Lakes* overturned the timeless immediacy of nature by filling the seemingly vacant land-scape of the prairie with traces of human occupation, power, and loss. Far more the political activist than Emerson, Fuller realigned his vision of self, society, and nature in order to make the tacit argument that a vision of *pristine* nature could not serve as the fulcrum for intellectual agency because it occluded the social shaping of every vista. Whereas Emerson thought that "the natural" had the possibility of transforming "the social," Fuller depicted nature as both the site of human power and the repository of loss.[48]

One might imagine Frederick Douglass remaining quiet during this early part of the conversation, until Emerson proclaimed, "I quit a society which is no longer one. I repudiate the false out of love of the true." The immediate rejoinder from Douglass was that he had not decided to "quit" society and locate himself on its boundary; the institutions of slavery had firmly placed him there. Unlike Emerson, Douglass could not assume that his writing would find acceptance in public life, and his autobiography announced "written by himself" to refute suggestions that a white abolitionist had ghostwritten the book. Among the principal themes of Douglass's *Narrative*, he developed most fully and consistently the illusory quality of perception, including the human capacity for self-delusion. This motif of illusion revolved especially around human misperceptions of freedom. Douglass may be said to have doubted Emerson's confident distinction between the false society and the true.[49]

Emerson had recommended in "Man the Reformer" (1841) what he called "the doctrine of the Farm," which would return the idealist to an elemental relation to nature and to labor.[50] Despite his own decision not to participate in the utopian experiment at Brook Farm, Emerson advocated agricultural work as a discipline whereby the intellectual could reestablish connections between creative thinking and the natural sources of productive human activity. By such personal experiment, society too might be rebuilt from the inside out, shedding the conventional husk of a social order rapidly passing away and adopting a form more consonant with human nature itself and with the times.

But for Douglass farm labor represented alienation, not redemption. In contrast to Margaret Fuller, who affirmed that there were no "walls" in "Eden" and dramatically portrayed the seemingly limitless prairie vistas of Illinois, Douglass depicted farmland bordered round by fences and hiding places. The slave overseer Edward Covey was a taskmaster whose "*forte* consisted in his power to deceive" his laborers. Having pretended to ride away on horseback, Covey—a veritable snake in the garden—would shortly afterward be seen "coiled up in the corner of the wood-fence, watching every motion of the slaves." "Poor man!" Douglass concluded, "such was his disposition, and success at deceiving, I do verily believe that he sometimes deceived himself into the solemn belief, that he was a sincere worshipper of the most high God." Douglass retrospectively recognized that self-deception regularly befell not only Covey but also Douglass himself. During the year he had been leased out to Covey, Douglass remembered looking out across the Chesapeake Bay, an open panorama of freely moving ships: "those beautiful vessels, robed in purest white, so delightful to the eye of freemen, were to me so many shrouded ghosts, to terrify and torment me with the thoughts of my wretched condition." He recalled that while watching the ships, he felt compelled to address them directly in his hope for freedom "'You are loosed from your moorings, and are free; I am fast in my chains, and am a slave!'" But this sharp contrast between freedom and slavery proved to be Douglass's own self-deception. Having learned ship caulking in the shipyards of Baltimore, he had hoped to find work in the northern shipyards of New Bedford after he achieved his freedom. However, when he sought a job as a caulker, "such was the strength of prejudice against color, among the white calkers, that they refused to work with me, and of course I could get no employment."[51] While acknowledging Emerson's skepticism about "society," Douglass found no evidence that nature was "unprofaned" or "unfallen" in the way that Thoreau and Emerson had described it, and he mistrusted any natural vista that held seeming promise of crossing over into freedom.

Emily Dickinson found her attention especially captured by one sentence from Emerson: "I went to Walden Pond this evening a little before sunset, and in the tranquil landscape I behold somewhat as beautiful as my own nature." She shared Emerson's aesthetic appreciation of nature's beauty. Yet buried in many of her vivid images—both her poetry and her prose—were signals of the loss and deception enunciated in the writings of Fuller and Douglass. Still more important, Dickinson joined Emerson in emphasizing the affective connection between nature and the attentively engaged observer. Yet, while Emerson gained revelatory insight from the immediacy of this connection, Dickinson instead focused on changes that occurred in a natural scene over the passage of time, the course of a day or the cycle of seasons. This focus on extended observation, in turn, drew her attention to a different set of emotions, those that entailed temporal duration: anticipation, desire, and remorse, for example. Her attentiveness to accumulated experiences, memory, and disposition of the self in time aligned Dickinson with features of the retrospective spiritual disciplines that had been cultivated by the Puritans and Jonathan Edwards. Recalling in one of her letters a beautiful spring day she had shared with her cousin John Graves, she reported both the seasonal return of that beauty and the evidence that death accompanied new life; in the

corners of the spring garden lay "wings half turned to dust that flut-
tered so last year."[52] And many of Dickinson's most distinctive poems
trained attention on the aftermath of experience, as in one that began,
"After great pain, a formal feeling comes – / The Nerves sit ceremoni-
ous, like Tombs" (F372). In a poem that began, "There's a certain Slant
of light," Dickinson displaced the benign and generative nature that
Emerson had encountered in late afternoon at Walden Pond, chang-
ing both the season in which the poem was set and the mood that it
evoked, while, in her own way, retaining Emerson's insistence on the
emotional mirroring of self and nature.

> *There's a certain Slant of light,*
> *Winter Afternoons –*
> *That oppresses, like the Heft*
> *Of Cathedral Tunes –*
>
> *Heavenly Hurt, it gives us –*
> *We can find no scar,*
> *But internal Difference –*
> *Where the Meanings, are –*
>
> *None may teach it – Any –*
> *'Tis the Seal Despair –*
> *An imperial affliction*
> *Sent us of the Air –*
>
> *When it comes, the Landscape listens –*
> *Shadows – hold their breath –*
> *When it goes, 'tis like the Distance*
> *On the Look of Death –*
>
> (F320)

Both Emerson's meditations at Walden Pond and Dickinson's stan-
zas on a winter afternoon depicted the effect of light—late in the day—
on the inner affective state of a solitary observer. Reminiscent of Emer-
son, Dickinson also alluded to a threatening society—especially in its

religious dimensions—by casting the landscape in terms of cathedrals and empires that oppress and afflict. Emerson's journal entry made the bare assertion of the reciprocity between the self and the natural scene that he beheld "a little before sunset." Dickinson, in contrast, created a compressed narrative in which the gradual process of sunset is carried through to its conclusion. In so doing, Dickinson reversed Emerson's emotional response, by representing a landscape whose beauty evoked not tranquility but despair. Like the anthropomorphic "Shadows" that will disappear when light departs, the reader holds her breath, just before expiring.

Throughout their "discussion," Emerson, Fuller, Douglass, and Dickinson concurred that attentiveness to natural surroundings included an affective relationship between the observer and what was seen. They also agreed that this perception generated new insight, even if this insight did not quite rise to the level of Edwards's transformative "sense of the heart." Fuller, Douglass, and Dickinson disagreed, however, with Emerson's invocation of an "unfallen" nature that held possibility of redeeming the human spirit. All three emphasized in various ways the illusory quality of pristine nature and the power exerted in nature by a pervasive human presence. The perception of nature remained fraught in Dickinson's poetry, even when she was celebrating nature's beauty and affective power.

In 1924, Martha Dickinson Bianchi, the daughter of Austin and Susan Dickinson, published *The Life and Letters of Emily Dickinson*, which included both a brief biography, with reminiscences of family and friends, and a chronological arrangement of selected letters. Bianchi chose to preface the book and conclude its biographical portion with two poems in which Dickinson reflected on the qualities of solitude as, on the one hand, withdrawal from society and, on the other hand, separation from the companion. Bianchi explained that she wrote to inform a public that, while increasingly fascinated by Dickinson's poetry, "misunderstood and exaggerated her seclusion." Despite this admonition, when Bianchi selected the prefatory poem, in which Dickinson "supplies the only clue to herself, the articles of her Faith," it was this.[53]

The Soul's Superior instants
Occur to Her — alone —
When friend — and Earth's occasion
Have infinite withdrawn —

Or she — Herself — ascended
To too remote a Hight
For lower Recognition
Than Her Omnipotent —

This Mortal Abolition
Is seldom — but as fair
As Apparition — subject
To Autocratic Air —

Eternity's disclosure
To favorites — a few —
Of the Colossal substance
Of Immortality

(F630)

With respect to the religious traditions of solitude, it is, of course, notable that the poem reiterated the "Soul's Superior instants" as both a withdrawal and an ascent to heights that were too distant for "lower Recognition," where eternity would disclose secrets to a favored few. In addition, I would emphasize that these "Superior instants" were "seldom." In the religious and literary background to Dickinson's solitude, the retreat into solitude was a regimen of reorientation, intended to set the moral compass for engagement with society. Solitude, on such terms, included its "Superior instants" in which it was captured by the "new sense" or by the currents of nature "whose floods of life stream around and through us." But such moments—clearly represented in this poem—did not lead Dickinson into social activism but rather into more continuous withdrawal and seclusion, the "renunciation" that Judith Farr has described so persuasively.

At the end of her biography, Bianchi quoted a single stanza that her mother, Susan Gilbert Dickinson, had used to conclude the obituary of Emily Dickinson that she had written for the *Springfield Republican*.[54]

> *Morns like these — we parted.*
> *Noons like these — she rose*
> *Fluttering first — then firmer —*
> *To her fair repose.*

(F18b)

In this poem of a bird (or a soul) fluttering to "her fair repose," Dickinson had drawn on another dimension of the traditions of solitude, one that I have illustrated through the evangelical piety of Jonathan Edwards. In this case, meditations on the meaning of solitude revolved around the desire for perfect intimacy with the companion or with God, and they portrayed mortal life as a separation—or series of separations—that did not diminish but rather heightened the desire for communion, including, for Edwards, the perfect communion of heaven. As Edwards's views implied and as Susan Dickinson clearly recognized, the paradigmatic form of solitude-as-separation was the separation imposed by death. As Dickinson continued the poem, the parting at death became a progressively stronger motif, a separation that compelled silence: the one who "parted" was "mute from transport," and the one who remained behind was mute "from agony." And a day unfolded, from morning, through noon, until evening neared, when a veil parted between two realms: "One the Curtains drew — / Quick! A sharper rustling! / And this Linnet flew!" Although the solitary ecstasy of the "Soul's Superior instants" made its appearance in many of Dickinson's poems, I think that this second connotation of solitude as separation and a sense of absence predominated. It may even be the case, as Michel de Certeau has suggested with respect to seventeenth-century spirituality, that the sensation of an absence or an empty space is what initially prompts the search in solitude. "The One is no longer to be found," writes Certeau, and the quest for what is missing fills solitude "with the story of his loss, the history of his returns elsewhere and otherwise, in ways that are the effect rather than the refutation of his absence."[55]

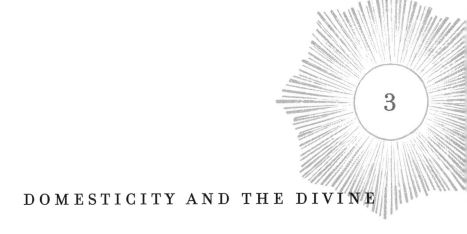

DOMESTICITY AND THE DIVINE

Whereas Emerson had sought artistic inspiration by venturing into the solitude of nature, Emily Dickinson gradually retreated into the solitude of her family home. Like Emerson and Thoreau, Dickinson took obvious delight in her natural surroundings and acutely observed natural forms and rhythms; her letters were crowded with flowers from her garden, birds, a whole collection of insects, excited reports on the transition from one season to the next, and youthful sleigh rides across New England's snow-covered landscape. And, like Emerson, she early developed a propensity for "strolling" in woods and meadows. "I think you would like the Chestnut Tree, I met in my walk," she wrote to Thomas Wentworth Higginson. But, as described in chapter 2, Emerson portrayed the person of "poetic sensibilities" leaving society, the village, and the house in order to enter a separate natural domain. In contrast, Dickinson wrote about nature as an integral part of her domestic surroundings. During the poet's lifetime, the Dickinson property amounted to a small farm of fourteen acres, including a barn, orchard, gardens, and a meadow.[1] Nature surrounded her as she worked in her garden; she composed it in displays of cut flowers; she watched intently from her window. Her practice of solitude, in short, accentuated the character of her daily life as seclusion in a domestic landscape. The house was her vantage point on nature.

Withdrawing into the Homestead established a space within which Dickinson could pursue her vocation as a writer. Ironically, however, when Dickinson "departed" from society to discover creative independence in house and garden, she did so at a historical moment when the wider culture was ever more carefully defining this domestic sphere and woman's role within it. Her pursuit of solitary creative space thus came into daily tension with the social fabrication of the domestic sphere and the ordered placement of women within that sphere. She had pursued freedom from social expectations into a domestic environment that overflowed with such expectations.

Even as conformity and creativity competed within this domestic arena, Dickinson's principal experiential resources for composing her poetry came from her engagement in household routines. Cooking, cleaning, gardening, playing the piano, reading, and writing letters organized her daily regimen. The house surrounded her with furnishings, interior spaces, and lines of sight: its windows and doors, walls and intimate corners, clocks and couches, flowers, and the play of light in late afternoon all became writing material. When she was unable to supply Thomas Wentworth Higginson with a portrait of herself, she improvised from her surroundings: she was "small, like a Wren, and my Hair is bold, like the Chestnut Bur—and my eyes, like the Sherry in the Glass, that the Guest leaves—Would this do just as well?"[2] Throughout the course of days and seasons, Dickinson was minutely observing the details of the house, its landscape, and the intimate friendships and sometimes difficult family relationships that occurred in this domestic terrain. She refracted these quotidian scenes through images that she drew from her expansive reading in newspapers, magazines, and current fiction. Dickinson's letters demonstrate that she read regularly in the King James Bible and Shakespeare, favored the poetry of the Brownings, and thoroughly absorbed novels by Longfellow, Hawthorne, and George Eliot. By the 1860s the family was subscribing to fifteen newspapers and magazines, ranging from the *Springfield Daily Republican* to *Harper's Magazine*.[3] She inventively combined household experiences and literary resources to create the metaphors and metonymies of her poetry. Even while declaring that she had "never seen 'Volcanoes,'" Dickinson imaginatively transformed their constrained explosiveness into a comment on interior pain: "the stillness is Volcanic / In the human face / When upon a pain Titanic / Features keep their place" (F165).

In sum, the nineteenth-century domestic sphere not only structured Dickinson's daily life but also supplied the repertoire of tropes and images she deployed as a writer. In her decision for solitude, she both inhabited the domestic sphere and resisted it. The middle-class prosperity and sense of civic duty that marked the Dickinson family not only afforded the privileged privacy within which Dickinson produced her poetry but also instilled an ethic of obligation to "improve" that private time in reading, writing, music, and reflection.[4] By pursuing her writing in the politically and socially active Dickinson household, Dickinson's domestic solitude was obviously quite different from the isolated cottages—rural utopias—that the writings of William Livingston, Charles Brockden Brown, Donald Grant Mitchell, and Henry David Thoreau portrayed as the ideal locale for solitary writing and reflection. For this reason, this chapter begins by exploring house and garden as a domain painstakingly ordered by the wider society to shape the daily life, public responsibilities, and sense of personal interiority of those who occupied it. Dickinson, like other women writers of her era, bent the social expectations of domesticity toward her solitary vocation as a poet, constructing solitary space for her poetry workshop and co-opting scenes from the domestic sphere for her poetic imagery. In so doing, Dickinson transformed the residential landscape into metaphors of the self and the work of writing poetry.

RELIGION WITHIN NEW ENGLAND'S DOMESTIC SPHERE

Household symbolism was, of course, no new thing in either poetry or religion. For generations, the house, interior spaces, and domestic routine had provided New England writers with a large repository of religiously inflected symbols and metaphors. Devotional poets of seventeenth-century New England such as Roger Williams, Anne Bradstreet, and Edward Taylor had commended private devotions and "secret prayer" through images of devotional seclusion derived from the "house well ordered, swept, and garnished" and the "closet" of prayer. To identify the human self as an instrument of divine purpose, Edward Taylor opened a poem entitled "Huswifery" with the appeal "Make me, O Lord, thy Spining Wheele complete."[5] When these Puritan poets turned from household images to employ symbols derived from nature, it was usually nature transformed by human agency: "husbandry spiritualized" in the grafting of fruit trees in an orchard or the tastes of a meal, or the bridal imagery of sexual relations transformed into a marriage covenant. Furthermore, since the conversion process had been absolutely central to the Puritan doctrine of the church, New England's classic platforms of church government similarly depicted the church member as a rough timber or stone, now hewn, shaped, and polished so as to fit into the spiritual edifice of the church.[6] By contrast, nature untouched by European craft and husbandry frequently represented to these seventeenth-century authors the wilderness of religious danger and privation, as in Mary Rowlandson's famous captivity narrative *The Sovereignty and Goodness of God* (1682).

Among New England poets of the early nineteenth century, Lydia Huntley Sigourney (1791–1865) perhaps most effectively revised the domestic symbolism that had characterized colonial meditative poetry in order to reflect a new economic and cultural situation. In her apostrophe "To a Shred of Linen," Sigourney announced in mock horror the offense against good housekeeping that had left this scrap of fabric littering the floor—the unfortunate consequence, no doubt, of a homemaker who spent too much time *"reading books"* or *"writing poetry."* Shifting her attention away from this feigned scandal, Sigourney wondered about the origin of the linen and the colonial woman whose "dexterous hand" had turned the spinning wheel, the woman whose cloth and butter "to the market borne" had contributed to the colonial economy. Sigourney transformed the linen scrap into the relic of a bygone domestic culture, the product of a spinning wheel that New England's middle-class refinement had now "quite displaced" in favor of a sofa and piano. "What was thy lot," Sigourney asked the shred of linen, after you were taken from the loom and bleached in the sun? Perhaps the linen had become a pillowcase that greeted notable visitors in "the best chamber" of the house or intuited from a "young beauty's restless sigh" her "tale of untold love." But, holding its memories in secret, the shred of linen was now fit only to be cast

> *Into the paper mill, and from its jaws,*
> *Stainless and smooth, emerge.—Happy shall be*
> *The renovation, if on thy fair page*
> *Wisdom and truth, their hallow'd lineaments*
> *Trace for posterity. So shall thine end*
> *Be better than thy birth, and worthier bard*
> *Thine apotheosis immortalize.*

With wit and a certain light-handed poignancy, Sigourney captured many of the themes of this chapter and those that follow: a nostalgic awareness of New England's transition to a new market economy, the implications of that new economy for women's domestic role, and the metaphorical parallels between the linen's resurrection—"renovation"—into writing paper and a writer's own striving toward immortality.[7]

During Lydia Sigourney's lifetime, from the 1790s to the 1860s, the economic transition from an era of household agricultural production to an industrial and commercial economy had gradually altered the domestic roles and responsibilities of men and women. Mechanized production of consumer goods not only drew men away from the household into wage labor but further separated the home from the economic realm by taking over many of its traditional tasks, such as weaving clothing and making shoes. In what Charles Sellers has described as a market revolution, "women lost their traditional status and authority as skilled producers of a vital half or more of family livelihood." By midcentury, commercially produced carpets, bookcases, clocks, and other household furnishings were readily transported by canal and railroad to meet growing domestic demand. Middle-class society was consolidating, and its daily patterns of living were becoming more comfortable, from the installation of cast-iron stoves that circulated heat more efficiently to the growing attention to fashionable clothing.[8] The spinning wheel of Sigourney's poem was fast becoming an antique. Meanwhile, even in a small town such as Emily Dickinson's Amherst, law, medicine, ministry, and the college professoriate were undergoing a gradual professionalization. Hence, although Dickinson and her contemporaries—both women and men—continued to use domestic imagery in their writings, they did so within a society in which domesticity was accumulating new and distinctive layers of religious and cultural meaning.

As Sigourney's "To a Shred of Linen" demonstrated, traditional domestic metaphors such as the spinning wheel and the weaving shuttle persisted in a revised form that addressed the nineteenth-century context. In the late seventeenth century, Edward Taylor's "Huswifery" had identified the human self as God's spinning wheel and loom, and Taylor prayed that God would "weave the Web thyselfe. The yarn is fine."[9] In 1855, Emily Dickinson employed this same trope—the woven threads of one's lifetime—in a letter to Susan Gilbert, about a year before Susan's marriage to Dickinson's brother, Austin. Referring generically to household chores, Dickinson promised, "I'll get 'my spinning done,' for Susie." She then shifted into meditative metaphor, remarking, "it steals over me once in a little while, that as my fingers fly and I am so busy, a far more wondrous Shuttle shifts the subtler thread, and when *that's* web is spun, *indeed my* spinning will be done."[10]

Alongside the classic religious metaphors, in which household labor represented the spiritual history of the self, an expanding market for consumer goods provoked the classic religious worries. Might the enjoyment of modern comforts dissipate into the spiritual hazards of luxury and worldliness? In sermons, advice literature, and edifying fiction, Dickinson's contemporaries cautioned against acquisitiveness and merely monetary evaluation of household goods. To combat these dangers, they advised that household furnishings should be cherished for the memories and enduring personal attachments they signified; "sentimental possession" would thus preserve the home from sheer acquisitiveness. In Harriet Beecher Stowe's fiction particularly, the house became a spiritually animated space, and consumer goods acquired a "quasi-spiritual significance" emblematic of the affective connections among friends and family, both living and dead.[11] Metaphorical identification between domestic furnishings and familial sentiment became commonplace, and Emily Dickinson readily employed these tropes in her letters. When, for example, she wrote encouraging her younger cousin Louise Norcross to pay a visit, Dickinson reminded Louise, "I keep an ottoman in my heart exclusively for you."[12]

Such transvaluations of consumer goods were accompanied by new ideas about residential architecture, which similarly translated domestic symbolism into a new cultural idiom. In the 1840s the popular magazine *Godey's Lady's Book*, together with other publications, began printing house plans. One such plan, from *The Architecture of Country Houses* (1850) by the prominent residential architect Andrew Jackson Downing, was adapted for the construction of Austin and Susan Dickinson's home, the Evergreens, a wooden Italianate villa built next door to the Dickinson Homestead in 1856. Downing had succinctly enunciated his principle of design: "a man's home translated his individual personality into a material statement." To accomplish this melding of person and residence, popular architectural patterns by Downing and others symbolically organized the middle-class house, especially its parlor and study, in ways that ascribed gendered meanings to privacy, intimacy, and hospitality. The study represented a man's solitary retreat. The parlor, by contrast, became a woman's space for cultivating the emotional bonds of family and welcoming guests, who would be drawn by "the magnetic force of the wife and mother's affections." Thus, in addition to the public-private boundary, equally important gendered divisions developed within the private sphere itself, delimiting women's domestic spaces by norms of hospitality rather than privacy. In the process of symbolically reinforcing gender roles and conceptions of privacy, midcentury residential designs functioned as metaphors for subjective interiority, communicative intimacy, and empathy.[13] In domestic spaces, issues of public and private, solitude and sociability, were being worked out simultaneously, and the tensions opened many avenues for literary elaboration. When Nathaniel Hawthorne's narrator began *The House of the Seven Gables* by observing that "the aspect of the venerable mansion has always affected me like a human countenance," his opening analogy set the stage for the novel's innumerable subsequent tropes connecting personal identity with the interior furnishings and external façade of a house.[14]

SELF-CULTURE

At the same time that ministers, educators, and journalists sought to codify women's roles in family and religion, they also identified domestic spaces—untainted by the public world of commerce and political faction—with possibilities for individual expression and the cultivation of a more authentic self. Domestic privacy, so these various advisers to the public culture declared, afforded opportunities for reading, letter writing, diary keeping, and close personal conversation that not only deepened self-awareness but also elevated the self into awareness of the ultimate and divine. Within limits, therefore, mid-century ideals of domesticity extolled the cultivation of individuality as the definitively religious labor that built a person who would contribute to civil society. In a famous public lecture in 1838, the Unitarian minister William Ellery Channing (1780–1842) defined this process as "self-culture."

Channing declared that self-improvement was within the reach of every person, since "the true greatness of human life" did not consist in the magnitude of public economic or political influence but rather "in force of soul, that is, in the force of thought, moral principle, and love, and this may be found in the humblest condition of life." He thought it likely that "the greatest in our city at this moment" labored in obscurity: "How often does the pious heart of woman mingle the greatest of all thoughts, that of God, with household drudgery!" Accordingly, Channing announced, he was addressing persons from every station of life on a subject of crucial importance: "Self-culture, or the care which every man owes to himself, to the unfolding and perfecting of his nature."[15]

Channing thought that two powers of the soul made self-culture possible. One was the capacity for self-searching, in which the mind turned in on itself, "recalling its past, and watching its present operations" in order to learn "what it can do and bear, what it can enjoy and suffer," and thereby discovering its distinctive nature and purpose. To this vestige of Puritan retrospective piety, he added a second, "still nobler power," the capacity for self-forming. In Channing's view, people vastly underestimated "the energy which the mind is created to exert on the material world. It transcends in importance all our power over outward nature. There is more of divinity in it than in the force which impels the outward universe." This self-forming energy was—at least latently—moral and religious. It revered "impartial justice and universal good-will," and it could not be content with "what we see and handle" but rather "seeks for the Infinite, Uncreated Cause" and "cannot rest till it ascend to the Eternal, All-comprehending Mind." Channing assured his audience that, in this never-ending pursuit of the eternal in and through the finite world, self-culture would discover that it simultaneously pursued the true self: "the beauty of the outward creation is intimately related to the lovely, grand, interesting attributes of the soul." When people recognized that the material universe was "the emblem or expression" of the soul, nature seemed "to lose its material aspect, its inertness, finiteness, and grossness, and by the ethereal lightness of its forms and motions seems to approach spirit."[16] This aesthetic elevation of self and nature toward the divine resonated with comparable themes in Jonathan Edwards and Ralph Waldo Emerson, especially in its emphasis on a distinctive spiritual attentiveness to "the outward creation." Self-culture transformed the person in large measure by transforming perception, awakening a vibrant reciprocity between the self and the natural order and, in the process, opening an avenue "to approach spirit."

Reading was the universally advised means of gathering self-culture's mental energies and directing them toward the improvement of society. Channing emphatically agreed. It was a signal condition of the times, he asserted, that books now circulated "through all conditions of society" rather than being "confined to a few by their costliness." This democratic accessibility was bringing about a "highly favorable" change of habits throughout American culture. Books were becoming "the true levelers" of a democratic society. "Instead of forming their judgments in crowds, and receiving their chief excitement" from the impassioned voices of their neighbors, "men are now learning to study and reflect alone." Solitary reading, Channing emphasized, enabled them "to follow out subjects continuously, to determine for themselves what shall engage their minds," and he forecasted that the result would be "a deliberateness and independence of judgment, and a thoroughness and extent of information, unknown in former times." Careful study of books thus instilled one of "the chief arts of self-culture," a capacity to welcome "light from every human being who can give it" combined with "manly resistance of opinions however current, of influences however generally revered, which do not approve themselves to our deliberate judgment." Despite his democratic affirmations, however, Channing imagined that the reading public would study a tightly defined canon "with fixed attention and a reverential love of truth." In his view, the aim of reading was "intercourse with superior minds," especially Milton, Shakespeare, Franklin, and the "Sacred Writers."[17] Since, in this ideology, the divine spirit harmonized all creation, it followed that individual souls caught up in "a reverential love of truth" were themselves on the path toward social harmony.

But Channing's assumptions were becoming antiquated as he spoke. In the early decades of the nineteenth century, readers were shifting from the intensive reading of a few texts to the extensive reading of many books, one after another. Extensive reading, Cathy Davidson has argued, "can signify a new relationship of audience to authority," since readers enjoyed expanded choices, and their demand for choice, in turn, propelled the expanded production of literary works. According to Davidson, the antebellum advocacy of reading as the foundation of domestic self-culture indirectly generated "an increased sense of autonomy and an education not necessarily grounded in theocracy but democracy."[18] Channing's list of recommended authors, it should be noted, did not include novelists. President Hitchcock of Amherst College shared Channing's skepticism about the moral value of fiction, and Edward Dickinson, to his chagrin, failed in his efforts to regulate the flow of novels smuggled into his home and read avidly by Austin, Emily, and Lavinia Dickinson.[19]

Thus self-culture aimed to foster the individuality of men and women but to do so within the limits of a broad cultural consensus.

Despite Channing's conviction that independence of mind was the bulwark of public order against the impassioned opinions of "crowds," his assumption that such socially harmonious independence arose from private reading and reflection inadvertently left numerous doors ajar for the entrance of diverse judgment and expression. This was especially the case for middle-class women. Both the earnest but rather haphazard approach to women's formal education and the self-education that occurred through reading, letter writing, diary entries, or reconsidering the morning sermon did not always follow the approved avenues of societal norms. Encouraged toward domestic practices of self-culture, women sometimes pursued Channing's advice more assiduously than he had intended. Harmonious agreement was not the result. Throughout the middle decades of the century, both the churches and the wider society ceaselessly debated the appropriate boundaries for women's public roles as social activists, public orators, and published authors. The home—as the symbolic matrix of both gender roles and individual self-culture—became central to these debates.

In the process of setting and testing these behavioral boundaries, Dickinson and her contemporaries related personal goals and desires to the socially approved norms of female behavior in various ways, and the range of these experiments could and did reshape the religious institutions and cultural conventions of the era. As the social theorist and scholar of comparative literature Michel de Certeau observed, the collection of ideas and symbols in a cultural system are by no means fully systematized. Thus those living within such cultural systems can engage in "dispersed, tactical, and makeshift creativity" that shifts the boundaries of "natural" behavior, redistributes power or influence from one group to another, or challenges the expected ways of using cultural symbols. In nineteenth-century America, tactical inventors of this sort usually made only modest departures from social expectation, devising what we might term a respectable individuality. But social activists, religious innovators, and writers sometimes recombined the inherited cultural symbols in ways that suggested these symbols' more radical possibilities. In the case of Emily Dickinson, domestic space included what Certeau described as a *"utopian* space," an imagined space that can become "a site of protest that is impregnable, because it is a nowhere, a utopia."[20] Like Thoreau's hut at Walden Pond, Dickinson's home could be as distant from Amherst "as many a region viewed nightly by astronomers." The domestic sphere inhabited by Emily Dickinson was thus composed of several layers of activity and symbolism: a culturally inscribed arena, which contained some built-in room for adaptive individual self-expression, and a utopian space in which one might imagine the possibility of absolute creativity. Inherent tensions among these layers propelled her creative aspirations as a writer. Conformity, adaptation, and utopian imagination intersected—and not infrequently clashed—in the *house* that functioned both as physical residence and as metaphor.

Since the nineteenth century provides a cornucopia of examples of religious innovation taking place *fully within* the overarching domestic ideology of "self-culture," I have selected two examples that illuminate the wider context in which Dickinson pursued her solitary vocation as a poet. The first example expands on the dictum of residential architect Andrew Jackson Downing that "a man's home translated his individual personality into a material statement." The second explores how innovations in popular religious practice could be justified by appealing to the commonplace assumption that the parlor was a place where women fulfilled their responsibility for domestic hospitality.

The residence as an extension of personal identity figured prominently in magazine columns that Henry Ward Beecher (1813–1887) wrote for the *New York Independent* and subsequently published as *Star Papers: Or, Experiences of Art and Nature*. One of the best-known Protestant preachers of the century, younger brother of Harriet Beecher Stowe, and member of a formidable family of religious writers and reformers, Beecher had graduated from Amherst in 1834 and returned afterward to preach and participate in the college's commencement exercises. In a *Star Papers* essay entitled "Building a House," Beecher asserted that "a house is the shape which a man's thoughts take when he imagines how he should like to live. Its interior is the measure of his social and domestic nature; its exterior, of his esthetic and artistic nature." Every man was, "in a small way, a creator," who sought to embody in material forms "our spirit—invisible and intangible."[21]

Believing that the vast majority of young men were "born poor, but determined to be rich," Beecher presented the process of building a house as the domestic analogue to public ambition. In the process of "making his fortune," the industrious man was also "making himself." Invoking the commonplace ideal of the self-made man, Beecher implied both that personal identity was consciously constructed and that, having successfully pursued self-improvement, such a man displayed his character through his achievements. In the same way that self-making was a process, making a house displayed in its exterior the interior character of its owner. With economic success, a house would grow organically according to the growing needs of a man and his family, and Beecher imagined each room added to meet a specific purpose and therefore exhibiting a "decided character." Beecher dismissed the merely "conventional houses" that resulted from "architect's plans" and "portfolios of what has been done." Instead, "a genuine house, an original house, a house that expresses the builder's inward idea of life in its social and domestic aspect, can not be *planned* for him; nor can he, all at once, sit down and plan it. It must be a result of his own growth." A genuine house displayed a personality with distinctive and diverse features: "doors should come upon you in unexpected places; little cosy rooms should surprise you in every direction." Such a house would embody "our fullest idea of comfort," and visitors would experience a "social largeness" when entering spacious halls that seemed "like open arms holding out a welcome." The individuality of an organically enlarging house, Beecher concluded, "never sprang full-grown from an architect's brain."[22]

Turning from the home's evolving design to its interior furnishings, Beecher identified "the great treasures of a dwelling." These objects bespoke the importance of generational continuity and intimacy: "the child's cradle, the grandmother's chair, the hearth and old-fashioned fire-place, the table, and the window." Although Beecher was ostensibly discussing the construction of a new house that expressed the expansive individual personality of a modern-day entrepreneur, his list of household "treasures" expressed something quite different: nostalgia for the spare simplicity of an "old-fashioned" earlier day, accommodating the generations around fireplace and table. The window seems to be the outlier on his list, but Beecher considered windows especially important: "they are designed to let the light in, and equally to let the sight out." Most important, they opened the house to the beauty of the natural order, and Beecher declared, "there are no such landscapes on canvas as those which you see through glass." Even though every human builder of a house was "in a small way, a creator," it was fitting that the house should look out onto nature, since all human construction (whether building a house or building a self) paled in comparison to the divine builder: "when all the works of man are ended, he has not approached the inexpressible beauty of God's architecture."[23] God, as absolute individuality, was his own architect whose "house" organically expressed himself.

At midcentury, conventional etiquette denominated the parlor and its hospitality the distinctive domain of women. Consequently, women not infrequently exerted their domestic authority by adapting this space of sociability to create opportunities for individual expression and religious innovation. In New York, the Methodist spiritual leader Phoebe Palmer (1807–1874) presided over an extraordinarily successful experiment with parlor piety. From 2:30 to 4:00 each Tuesday afternoon, Palmer welcomed the "Tuesday Meeting for the Promotion of Holiness" to the second-floor parlors of her home on Rivington Street. Between fifty and 150 persons, including men and women from several Protestant denominations, attended the weekly prayer meetings, where Palmer was assisted by her husband, the physician Walter Palmer, and by her sister, Sarah Langford. Although the prayer meetings were most notable for the active engagement of laity, several members of the clergy were generally present, and the prominent Methodist minister Nathan Bangs (1778–1862) frequently led the opening exercises, after which all present were "at liberty to speak, sing, or propose united prayer." Palmer's message stressed interior spirituality, and she maintained a close collaboration and friendship with Thomas C. Upham (1799–1872), the Congregationalist minister, educator, and poet whose *Principles of the Interior or Hidden Life* disseminated the experiential theology of the seventeenth-century French mystic and visionary Madame Guyon. By 1872, Palmer could look back across more than thirty years and record in her diary that the Tuesday meetings had drawn participants internationally and from every region of the United States. Manifestations of divine presence had been "glorious, beyond description," and God seemed to have taken up residence in Palmer's parlor: "Who am I, or what was my Father's house, that the ark of the Lord should so long abide in our house?" At the Tuesday meetings, Palmer recorded, "the old, yet ever new story of Jesus and His love" continued to be "told with unabated power," and in response "hearts glow with hallowed fire, and eyes are suffused with joyous tears." In her parlor, home and holy emotion combined. Songs of praise seemed a foretaste of "millennial glory" as they rose from "the hallowed spot" and blended "with the melodious hymns of those who have passed from its precincts to the city of our God,—Jerusalem the golden." Palmer's discrete leadership had expanded commonplace notions of the home as a religious haven centered on female devotion into a setting for women's religious agency. Her prayer meetings balanced the populist religious zeal of Methodism's early history with middle-class decorum, producing what the historian Kathryn Long has aptly described as "consecrated respectability."[24]

Phoebe Palmer's Tuesday Meeting was not a singular phenomenon. Parlor gatherings took various forms and readily adapted to a whole spectrum of religious styles and purposes within middle-class Protestant culture. Palmer's nineteenth-century biographer Richard Wheatley cited a Congregationalist journal in order to describe the informality of Palmer's prayer meetings and to distinguish them from comparable gatherings of less evangelical tenor. "The children of this world have their social gatherings, where, in intelligent, social converse, heart meets heart in unrestrained fellowship," Wheatley explained, and anyone could readily "conceive how undesirable any set forms would be under such circumstances." Comparing these gatherings to the Tuesday Meeting, Wheatley drew the analogy that Palmer's "social gathering is designed to be, in the religious world, answerable to this want of our social nature as children of the kingdom."[25] Although it would be anachronistic to assume that Wheatley understood these more "worldly" social gatherings as *secular*, they did reflect modes of Protestant religiosity at some remove from Palmer's vision of Christian fellowship. For example, Joan Hedrick, in her biography of Harriet Beecher Stowe, has portrayed the literary clubs that were a feature of Catharine and Harriet Beecher's youth in Litchfield, Connecticut, and later in Cincinnati, Ohio, where their father, Lyman Beecher, had assumed the presidency of Lane Seminary. In distinction from Palmer's emphasis on devotional practices, "men and women gathered in the parlor and read aloud their essays and poems," Hedrick comments, and "these literary gatherings provided entertainment, sociability, and a stimulus to amateur authors."[26]

Organized gatherings of this sort—the Semi-Colon Club of Cincinnati met every Monday evening at 7:30—built on the informal parlor routines of family life: singing, playing the piano, or reading letters and poems. The Beecher sisters composed prose and verse for club meetings as well as family gatherings, and these writings circulated among members of the family's social circle. What Hedrick has termed *parlor literature* was thus "an integral part of polite society and domestic culture." Providing an avenue from parlor performance to authorship, the literary club became "an important institution mediating between oral tradition and print culture."[27] As a young woman, Dickinson had participated in a "Reading Club," and such literary clubs remained active well after the Civil War. In contrast to Dickinson's gradual retreat into seclusion, her cousins Louise and Frances Norcross actively involved themselves in a range of social activities, including suffrage organizing, especially after they moved to Concord in 1874. There, they became members of the Concord Saturday Club, which regularly read together from unpublished literary manuscripts, although there is no record that the Norcross sisters shared any of Dickinson's writings with the club.[28]

There were limits to women's religious leadership in and through the hospitality of the parlor, and these boundaries varied according to region, social class, and religious affiliation. Although the parlor opened toward public life and civil society, it was not itself a fully public space. When women stepped directly into civil society, through preaching, social activism, or publication, they engendered controversy. Precisely to guard against such controversy, Palmer carefully pointed out that, when "addressing the people previous to the prayer-meeting services," she did not preach, "that is, not in a *technical* sense."[29] Since the 1830s, mainline ministers had objected to women preaching or even engaging in public prayer when men were present. Asahel Nettleton was among those clergymen who feared that women's praying in public "made an inlet to other innovations." These other innovations were indeed arising in multiple forms during the middle decades of the century, and the spectrum of controversial practices ranged from female preachers to women activists who became "platform speakers" on behalf of public causes, most controversially woman's rights and the abolition of slavery.[30]

Just as different Protestant groups set different boundaries for women's public speech, so they also held a range of views about the propriety of women's moving beyond the literary enterprises associated with parlor hospitality to engage in print publication. Phoebe Palmer entered the growing market for women's magazines in 1841, when she became the founding editor of the *Ladies' Repository*. Nonetheless, she placed strict limits on publishing her own prose and poetry: "I have never dared to give anything to the public, other than I have cause to believe would be for the glory of God." By contrast, equally ardent Protestant women such as Harriet Beecher Stowe, Susan Warner, and Elizabeth Stuart Phelps published novels that enjoyed striking popular success. Palmer's ambivalence about popular fiction was evident when she met Stowe and expressed uneasiness that Stowe would attempt to promote Christian holiness through the publication of novels. Despite Palmer's stated abhorrence of slavery, and especially of the atrocities "permitted by the North" under the Fugitive Slave Law, she recorded in her diary, in reference to a "religious interview" with Stowe in the summer of 1857, "I have always had misgivings in regard to Mrs. Stowe's fictitious writings, presenting as they do, in many portions, religious experiences in a fictitious garb. It always seems to me like doing evil that good may come." Thousands of religiously conscientious people, Palmer lamented, "now attend the theatre, who, before the appearance of 'Uncle Tom's Cabin,' would have abhorred the thought, as utterly at variance with their religious profession."[31]

Emily Dickinson and other contemporary women writers resisted, in various ways and to varying degrees, the expectations of the domestic sphere and the obligations for literary performance that accompanied parlor sociability. Joan Hedrick has noted, for instance, that in nineteenth-century America the writing and reading of letters constituted a "more public act" than might be recognized today, since letters were often read aloud in the parlor to audiences of family, friends, boarders, and servants. "Correspondents took pains to make their letters entertaining, literary, amusing, and fit for such semipublic occasions," Hedrick writes, and the evidence strongly suggests that letters acquired a self-consciously literary form. Letters delivered vividly detailed portraiture of persons in their domestic surroundings and in so doing "became more novelistic and more firmly established within the domain of parlor literature." Since the parlor was also frequently the place for writing letters, "women often peopled their first paragraph with those among whom they sat" as they wrote.[32]

These self-consciously literary—even novelistic—features of the familiar letter are quite evident in the early letters and Valentines of Emily Dickinson.[33] But she did not hesitate to tweak the overly artful letter writer. In a gentle parody of the convention of naming the parlor companions among whom one wrote, Dickinson sometimes "peopled" the opening paragraph of her letters with her dog Carlo, "three or four Hens," "my books," or "Violets" as the companions by her side.[34] And one witty poem elaborately described the extreme length to which the recipient of a letter might go, in order to savor its contents privately and avoid reading it as a parlor performance.

> *The Way I read a Letter's — this —*
> *'Tis first — I lock the Door —*
> *And push it with my fingers — next —*
> *For transport it be sure —*
>
> *And then I go the furthest off*
> *To counteract a knock —*

Then draw my little Letter forth
And slowly pick the lock —

Even then, before it was safe to begin reading, the poet must closely
inspect the floor to be certain that an intrusive mouse did not lurk and
violate her privacy. Now assured of her solitude, the poet addressed
her final stanza directly to the reader of the poem, not to disclose the
content of the letter but, triumphantly, to withhold it.

Peruse how infinite I am
To no one that You — know —
And sigh for lack of Heaven — but not
The Heaven God bestow —

(F700)

The act of reading a letter in this poem paralleled the acts of domestic
intimacy that Dickinson imaginatively portrayed in her letters. She did
not depict instances of parlor sociability but, on the contrary, confi-
dential exchanges that emphatically resisted social circulation. A letter
to Susan Gilbert in 1852 narrated this confidentiality: "I am going out
on the doorstep, to get you some new—green grass—I shall pick it down
in the corner, where you and I use to sit, and have long fancies." Dick-
inson proceeded to speculate that "perhaps the dear little grasses were
growing all the while—and perhaps they heard what we said, but they
cant *tell*!" Having retrieved the blades of grass, Dickinson continued,
"I have come in now, dear Susie," having found the grass "not quite
so glad and green as when we used to sit there." Perhaps the "sad and
pensive" grass mourned over Susan Gilbert's absence from Amherst,
but, in any case, Dickinson insisted that no grassy gossip destroy the
privacy between correspondents![35]

Like many nineteenth-century women writers, Dickinson was of
two minds about the reciprocal shaping of domestic interior and per-
sonal interiority. At times, she elaborated religious metaphors of the
redemptive powers of home. Thus, Dickinson was by no means unusual
in writing to her brother in Boston that, as "our fire burned so cheer-
fully" in Amherst, she wished he would suddenly stride through the

doorway: "home is a holy thing—nothing of doubt or distrust can enter it's blessed portals. I feel it more and more as the great world goes on and one and another forsake, in whom you place your trust—here seems indeed to be a bit of Eden which not the sin of *any* can utterly destroy."[36] But Dickinson could also challenge such Edenic portrayals of home and resist norms of womanly comportment, especially if the "blessed portals" admitted visitors rather than members of the immediate family. Her resistance against parlor etiquette sometimes displayed a madcap quality. In the winter of 1859 she and her friend Catherine Scott fled—"like culprit mice"—from answering the front door when two gentlemen arrived for a business meeting with her father. "Since the dead might have heard us scamper," she explained in a letter to Elizabeth Holland, there was nothing to be done but reenter the room and offer an embarrassed apology: "the gentlemen simply looked at us with a grave surprise." Dickinson now made her confession to Elizabeth Holland, with the admission, "'Father, I have sinned.'" She planned to write a letter of apology, but if it were not accepted and Mrs. Holland next came to visit her in prison, "know that I was a loving felon, sentenced for a door bell."[37]

At other times, Dickinson adopted the manner of Emerson and questioned underlying presuppositions about the natural "rightness" of conventional behavior. In a poem written a few years after the incident of the culprit mice, she asserted that "a discerning Eye" would not only see "divinest Sense" in behavior that society declared madness but also perceive "the starkest Madness" in the arbitrary constraints of common sense.

> 'Tis the Majority
> In this, as all, prevail —
> Assent — and you are sane —
> Demur — you're straightway dangerous —
> And handled with a Chain —
>
> (F620)

Other women writers of the era, likewise, did not permit images of a redemptive domestic sphere to go uncontested, and the contest itself evoked an alternative cascade of domestic metaphor. Antebellum advocates of women's rights such as Sarah Grimké and Elizabeth Cady Stanton countered sentimental images by depicting domesticity as a realm of female constraint, a "vast prison" in which women were "born slaves," or, as Dickinson put it, "handled with a Chain." Elizabeth Akers Allen (1832–1911) and Sarah Morgan Piatt (1836–1919), poets who were Dickinson's contemporaries, published verse that expressed disillusionment with the isolation, emptiness, and tragedies of marriage.[38] Beyond questioning customs that enjoined womanly submission, these writers extended resistance more broadly to challenge the metaphysical or theological justifications for these institutionalized norms. Thus Piatt wrote "Giving Back the Flower" as a lamentation over a husband killed in the Civil War: "When I saw your corpse in your coffin, I flung back your flower to you." Casting doubt on platitudes about God's loving care, the widow voiced her angry sorrow directly to her dead husband.

> Ah? so God is your witness. Has God, then, no world to
>   look after but ours?
> May He not have been searching for that wild star, with
>   the trailing plumage, that flew
> Far over a part of our darkness while we were there by the
>   freezing flowers,
> Or else brightening some planet's luminous rings, instead
>   of thinking of you?[39]

When the ideology of the domestic sphere built constraints through mutually reinforcing models of human nature, society, and cosmos, Dickinson and her contemporaries did not simply balk at personal constraint but, in the process, questioned the social and religious theory that authorized the constraint.

From the 1850s onward, sometimes playfully, at other times in utmost seriousness, Emily Dickinson summarized the contest between social comportment and solitary creativity by contrasting the sober life of prose to the imaginative life of poetry. In 1851 she lamented to Austin regarding the Dickinson household, "We don't *have* many jokes tho' *now*, it is pretty much all sobriety, and we do not have much poetry, father having made up his mind that its pretty much all *real life*." In mock relief, she reassured Austin that, while "fathers real life and *mine* sometimes come into collision," they "as yet, escape unhurt!" In a similar spirit, a confiding letter from Dickinson to Susan Gilbert remarked that the two of them "please ourselves with the fancy that we are the only poets, and everyone else is *prose*."[40] Late in 1862, Dickinson shaped the contrast into a poem of imaginative freedom overcoming constraint.

> *They shut me up in Prose –*
> *As when a little Girl*
> *They put me in the Closet –*
> *Because they liked me 'still' –*

But the fruitlessness of this restraint would have been evident if they had "seen my Brain – go round." Parents might as easily have sought to restrain the flight of a bird who willed to soar, "And easy as a Star / Look down opon Captivity" (F445). Seclusion imaginatively elevated Dickinson into a utopian space from which she could "Look down opon Captivity" from the empyrean of freedom.

Sandra Gilbert has astutely argued that when Dickinson—resisting the prose of prosaic life—appropriated the persona of the poet, she used "all the materials of daily reality, and most especially the details of domesticity, as if they were not facts but metaphors, in order to recreate herself-and-her-life as a single, emblematic text, and often, indeed, as a sort of religious text" that might be termed an "ironic hagiography."[41] Dickinson's fascination in the early 1850s with Henry Wadsworth Longfellow's brief novel *Kavanagh* (1849) provides a lens through which to view these efforts to recreate her life "as a single, emblematic text." It must be said that Longfellow's novel provided little in the way of plot. The young minister Arthur Kavanagh arrives in a New England village with a new style of preaching that contrasts agreeably with the fire and brimstone of his predecessor, makes new friends, and eventually marries a local belle, Cecilia Vaughan. At the end of the novel, the couple, quite improbably, embarks on a three-year honeymoon to Italy. Dickinson's interest, I suspect, focused not on the plot but on the character types that Longfellow portrayed. The local schoolmaster, Mr. Churchill, had great plans for writing a romantic novel, but very easily permitted himself to be distracted from this artistic endeavor by claims to attention from his family, friends, and the duties of his office, such that he constantly "postponed the great designs, which he felt capable of accomplishing, but never had the resolute courage to begin."[42] Kavanagh himself was "descended from an ancient Catholic family" but, while retaining his love for the legends of the saints, had gradually converted to Protestantism. Soon after arrival in his new parish, Kavanagh discovered a vacant room in the church tower, which he converted into a study. There, he could meditate in solitude on "the great design and purpose of his life" and pour himself into sermonic "discourses, with which he hoped to reach and move the hearts of his parishioners." From the tower's "four oval windows, fronting the four corners of the heavens," Kavanagh experienced "that peculiar sense of seclusion and spiritual elevation, that entire separation from the world below, which a chamber in a tower always gives."[43] Most important for Dickinson, perhaps, Longfellow portrayed the intimate friendship between Cecilia Vaughan and Alice Archer, who "wrote long and impassioned letters to each other in the evening" and who trained a carrier pigeon to deliver these epistles back and forth between their homes.[44] By the conclusion of the novel, Cecilia and Kavanagh are engaged and Alice, who had secretly fallen in love with Kavanagh, has died of a sudden fever. Alice's "long domestic tragedy was ended," Longfellow concludes; "she was dead; and with her had died her secret sorrow and her secret love." Not only did Kavanagh never learn of her "wealth of affection for him," or Cecilia recognize "what fidelity of friendship" had gone with Alice to the grave, but also, and ironically, Schoolmaster Churchill never knew that the romance he had longed to write "had really occurred in his neighborhood, among his own friends."[45] As Virginia Jackson has commented in *Dickinson's Misery*, between approximately 1840 and 1880, the suffering of a secret sorrow, borne silently within a private world, became a commonplace of both poetry and fiction, establishing the fictive persona of "the poetess." But, Jackson points out, this "secret sorrow" of the poetess was not actually secret at all: "since this burden is also the occasion for the poem, 'the secret sorrow' is an open secret."[46] Although when she read *Kavanagh* Dickinson's career as a poet lay almost entirely ahead of her, vicarious identification with an isolated study elevated above the landscape, with hidden sorrow, and with a suffering poetess provided Dickinson fictive personae that she would actively appropriate for later poems of solitary observation, secret longing, and desire. The characters of Longfellow's novel portrayed alternative versions of life as "a single, emblematic text" through which to imagine what she might accomplish and become.

BECOMING A WRITER

"A writer can only become a writer," Richard Brodhead has remarked, "by first constructing some working idea of what a writer is and does. Such definitions in turn are never merely self-generated but are formed in and against the understandings of this role that are operative in a particular cultural space." For this reason, "the history of American literature needs to be understood not as the history of literary works only but also as the history of literature's working conditions— the history of the diverse and changing worlds that have been constructed around writing in American social life." In his book *Cultures of Letters*, Brodhead proposes a chronology for understanding these "changing worlds" of writing and authorship in nineteenth-century America. A "domestic culture of letters" had consolidated in the 1830s and 1840s, but the segmentation or fracturing of this cultural field "brought a distinctly demarcated high-literary culture into existence in the 1860s and after."[47] Dickinson was, of course, writing in the midst of this very transition, and Lawrence Buell has observed that the breakdown of the earlier ideal of literature as an instrument of cohesive civic culture opened the way for Dickinson and others of her generation to pursue "anticonventional, risk-taking commitment to their expressive gift at the cost of forfeiting any chance of integration into the ranks of the socially proper." Both Thoreau and Dickinson "cultivated a sense of their differentness," Buell says, and "in their more confident moments, positively rejoiced in the thought that their writings were caviar to the general."[48]

Some more specific connections between Dickinson's self-understanding as a poet and these transitions in American literature become evident when we compare two famous nineteenth-century essays on writing and authorship. The first, written by Ralph Waldo Emerson for the October 1840 issue of the *Dial*, celebrated what Emerson termed *"Verses of the Portfolio."* Some twenty years later, in 1862, Thomas Wentworth Higginson wrote "A Letter to a Young Contributor" for the *Atlantic Monthly*, addressing himself to writers seeking advice about publication. Higginson's essay caught the eye of Emily Dickinson, who responded to it with a letter that launched a long friendship, mainly through correspondence, between the two.

The "democratical" tendencies of the times had extended to oratory and literature, Emerson announced, and soon there would be neither pulpit nor platform in any church or meeting hall. Instead, "each person, who is moved to address any public assembly, will speak from the floor." To the same democratic effect, books were circulating through "every house," the practice of keeping diaries was becoming general, and "a wider epistolary intercourse ministers to the ends of sentiment and reflection than ever existed before." In this democratic climate of confidence in personal voice, a new style of poetry had emerged: *"Verses of the Portfolio."* Often lacking the polished "workmanship" of verse intended for publication, these more spontaneous effusions, with sometimes "halting rhymes," represented "the easy and unpremeditated translation" of personal thoughts and feelings. They attempted "to throw into verse the experiences of private life." More important, in Emerson's estimation, "men of genius" were largely incapable of highly polished productions, because for them public influence was "always a secondary aim." Instead, verses of the portfolio came from self-interrogating writers "whose worship is toward the Ideal Beauty, which chooses to be courted not so often in perfect hymns, as in wild ear-piercing ejaculations, or in silent musings." The result was an absence of "all conventional imagery" and a "bold use" of what "the moment's mood had made sacred to him, quite careless that it might be sacred to no other." Responding to the spontaneous daring of such writing, Emerson concluded that a new taste for "private and household poetry" had arisen, certainly in himself and probably in the wider society.[49]

Higginson's "Letter to a Young Contributor" took up the quite different matter of writing for commercial publication. He forthrightly, if ironically, laid out the interests of midcentury publishing. An editor, Higginson explained, was "a bland and virtuous man, exceedingly anxious to secure plenty of good subscribers and contributors, and very ready to perform any acts of kindness not inconsistent with this grand design." Editors and potential contributors thus shared a common goal: "No editor can ever afford the rejection of a good thing, and no author the publication of a bad one. The only difficulty lies in drawing the line." Given his focus on publication, Higginson addressed precisely those aspects of writing that Emerson had swept aside in order to extoll the spontaneity of "private and household poetry." Higginson emphasized the physical appearance of the submission, the careful deliberation of each word and phrase, and the polish that would obviate any need for "the slightest literary revision before printing." The well-crafted literary production, Higginson concluded, was "attar of roses, one distilled drop from a million blossoms." Quite unlike Emerson's imagined writer of portfolio verse, Higginson presumed that literature's public influence was the primary, not secondary, consideration. He applauded the development of "American literature" and encouraged the use of a distinctively American "vocabulary so rich and copious as we are acquiring" through "new felicities of dialect" contributed from Ireland, Scotland, Germany, and Africa ("even China is creeping in"). Hence the American writer was like a "sea-captain amid his crew: a medley of all nations, waiting for some organizing mind to mould them into a unit of force." Despite this grandiloquent metaphor of seafaring command, Higginson concluded by discounting the transitory glories of war and politics. While "great American politicians of the last generation" were on "the path to oblivion," Higginson assured the young contributor that a great book was "immortality." The aspiring author should not succumb to despair: "Who cannot bear a few disappointments, if the vista be so wide that the mute inglorious Miltons of this sphere may in some other sing their Paradise as Found?" Ending on a fanciful note, Higginson wondered whether "in some other realm of existence we may look back with a kindly interest on this scene of our earlier life, and say to one another, 'Do you remember yonder planet, where once we went to school?'"[50]

Although the working conditions of authorship were changing rapidly in the middle decades of the nineteenth century, the idea of being a writer, especially when the writer was a woman, inevitably raised the relationship between privately circulated parlor literature and the public world of commercial print. In the course of their correspondence, Dickinson declared to Higginson in 1862 that the idea of publishing her poetry was as "foreign to my thought, as Firmament to Fin," but this disavowal certainly did not mean that she regarded poetry as a pastime for idle hours or an ornament of feminine refinement. How, then, might we situate Dickinson's disinclination to publish in the gap between the differing proposals of Emerson and Higginson? One way to place Dickinson in the spectrum of nineteenth-century ideas about being a writer is to begin by noting that Emerson and Higginson held different conceptions of the writer, each of which resonated with aspects of Dickinson's sense of her vocation.

Emerson emphasized the creative process and fastened on the writer's spontaneity, unconventional phrasing, and pursuit of an unattainable "Idealized Beauty." In all of these dimensions, the act of writing, for Emerson, represented the welling up of an inner impulse, which sought its fulfillment through writing. In part, this was the Romantic reinvention of Puritan and evangelical traditions of writing as a spiritual discipline, in which poetry, autobiographical narrative, and diaries represented crucial practices of vocational self-understanding that formed the self in light of a transcendent norm. As described in chapter 2, the evangelical leader Sarah Osborn had understood herself as a writer not because of the one small pamphlet published during her lifetime but because of her lifelong production of exegetical and devotional diaries. Verses of the portfolio were also examples of nineteenth-century parlor literature, as described by Joan Hedrick, and linked the act of writing to the formation and maintenance of friendship and family affection. Finally, Emerson's conception of the writer resonated with the spontaneous musings of rural retreat, idealized in the writers of reverie: Charles Brockden Brown's rhapsodist and Donald Grant Mitchell's Ik Marvel. None of these writers—whether devotional diarists or fictive solitaries—pursued publication as the central purpose of writing, though it might be a secondary result. The writer's identity was bound up in the act of writing. To the extent that *"Verses of the Portfolio"* addressed an audience, Emerson primarily commended them to the readers of the *Dial* as acts of *intimate* communication that explicitly aligned art with the diary and the familiar letter. For Dickinson, this broad ambit of noncommercial understandings of being a writer buttressed her personal desire to write unencumbered by the expectations surrounding published verse—especially women's verse—in the nineteenth century.

In contrast to Emerson, who dwelt on the spontaneous effusion of ideas from which the act of writing commenced, Higginson considered writing preeminently an act of craftsmanship culminating in a fully finished product. Hence the most compelling image in Higginson's essay described a finished composition as "attar of roses," carefully distilled from innumerable preceding drafts. In chapter 4, I indicate how this image seemed to stick with Emily Dickinson and influence her self-presentation as a poet. In her initial letter to Higginson, however, she asked not whether the four poems she had enclosed displayed the high polish achieved through many revisions. She asked if they were "alive" and "breathed." Perhaps this choice of words or perhaps the poems themselves led Higginson to characterize the writing as "spasmodic," a reference to the Spasmodic School of Victorian poetry associated especially with the Scot Alexander Smith (1830–1867) and noted for its unrepressed, impassioned imagination. Certainly, Dickinson was familiar with Smith's major collection, *A Life-Drama and Other Poems*, which Austin Dickinson sent to her in 1853, the year of its publication. And she admired Smith's work, despite (like many contemporary critics) giving the poems a mixed review: "they are not very coherent, but there's good deal of exquisite frenzy, and some wonderful figures, as ever I met in my life."[51] Still, "exquisite frenzy" is not the first phrase that comes to mind when seeking to describe Dickinson's poetry, and I think it was Higginson's stress on craftsmanship that most strongly resonated with her developing conception of the poet's task.

Much earlier in her life Dickinson had remarked to Abiah Root that she found herself "so easily excited" that she avoided attending revivals out of fear that she might be self-deceived by the emotions of the moment.[52] Higginson's letter of advice in the *Atlantic Monthly* may thus have confirmed her own predisposition toward writing. The labor of carefully choosing her words disciplined or distilled the immediacy of emotion. This self-discipline was not incompatible with the interrogative and questing purpose of writing from Edwards to Emerson, from Osborn to Palmer. But it drew back from the spontaneous ardor that Emerson had commended in verses of the portfolio and inclined instead toward an abstract analysis of emotional states, including a self-distanced analysis of her own excitability. Perhaps Higginson's fanciful conclusion to his "Letter to a Young Contributor," in which he imagined life on earth as a preparatory "school," captured Dickinson's desire to make the composition of poetry a tactic of self-composition. She said as much in one of the poems she enclosed in her first letter to Higginson, which represented the poet as something like an apprentice jeweler, who was moving from costume fashion to more precious materials.[53]

> *We play at Paste —*
> *Till qualified, for Pearl —*
> *Then, drop the Paste —*
> *And deem ourself a fool —*
>
> *The Shapes — though — were similar —*
> *And our new Hands*
> *Learned Gem-tactics —*
> *Practising Sands*

(F282)

Apprentices need teachers. Admitting to Higginson, "I have none to ask," Dickinson wrote him five letters between April and August 1862, enclosing thirteen poems and incorporating a fourteenth into the body of one letter.[54] Having retreated into solitude, she sought a "preceptor" who—from a distance—could be an interlocutor as she developed her craft. Her reply to Higginson's initial recommendations, however, seems more an ironic rebuttal, not quite striking the note of grateful obedience one might anticipate from an author in search of a preceptor: "You think my gait 'spasmodic'—I am in danger—Sir—You think me 'uncontrolled'—I have no Tribunal." What motives were at work here? Since childhood, Dickinson had admired her teachers and described older individuals who shared her interests as preceptors. After her death, the family discovered three drafted letters (apparently never mailed) to an anonymous "master," and Dickinson's biographers have devoted considerable detective work to the possible identity of this correspondent.[55]

My own speculations about the relation of "preceptors" to her vocation as a writer are easier to state. First, since writing was a discipline that crafted her vocation and sense of self, Dickinson wanted to know if her writing was "alive," if it "breathed," if it was "true." The old Puritans had not written their personal narratives in order to file them away but in order to deliver testimony and have that testimony appraised by their community. Unlike the Puritans, Dickinson did not feel beholden to the judgment of her surrounding religious and literary communities; to this extent, she sought Emerson's experimental life. But like the Puritans, she did want to hear whether or not writing that arose from her own life resonated with the lives of others, whether it vivified the human circumstance for her time. Second, the observations of Sandra Gilbert about Dickinson's desire "to recreate herself-and-her-life as a single, emblematic text" are important for understanding what Dickinson thought it meant to become a writer. When Dickinson announced herself as a poet in search of a mentor, she assumed a familiar persona from nineteenth-century fiction. Longfellow's *Kavanagh* included an advice-seeking young writer, Clarissa Cartwright, who hoped to publish her poems under the title "Symphonies of the Soul." And Stacey Margolis has pointed out that a hallmark of Susan Warner's novels, especially *The Wide, Wide World*, was the young woman seeking an "ideal mentor" who would "give her some idea of her proper role in the world."[56] Novelistic portraits of the Clarissa Cartwright figure frequently implied that uncritical acceptance of advice from preceptors was foolish or naïve. In seeking advice, Dickinson was engaged in a deeper search for critical independence, which entailed the receipt of honest criticism. "Men do not call the surgeon," she reminded Higginson, "to commend—the Bone, but to set it, Sir, and fracture within, is more critical."[57] In both the piety and the fiction of the era, writing was a route to self-knowledge, and confidants who appraised the writing were also entrusted with appraising the writer—whether or not the writing found its way into print.

THE POETIC CONSTRUCTION OF A HOUSE

The house became a multivalent metaphor in Dickinson's poetry. It signified self, society, nature, and cosmos, and these significations often overlapped and intertwined in individual poems. Dickinson moved freely and imaginatively back and forth between the house and the order of nature. The house might become a ship with "magic Planks," sailing on "A Sea of Summer Air," captained by a butterfly and counting "an entire universe" for its crew (F1199). Or nature might assume the domestic duties of a mother. On a summer afternoon, nature engaged in charming conversation amid "Her Household," which at sundown became "Her Assembly" in a church with "Aisles," where her voice incited the "timid prayer" of cricket and flower. And after her children had fallen asleep, nature turned from them to "light Her lamps" and then, "bending from the Sky,"

> *With infinite Affection —*
> *And infinite Care —*
> *Her Golden finger on Her lip —*
> *Wills Silence — Everywhere —*
>   (F741)

The metaphorical system that Dickinson elaborated around the image of *a house* was an array that ranged from the utopian to the terrifying, and I explore it further in chapters 4 and 5. But this chapter concludes by focusing on the way in which Dickinson accentuated the reciprocal relationships between a house and its immediately surrounding landscape, in order to articulate an understanding of both herself as a poet and the work of writing poetry.

The raw materials for portraying the metaphorical relationships among house, self, and nature were readily available to Dickinson from the surrounding religious culture. Henry Ward Beecher had drawn the analogy between building a house and building a self, proposing that a house was "the shape which a man's thoughts take when he imagines how he should like to live." As I have indicated, when Dickinson imagined how she "should like to live," her house took the shape of poetry, not prose.

> *I dwell in Possibility –*
> *A fairer House than Prose –*
> *More numerous of Windows –*
> *Superior – for Doors –*
>
> *Of Chambers as the Cedars –*
> *Impregnable of eye –*
> *And for an everlasting Roof*
> *The Gambrels of the Sky –*
>
> *Of Visitors – the fairest –*
> *For Occupation – This –*
> *The spreading wide my narrow Hands*
> *To gather Paradise –*

(F466)

In William Ellery Channing's vision of "self-culture," when persons recognized that "the outward creation" was "the emblem" of the soul, nature seemed "to lose its material aspect" and disclose its identity with spirit. Dickinson's house of "Possibility" had similarly ethereal construction materials; passing through one of its numerous doors, the visitor entered rooms of everlasting cedar and gazed upward to an "everlasting Roof," the sky. However uncomfortable Dickinson may have been with the parlor hospitality of a Phoebe Palmer or Harriet Beecher Stowe, when she imagined "spreading wide my narrow Hands / To gather Paradise," she drew from the same reservoir of religious symbols as Palmer's image of parlor devotions that gave her visitors a foretaste of "Jerusalem the golden."

For Dickinson, writing began with attentive perception, and that attentiveness included an affective connection between the observer and the scene being observed. But whereas Emerson had stressed the intuitive immediacy of this connection, Dickinson puzzled over perceptions that evolved through time and the changing emotional responses that accumulated during that temporal process. Repeated views through the same window could provide a framing device for such accumulating perceptions. Henry Ward Beecher had considered windows an extraordinarily important feature of a house not simply because they let in light but because they "let the sight out" onto "the inexpressible beauty of God's architecture." No landscape paintings, Beecher asserted, could match those "you see through glass." Since Emily Dickinson's house of possibility was "More numerous of Windows," it offered many vantage points that "let the sight out" onto the landscape. A poem she wrote in the summer of 1863 specified the difference between a canvas landscape and a landscape seen "through glass." Beecher, not unlike Emerson, had implied that the divine architecture of nature was quite separate from human architecture, but in Dickinson's poem the view from a bedroom window intermingled both natural features and humanly constructed ones, a chimney, weathervane, and steeple, as well as tree and hill. And the effect of the poem depended on its representation of a landscape that disclosed its meanings not on a single viewing but by sustained observation through the passage of time, "every time I wake."

> The Angle of a Landscape –
> That every time I wake –
> Between my Curtain and the Wall
> Opon an ample Crack –
>
> Like a Venetian – waiting –
> Accosts my open eye –
> Is just a Bough of Apples –
> Held slanting, in the Sky –

The Pattern of a Chimney —
The Forehead of a Hill —
Sometimes — a Vane's Forefinger —
But that's — Occasional —

The Seasons — shift — my picture —
Opon my Emerald Bough,
I wake — to find no — Emeralds —
Then — Diamonds — which the Snow

From Polar Caskets — fetched me —
The Chimney — and the Hill —
And just the steeple's finger —
These — never stir at all —

$\qquad\qquad\qquad\qquad\qquad\qquad$ (F578)

The picture through the window changed in the course of the seasons, and the bough of the apple tree "Accosts" Dickinson's waiting eye with a treasure trove, first of emeralds and then of diamonds. "To the living senses," Helen Vendler writes, "even a 'Crack' is wide enough to manifest all the wealth that the eye could desire."[58] As the seasons shifted, from the arrival of apples to the arrival of snow, different features of the landscape attracted the observer's attention; Dickinson's repeated "I wake" marks the observer's changing focus. Her first three stanzas emphasize the slant of the living bough, bearing apples and "emerald" leaves. The final two stanzas return to the chimney and hill noted earlier in the poem and now recognize they have persisted through all the seasons: "These—never stir at all." Two features of human architecture symbolize the difference between these enduring features of the landscape and those that, because they were alive, are transient. The weathervane's "Forefinger" was occasionally visible in spring as it turned horizontally to report the changing winds around the house; by contrast, the church steeple's vertical "finger" pointed in only one direction, unmoving and starkly prominent in the winter air.

Beginning in the early 1850s, Dickinson increasingly absented herself from church in order to write letters or enjoy her own alternative worship service on the Homestead's lawn. She had come to relish the solitude afforded by her inability in good conscience to join the church, which would have made her eligible to stay beyond the morning service for Communion. "It is Communion Sunday," she wrote her brother in October 1851, "and they will stay a good while—what a nice time pussy and I have to enjoy ourselves!" In an 1852 letter to Susan Gilbert, Dickinson transmuted solitary time into a religious service of mutual interiority: "the bells are ringing, Susie, north, and east, and south, and *your own* village bell," calling people to Sunday meeting. But, Dickinson appealed, "dont *you* go Susie, not to *their* meeting, but come with me this morning to the church within our hearts, where the bells are always ringing, and the preacher whose name is Love—shall intercede there for us." Dickinson luxuriated in "*this* solitude, this sweet Sabbath of our's," as she sat on the lawn "alone with the winds and you."[59] On such solitary Sundays, birds became metaphorical "choristers," and one brief poem offered a Trinitarian benediction in the name of the bee, the butterfly, and the breeze, "Amen" (F23).

Dickinson elaborated this metaphorical transformation of her garden into a church-beyond-the-church in one of the poems she enclosed in her initial flurry of letters to Higginson during the summer of 1862.[60]

> Some — keep the Sabbath — going to church —
> I — keep it — staying at Home —
> With a Bobolink — for a Chorister —
> And an Orchard — for a Dome —
>
> Some — keep the Sabbath, in Surplice —
> I — just wear my wings —
> And instead of tolling the bell, for church —
> Our little Sexton — sings —
>
> "God" — preaches — a noted Clergyman —
> And the sermon is never long,
> So — instead of getting to Heaven — at last —
> I'm — going — all along!
>
> (F236)

In addition to its sheer delight in natural beauty, this poem contained at least two further features that illuminate the religion around Emily Dickinson. First, Dickinson did not discard the material forms, language, and symbolism of the church. She transposed them into her own distinctive key, as symbols—even allegories—of human intimacy, reflective interiority, and participation in the order of nature. The natural landscape had acquired the architecture, furnishings, and functions of a church; the orchard was its dome; wings served as ecclesiastical vestments; birds were choristers; and the brief sermon's natural theology did not simply direct the auditor toward heaven but disclosed that she was "going—all along." The poet fully identified with the natural scene; as one of the celebrants in the service she did not don a surplice but, becoming a bird, "just wear my wings." Second, by identifying church with nature, Dickinson allowed additional connotations to enter her celebration. A church's sexton—in this scene, singing—also performs the duties of parish gravedigger. The tolling bell calls the faithful not only to Sunday services but also to funerals. Angels as well as birds wear their wings. Taken as a whole, the affirmation that the poet was going to heaven "all along" suggested, simultaneously, vibrant immersion in the natural order and awareness that mortality pervaded it throughout.

The poetic construction of a house—the act of writing—thus posed for Dickinson the question of whether the solitary labor of writing poetry had any enduring significance. From the personal testimonies of the Puritans to the verses of the portfolio extolled by Emerson, the act of writing had "edification," the construction of the self, as its preeminent purpose. Although the Puritans conceived these spiritual labors to be aimed at immortality in its explicitly religious connotation, this focus on writing as self-composition deflected another connotation of immortality, the endurance of classic works of art in cultural memory. Dickinson's disinclination to publish thus brought into collision the two different connotations of the immortality that a writer might seek through writing. The question of the enduring significance of any individual life and its accomplishments had prompted Emerson to remark, about the details of daily life, "it is out of this sad lint and rag fair that the web of lasting life is woven."[61] And Higginson's

"Letter to a Young Contributor" had urged the aspiring author to bear up under disappointment, since in the wide vista of history, "the mute inglorious Miltons of this sphere may in some other sing their Paradise as Found." Having elected to pursue her poetic vocation in domestic solitude, Dickinson felt the force of this tension between "the web of lasting life" and transience as both woman and poet. Confronting the likelihood that her poetry would be buried with her, Dickinson also confronted the question whether any woman's labors and interior life would be known or remembered after death.

> How many times these low feet staggered –
> Only the soldered mouth can tell –
> Try – can you stir the awful rivet –
> Try – can you lift the hasps of steel!
>
> Stroke the cool forehead – hot so often –
> Lift – if you care – the listless hair –
> Handle the adamantine fingers
> Never a thimble – more – shall wear –
>
> Buzz the dull flies – on the chamber window –
> Brave – shines the sun through the freckled pane –
> Fearless – the cobweb swings from the ceiling –
> Indolent Housewife – in Daisies – lain!
>
> (F238)

Reading this poem, I imagine myself having entered the interior dialogue of a mourner, seated in a parlor next to a casket. As the mourner looks into the casket and around the room, an inner voice—somewhat distant, gently ironic—presses the mourner to confront her friend's death, indirectly foreshadowing her own. In the first stanza, this inner voice recognizes how many events in a lifetime of labor will remain unknown, permanently closed with solder, rivet, and "hasps of steel" in the body identified now with its closed coffin. The urge to touch her body evokes contrasts; fingers once nimble with thimble and thread are now "adamantine." Gazing absently around the parlor, the mourner sees that flies and spiders have continued the natural course of their living, creating the spots and webs that the now "Indolent Housewife" had so recently and so industriously swept away.

Two other poems of the early 1860s applied to the poet and her writing this same question of whether any part of personal labor would outlast death. In the first, Dickinson delivered her poem as an open letter to a world that had not yet displayed interest in striking up regular correspondence.

> This is my letter to the World
> That never wrote to Me —
> The simple News that Nature told —
> With tender Majesty
>
> Her Message is committed
> To Hands I cannot see —
> For love of Her — Sweet — countrymen —
> Judge tenderly — of Me
>
> (F519)

For the purposes of this chapter, the accent falls on the second stanza, in which the solitary writer entrusts her poem to readers she "cannot see." It is noteworthy that she does not present the letter's message as her own. It is, instead, "simple News that Nature told," which she has now "committed" into the hands of an unknown audience. Nature's willingness to disclose its message to attentive listeners had been a pivotal idea of Emerson, the Transcendentalists, and other writers influenced by Romanticism. Dickinson's invocation of nature's "tender Majesty" also bore traces of Jonathan Edwards's depiction of nature as the handiwork of God, displaying "a sweet and gentle, and holy majesty; and also a majestic meekness; an awful sweetness; a high, and great, and holy gentleness." In both Romanticism and the theology of Edwards, the message of nature and nature's God became audible when it passed through the transformed attentiveness of an individual devotee, and, reflecting this assumption, Dickinson had not written nature's letter to the world but "my letter to the World."

Dickinson composed "This is my letter to the World" before beginning her correspondence with Higginson, but a second poem, written early in 1865, perhaps suggests the influence of his "Letter to a Young Contributor." Higginson had urged that writers not despair over lack of recognition in their own time. And this poem acknowledges that, although poets "Themselves—go out," the light of their work might endure, focused and disseminated through the "Lens" of other and later eras.

> *The Poets light but Lamps —*
> *Themselves — go out —*
> *The Wicks they stimulate*
> *If vital Light*
>
> *Inhere as do the Suns —*
> *Each Age a Lens*
> *Disseminating their*
> *Circumference*
>
> (F930)

Having elected solitude rather than pursuing print, Dickinson confronted the very real possibility that her poetic "Circumference," if by that she meant influence, would be slight indeed. But Dickinson registered a crucial qualification to the possibility that the poets' "Lamps" would illuminate later ages. Their "Circumference" would be enlarged, "If vital Light // Inhere as do the Suns." The necessity of a poet's inherent "vital Light" had earlier impelled Dickinson to inquire of Higginson whether her poems were "alive," whether they "breathed." In the summer of 1862, Dickinson corresponded about her "business" as a poet in ways that have a bearing on this idea of "Circumference." To Higginson she acknowledged, "perhaps you smile at me. I could not stop for that— My Business is Circumference." She reiterated these observations in a letter to Josiah and Elizabeth Holland, but borrowed a line from Josiah Holland's novel *Miss Gilbert's Career* in order to change the designation of her business from circumference to love: "Perhaps you laugh at me! Perhaps the whole United States are laughing at me too! *I* can't stop for that! *My* business is to love."[62] In these statements, the matter of knowing one's "business" seems to involve understanding its inherent "vital Light" more than measuring the perimeter to which the light was cast. If that is the case, then the *circumference* primarily represented for Dickinson a place at the edge or margin of her life at which to stand and view "the self's becoming what it is."[63] She explained her sense of vocation to the Hollands through an analogy to a solitary songbird she had encountered that morning "down—down—on a little bush at the foot of the garden." Dickinson questioned the bird: "wherefore sing, I said, since nobody *hears*?" In reply, the bird declared, with "one sob in the throat, one flutter of bosom—'*My* business is to *sing*'—and away she rose! How do I know but cherubim, once, themselves, as patient, listened, and applauded her unnoticed hymn?"[64]

AN INTIMATE ABSENCE

Emily Dickinson held tightly to the world, demanded much from her friends, and feared that departures would become permanent. As she remarked in a letter to her close friend Samuel Bowles, the editor of the *Springfield Republican*, "my friends are my 'estate.' Forgive me then the avarice to hoard them!"[1] Perhaps surprisingly, her decision for seclusion did not diminish but instead accentuated this powerful attachment to those from whom she found herself separated by distance, by her own design, by death. In her writing, Dickinson imaginatively amplified the experiences of absence, separation, and loss and set them in tension with experiences of presence, intimacy, and reunion. Solitude—whether at the writing desk or in the garden—became imagined intimacy with a separated, perhaps unattainable, object of desire. Indeed, separation heightened desire. Dickinson accentuated this simultaneity of separation and presence, intimacy and absence, by exploiting the metaphorical possibilities of the nineteenth century's most widely practiced form of writing: the letter.[2]

Among the spiritual disciplines of solitude, journals and diaries typically created private reservoirs from which writers subsequently drew material either for personal reflection or for revision into public writing and oratory. As I discussed in chapter 2, the eighteenth-century New England evangelicals Jonathan Edwards and Sarah Osborn regularly reviewed their diaries as a spiritual exercise, and Ralph Waldo Emerson kept carefully indexed journals as storehouses of ideas for revision into lectures and essays. Lavinia Dickinson kept a diary, but Emily Dickinson did not.[3] Letters, on the other hand, were composed for the express purpose of connecting the writer to family, friends, and the intimate circle within which the letters would be read aloud and circulated. Following standard conventions in the long cultural history of the familiar letter, nineteenth-century correspondents portrayed their letters as bridges, spanning absence, loss, or separation, including, symbolically, the separation of death. As they traveled from one household to another, letters thus mediated intimacy, and handwriting became the emblem of writers touching across distance. Furthermore, when the nineteenth-century letter traveled, it typically traveled with luggage. Enclosures—locks of hair, pressed flowers, or sentimental trinkets—were integral to the handwritten text and its meaning. These epistolary commonplaces framed Emily Dickinson's practices of including copies of her poems with her letters, incorporating verse into the body of a letter, and enclosing a pressed flower, a leaf, or other small memento as tangible emblems of connection between correspondents. Paradoxically, in the very act of conveying intimacy and physical objects emblematic of intimacy, the familiar letter accentuated the reality of absence. William Merrill Decker, in his excellent historical study of letter writing in America, has identified a pervasive apprehension on the part of separated, perhaps lonely letter writers that "death will intervene before the parties can reunite."[4]

These long-standing conventions of the familiar letter implied that separation was permanent, that reunion might never occur, and that only the traces of a lost intimacy would remain. Or they raised the possibility that the desire for intimate communication would remain forever unfulfilled. The notion that the object of her desire—indeed, human desire—was irretrievable or unattainable fascinated Dickinson, and in order to explore its implications for the conduct of her life, she turned to religious language. In particular, she appropriated and revised the venerable idea, exemplified in Jonathan Edwards, that the unimpeded communication of perfected love was desired in this life but deferred to heaven. As she playfully explained in a poem written early in 1862 (F310), "'Heaven'—is what I cannot reach!" In this case, Dickinson had directed her desire toward an apple dangling from a branch beyond her grasp: "Provided it do hopeless—hang—/ That—'Heaven' is—to Me!" It was one of numerous instances when indispensable artistic and intellectual labor was performed in Dickinson's poetry by terminology of "the afterlife": heaven, immortality, and eternity. This chapter explores the implications of her theological vocabulary, not only for Dickinson's poetry but also for the ways in which it illuminates broader currents in nineteenth-century American religion. First, the chapter examines Dickinson's letters in order to illustrate how the intersection of intimacy, absence, and desire prompted Dickinson to interpret *memory* through religious ideas about death and eternity. The chapter then argues that Dickinson's highly personal representations of memory, loss, and bereavement interacted with religious rituals of mourning and broader cultural patterns of nostalgia and memorialization. The chapter concludes by exploring the ways in which Dickinson incorporated the experience of enduring loss into her understanding of the work of creating poems.

LOSS, DESIRE, AND MEMORY IN DICKINSON'S LETTERS

Departures from Amherst required letters. Nineteenth-century epistolary etiquette presupposed that correspondents had a mutual obligation to maintain connection. Friends moved away; family traveled; visitors came and went. In the early 1850s, Austin Dickinson taught in Boston and attended Harvard Law School. At the end of the decade, Lavinia Dickinson was away from Amherst in Boston, caring for their ill aunt, Lavinia Norcross, who would die in 1860. And letters filled the gaps between visits, for example, in Emily Dickinson's long friendship and correspondence with Elizabeth Holland and her husband, the journalist and sometime poet Josiah G. Holland. In her letters, Emily Dickinson elaborated strong narratives of absence and desire, in which she not only celebrated past moments of face-to-face presence but also savored the experience of loss. As Dickinson's biographer Alfred Habegger has remarked, "she loved seeing the chosen few and thinking about them in their absence; indeed, the point of staying home alone was partly to commune more intensely over a distance."[5] Thus, in August 1858, when Mary Haven moved from Amherst with her husband, Joseph, who had accepted a faculty position at Chicago Theological Seminary, Dickinson wrote Mary, "permit us to keep you in our hearts, although you seem to outward eye, to be travelling from us! That is the sweet prerogative of the left behind!"[6]

This "sweet prerogative" of enjoying the sentiments that surrounded absence was a regular feature of Dickinson's letters. Several years earlier, when Austin was teaching school in Boston, Dickinson declared, "we miss you more and more, we do not become accustomed to separation from you." But, she quickly added, the unavoidable separation had its attractions: "and then again I think that it is pleasant to miss you if you must go away, and I would not have it otherwise, not even if I could."[7] One would not be missed if one were not loved. And this epistolary reassurance to the person who had gone mirrored emotion in the person who had stayed, that is, Emily Dickinson. A few months after Dickinson's close friend Emily Fowler Ford married and left Amherst, Dickinson wrote her that "your home looks very silent—and I try to think of things funny, and turn the other way when I am passing near, for sure I am that looking would make my heart too heavy, and make my eyes so dim." How she longed to see Emily Ford once again "at twilight sitting in the door." These sights and memories while walking home from church had prompted Dickinson to write, "I have just come home from meeting, where I have been all day, and it makes me so happy to think of writing you that I forget the sermon and minister and all, and think of none but you." Then, in a characteristic move, Dickinson transferred her sense of loss to a personified nature: "But nothing forgets you, Emily, not a blossom, not a bee; for in the merriest flower there is a pensive air, and in the bonniest bee a sorrow—they know that you are gone, they know how well you loved them, and in their little faces is sadness and in their mild eyes, tears."[8] In her youthful letters, these interconnections of presence, separation, and desire could veer toward sentimental cliché, but Dickinson continued to deepen her thinking and to experiment with ever more daring metaphors, and this nexus of emotions became central to many of her most important poems.

Her flights of imagination—Ik Marvel's reveries—sometimes took the form of imaginary letters. She declared to Josiah and Elizabeth Holland in November 1854, "I write you many letters with pens which are not seen. Do you receive them?" Continuing her actual letter, Dickinson reported that, just before her father awakened her with his customary early-morning rap on the bedroom door, she had been dreaming of gathering roses with the Hollands from a "wonderful garden" in a basket that never filled: "God grant the basket fill not, till, with hands purer and whiter, we gather flowers of gold in baskets made of pearl; higher—higher!"[9] Dickinson concluded the letter by juxtaposing departed "days with you last September" and the "delightful" prospect of meeting and sitting together in the near future. In the interim of memory and hope, she would "not repine, knowing that bird of mine, though flown—learneth beyond the sea, melody new for me, and will return."[10] Metaphorical constellations of idyllic gardens, heavenly landscapes, and the seasonal return of migratory birds became a common vocabulary of imagined intimacy in Dickinson's letters. They frequently, as in this case, carried the religious connotation of the flight of souls toward reunion in paradise. In chapter 1 I cited a letter to Elizabeth Holland in which Dickinson reported reading passages in Revelation "where friends should 'go no more out'; and there were 'no tears,' and I wished as a I sat down to-night that we were *there*—not *here*—and that wonderful world had commenced." Scripture's promise of heavenly intimacy led Dickinson to imagine, citing Revelation once again, that rather than writing across distance, she and Elizabeth were eternally engaged in heavenly conversation, only hoping that "the 144,000" would not be so boisterous in their praise of God as to disturb this everlasting companionship.[11]

Dickinson's letters to Susan Gilbert were intimate affairs in the early 1850s, reminiscent of the carrier pigeon epistles between Cecilia Vaughan and Alice Archer in Longfellow's *Kavanagh*. In March 1853, Dickinson lamented her separation from Gilbert. To convey her emotions, Dickinson inverted an old idea that I illustrated in chapter 2 through Jonathan Edwards's "sense of the heart," through which Edwards perceived the world differently because of his awareness of the divine presence. Now, for Dickinson, it was *absence* that altered perception. "Your absence insanes me so—I do not feel so peaceful, when you are gone from me," she declared to Susan; "all life looks differently, and the faces of my fellows are not the same they wear when you are with me." In her letter, "dear Susie" became the artist through whom Dickinson saw the world: "you sketch my pictures for me, and 'tis at their sweet colorings, rather than this dim real that I am used, so you see when you go away, the world looks staringly, and I find I need more vail." Characteristically, Dickinson moved easily from the "sweet colorings" with which Susan Gilbert's presence tinted her Amherst surroundings to a religious projection of everlasting companionship: "Bless God that we catch faint glimpses of his brighter Paradise from *occasional* Heavens *here!*"[12]

In late April 1856, when Dickinson was twenty-five and about to assume her poetic vocation, she drew together these various epistolary motifs in an artfully composed letter to a cousin of her own age, John L. Graves, who had visited the Dickinsons regularly during his student years at Amherst and who afterward was ordained to the Congregationalist ministry and then entered business in Boston. On a Sunday when "all have gone to church," Dickinson, followed by "three or four Hens" who now sit beside her, has "come out in the new grass to listen to the anthems." Thus placed, she describes what she sees and wishes that Graves could see. "You remember the crumbling wall," she writes, "that divides us from Mr. Sweetser—and the crumbling elms and evergreens—and *other* crumbling things—that spring, and fade, and cast their bloom within a simple twelvemonth—well—*they* are *here*, and skies on me fairer than Italy, in blue eye look down—up—see!— away—a league from here, on the way to Heaven!" Dickinson could show Graves "much that is gay," robins, crows, jays, even an early bumblebee, "if you were here with me, John, upon this April grass." But amid these living things, Dickinson also observes "*wings* half gone to dust, that fluttered so, last year." An elegiac verse almost begins, "Where last year's flies, their errand ran, and last year's *crickets fell!*

We, too, are flying—fading, John . . ." but abruptly ends "and the song 'here lies,' soon upon lips that love us now—will have hummed and ended." Immediately continuing, "To live, and die, and mount again in triumphant body, and *next* time, try the upper air—is no schoolboy's theme!"[13]

Throughout, Dickinson tied her letter together with images of song, beginning with the anthems she went out onto the grass to hear. Were these "anthems" ones that Dickinson overheard from the church? Were they the natural sounds of jays and bees? Were they tones from the Aeolian harp that Graves had built for her in April 1853?[14] Were they also dirges? They became so, later in the letter, for her and for John. She and John were themselves "a roundelay," combining both mortal and resurrected bodies in a round repeated now here in time, now there in eternity. The entire scene she so vividly portrayed for John (and for herself) was like an old, memory-laden song heard from a passing troubadour, remembered just as she now remembered John's old songs of "grief and fun," from a time together two Aprils past. Amid the visible presence of death and decay as she sat on the "April grass," Dickinson fixed in memory that earlier spring, which thereby partook of eternity; it was both "far from us" and had gotten "to heaven first." And thus the letter itself became a song and Dickinson herself the troubadour, employing memory to glimpse and ponder eternity. "How far from us, that spring seems—and those triumphant days—Our April got to Heaven *first*—Grant we may meet her there—at the 'right hand of the Father.'" Dickinson concluded with a gentle admonishment to Graves: "Remember, tho' you rove—John—and those who do *not* ramble will remember you."

In Dickinson's letter to John Graves, *memory* became the connective tissue of the scene she had so vividly depicted. And the scene was not, of course, simply the scene of Dickinson on the lawn with her hens. Memory, as Michel de Certeau has put it, introduces "a heterogeneous element" into what is already a cohesively formed space: Dickinson's Sunday morning on the lawn. When Dickinson incorporated fragments of the past—birds and insects, sounds and songs from a past April—into her immediately surrounding space, she thereby altered her letter's portrait with "a supplementary stroke" that was "so well-placed as to reverse the situation."[15] The present world was freshly perceived when memory insinuated new (yet departed) features into it. Her act of retrieval was simultaneously an act of imagination. Having transported past events into the present, she could also project that past into a future reunion, in which the memory had passed on ahead of her and Graves and arrived in "heaven" before them. Dickinson's portrayal of what she saw stretched backward and forward in time and lengthened out metaphorically to transcend temporal sequence and encompass eternity. A letter became an act of memory. More precisely, a letter became an act of remembering and not forgetting; correspondence became a bulwark against being forgotten, a worry she voiced to Graves and many of her correspondents. Memory created the common space of friendship that Dickinson invited Graves to reenter, with her, in shared memory. Here and elsewhere in her poetry and correspondence, memory recalled past times when the correspondents were directly present to one another, and memory evoked images of a future reunion.

William Merrill Decker has observed that anxiety about the possibility of loss "commonly generates a nostalgic or otherworldly fantasy of future reunion," prompting letter writers to construct "utopian scenes that restore the full presence of the lost or absent friend."[16] Dickinson's version of this pervasive motif regularly employed a familiar Protestant theological vocabulary to depict the utopian scene: heaven, paradise, and immortality. Memory had stabilized or fixed a past moment, abstracted it from the temporal flow, and transported it to another, future location. To represent her sensation that memory thus invested past events with a kind of permanence, Dickinson adapted religious language of the afterlife. Barton Levi St. Armand has remarked of this use of language that Dickinson "italicizes" images by taking commonplace terminology or everyday scenes and setting them off in a bold, startling, and structurally independent way. Her form of originality "selected, transformed, and inverted motifs rather than inventing new ones."[17] At the end of this chapter, I return to the way her introduction of religious language to interpret psychological responses to separation, departure, or loss created multivalent metaphors in which the lost object of desire might be construed as a person, God, or a poem that she had created and then "let go" as an enclosure in a letter.

THE CULTURAL WORK OF MEMORY IN NINETEENTH-CENTURY AMERICA

Memories, like letters, necessarily entail absence, distance, and separation. They retrieve a space from the past and recall events, objects, and persons that occupied a now-departed scene. As these illustrative letters from Emily Dickinson demonstrate, memory seldom if ever retrieves temporal duration. Instead, it recollects a celebratory meal with a cluster of friends, a cataclysmic event that changed the course of life, or a landscape seen from a specific window and the mood that view evoked. "In the theater of the past that is constituted by memory," writes Gaston Bachelard, "the stage setting" that stabilizes our memories of persons and events is provided by specific spaces. These spaces may be thought of as "fossilized duration," in the sense that through them the past is "fixed in space."[18] The space may be a physical repository of memory: house, forest, tomb, photograph, book. Or memory may take narrative form as the celebration of an anniversary, or the visit to a grave, or the return home. In either case, once "fossilized," the space moves through time with the person who remembers, and, in the case of Emily Dickinson under the influence of Christian theology, persists as a form of future possibility. It "got to heaven first." Although many would emphasize memory's malleability as it alters, conflates, or becomes confused with the passage of time, Dickinson chose instead to underscore memory's enduring influence on present emotions and perceptions and the longing it provoked for a future restoration. As she wrote to Austin in the autumn of 1851, "dont think of the present—the present is unkind" because of the separations it imposes, "but the future loves you—it sees you a great way off and runs to meet you," exclaiming in the father's joyful words from the parable of the prodigal son, "my son was dead, and lives again—he was lost and is found!"[19]

By focusing on departed spaces and the objects, persons, and incidents that occupied them, personal memories incline toward memorialization; that is, we attach a memory to an objective emblem like a ring, a photograph, or a favorite chair. As I discussed in chapter 3, nineteenth-century literature of domesticity advised that household objects in general ought properly to be viewed through this lens of sentimental attachment. In this way, loss and bereavement constituted one layer of the meanings ascribed to the pitcher on the table or the clothes in the closet that were encountered in the course of daily life. At the same time, certain objects may be singled out for this memory work or even designed to serve as the containers of memory. Cultures, especially the religious aspect of cultures, take a strong interest in shaping this process of memorializing, a process that occurs in moments of private bereavement, in publicly performed rituals such as funerals, and in public memorials constructed to commemorate the definitive events of corporate identity. Hence personal, familial, and public recollections of the past are thoroughly intertwined. Indeed, public memorialization derives its power from the fact that it resonates so deeply at the personal level, even as it attaches personal identity to the national, communal, and universal.

Like the symbolism of separation and desire for reunion that was implicit in the familiar letter, this intertwining of the personal and the public in rituals of mourning prompted Dickinson to employ the religious vocabulary that linked life and afterlife. These ritual processes took three principal forms, which I take up in turn. First are the keepsakes and memorials, both private and public, to which I have already referred. Second is nostalgia for a rapidly receding past. Third is the elaborate Victorian social ritual surrounding bereavement and consolation. Looking beyond Emily Dickinson to the broader patterns of nineteenth-century society, these three modes of ritual shared an emphasis on continuity, both the transmission of cultural identity in an era of national expansion and the continuity of personal identity across the unknowable chasm of death. Nostalgic public preoccupation with preservation from loss and personal worries about the eclipse of the self were closely related. Hence, during an era when an increasingly mobile commercial society applied disruptive pressure to traditional social continuities, religious leaders sought to maintain or reinvent the affective ties that bound together communities and families. At the same time, with respect to the continuity of the self, the era also displayed a ubiquitous fascination with spiritualism, the séance, communications from the dead, and the possibility that science might offer confirming evidence for the existence of the soul. I want to know how Dickinson's writing both adopted and adapted these cultural preoccupations.

My exploration begins with the keepsakes of personal memory. Emily Dickinson followed the common practice of collecting sentimental objects in a memory box. Since letters (and objects enclosed with letters) conveyed a physical trace of the writer that could be preserved beyond the writer's death, they often found their way into such boxes as reminders of departed persons and past occasions. The chain of associations that linked the memory box to love, separation, and death is evident in a letter that Dickinson wrote to Susan Gilbert in January 1855, about a year and a half before Susan married Austin. Dickinson declared that her love for Susan Gilbert remained as firm as the place where "love first began, on the step at the front door." But now, with Gilbert living in Michigan, Dickinson was stricken that Gilbert did not answer her letters; "it breaks my heart sometimes," she implored, that "not one word comes back to me from that silent West." If love had ended between them, Gilbert must tell her, and Dickinson would "raise the lid to my box of Phantoms, and lay one more love in." Preserved in her memory box, the love that had connected her to Susan would not be lost, even when they, their sisters, and Austin "are marble—and life has forgotten us!"[20] The letter placed love in multiple locations, at the front step, in Dickinson's memory box, and enduring beyond death in the mortuary stone—marble, impervious even to the world's forgetfulness. Dickinson also emphasized this endurance of love through memory and the keepsakes of memory in letters to John Graves and Mary Haven, when she assured them that her memories of them had been carefully laid away in her "box of Phantoms" to be preserved "unto the Resurrection." Another letter even suggested that the bonds of affection, thus preserved, remained vibrant: "have you the little chest to put the Alive—in?"[21]

It is perhaps in this context that we should interpret Dickinson's later remark to Thomas Wentworth Higginson: "a letter always feels to me like immortality because it is the mind alone without the corporeal friend. Indebted in our talk to attitude and accent, there seems a spectral power in thought that walks alone."[22] The immediately striking feature of Dickinson's observation is the separation of mind from body. And, of course, this emphasis on absence or the lack of physical presence constituted the central symbolism of Dickinson's representation of the letter, the memory box, and memory itself. On rereading, however, the materiality of the letter also mediated a different, longer-enduring presence of the correspondent—"immortality"—a presence in and through the letter that had its own "spectral power" and thus its own kind of quasi-physical life that "walks alone" whenever the letter is read. "Talk," with its attitudes and accents, begins to seem ephemeral and "the corporeal friend" mortal. Preserved in the letter or preserved in memory, this "spectral" thought differed from direct speech in yet another way; its "immortality" came, in part, from the fixity of a written form that captured or held a moment of the mind's activity rather than its ongoing process of thinking. The letter lifted from the memory box did not simply retrieve a mind's ideas but enlivened, albeit in "phantom" form, the active thought of one now absent. Dickinson's image of a letter's "spectral power" thus came close to Thoreau's observation that "a written word is the choicest of relics. It is something at once more intimate with us and more universal than any other work of art. It is the work of art nearest to life itself."[23]

Dickinson recognized and exploited the iconic capacity of such keepsakes to condense or focus a range of associated memories and to suggest metaphorical meanings of the object. Her poem "In Ebon Box, when years have flown" (F180) imagined "reverently" peering into an ebony box after the passage of years and finding there a letter "Grown Tawny now with time," whose contents had once "quickened us like Wine!" Sorting further through the memory-laden box, the investigator might come upon a shriveled flower plucked on a distant morning by a now "mouldering hand," a curl from a forehead "Our Constancy forgot," and even "an Antique trinket" set in "vanished fashions." Having cleaned away "the velvet dust" accumulated over intervening summers, not only the remembrances but also the "quickening" emotions they evoked were quietly laid back in place, "As if the little Ebon Box / Were none of our affair!" Perhaps because of the emotional content we add to its store, Bachelard has remarked that a closed box is always more full than an open one.[24]

Memory often served as its own memory box. Not long after her father's death in June 1874, Dickinson composed a poem in which memory was a closet stored with emotionally evocative and even surprising contents (F1385), the sorts of things one would be likely to find after a death in the family. The bittersweet poignancy of her letter to John Graves has been replaced, in this poem, by images of remembering as a somewhat hazardous process that often arose unbidden from an area somewhere beyond or below conscious reflection.

> *That sacred Closet when you sweep –*
> *Entitled 'Memory' –*
> *Select a reverential Broom*
> *And do it silently –*

Since it was "when you sweep," not "if you sweep," Dickinson assumed the necessity of rearranging and storing, but she urged caution: "August the Dust of that Domain – / Unchallenged – let it lie." She also thought that memory, unlike most other closets, could not simply have its contents boxed up and discarded. The present self could not supplant the self constituted by memory and memory's jumbled accumulation of friendship and disappointment, loss and ecstasy: "You cannot supersede itself, / But it can silence you." In a poem written a dozen years earlier (F445), which I discussed in chapter 3, a child's busy imagination had easily escaped the "closet" of parental expectations for proper behavior. But now the closet of memory formed and constrained the poet from within; it was closer in meaning to the old Puritan "closet" of prayer and self-interrogation.

Natural scenes, as Dickinson's letter to John Graves had emphasized, also stored memories and contained emblems of loss. Writing to Mary Bowles as winter was arriving in December 1859, Dickinson translated her natural surroundings into a graveside memorial service: "my garden is a little knoll with faces under it, and only the pines sing tunes, now the birds are absent." In the autumn of 1859, Dickinson had employed the late-blooming purple gentian to develop a more extended metaphor in a letter to Josiah and Elizabeth Holland. Dickinson described the September blossoms as "a greedy flower" that "overtakes us all"; she used the gentian, in short, as a metonymy for life at the boundary marked by the onset of autumn. Judith Farr has thus suggested that, in one of Dickinson's late poems, the gentian was the enticing purple flower growing on the opposite bank of a stream reachable only by children who dared to leap across and "clutch it" (F1588). In her letter to the Hollands, the gentian's autumnal fore- shadowing of winter prompted Dickinson to remark, "indeed, this world is short, and I wish, until I tremble, to touch the ones I love before the hills are red—are gray—are white—are 'born again'!" To extend this metaphor of intimacy threatened by the seasons of mortal life, Dick- inson shifted flowers, making a buried bulb her symbol of loss: "If we knew how deep the crocus lay, we never should let her go." Memory was like the "mounds whose gardeners till in anguish."[25]

MEMORY AS MEMORIAL

Personal questions of loss and memory were transposed into social practice and civic landscape by the "rural cemetery" movement. The move toward the landscaped cemetery on the edge of town had begun in the early 1830s, in part owing to health concerns in rapidly expanding America cities. Equally important, cemeteries designed as landscaped gardens encouraged mourners to visit graves, not only to remember deceased loved ones but also to contemplate in a natural setting.[26] The movement, and the sentiments it represented, spread rapidly across the nation. The most famous of these cemeteries, Mount Auburn in Cambridge (1831), Laurel Hill in Philadelphia (1836), and Greenwood in Brooklyn (1837), became models for numerous others around the country. The design encouraged not only visits by bereaved family members but also a sort of contemplative tourism along winding paths. A tower atop Mount Auburn afforded a view of the cemetery and the surrounding countryside, and a tour through Greenwood guided vis- itors past principal graves and vistas. By 1856, when Oak Dale Cem- etery was designed in Urbana, Ohio, the plan aimed to create a space of spiritual uplift, including lanes with pastoral names, benches for contemplation, a "poet's bower," and spaces designated for unbroken views across the landscape.[27] In 1848 the *Christian Review* published an article explaining that Christianity had dispelled the "cold and cheerless horrors" of the burying ground and made the landscaped cemetery "a place of calm and serene repose, a house of expectation, where mortal relics await a promised immortality."[28] Changing rituals surrounding death and mourning in the middle decades of the nineteenth century were gradually reshaping the ways that individuals and families experienced and performed intimate acts of grief and commemoration. These trends traversed the Protestant spectrum from Unitarianism to the evangelical Protestant communities and, as historian Gary Laderman has explained, "shifted their focus away from the corruptibility of the dead body and graphic descriptions of it in the process of disintegration—a common theme in Puritan sermons—and instead set their sights on the life of the spirit."[29] Gathering at the cemetery before the "mortal relics" was intended to remind the visitor less of mortality than of immortality.

Running parallel to these new approaches to commemoration of the dead, public acts of memorialization were consolidating national identity around the figures and events of the revolutionary era. George Washington, in particular, came to personify the foundational virtues of the Republic, and writers of the era composed extended analogies comparing Washington to Moses.[30] As part of this commemorative process, Mount Vernon became a national shrine, and right up to the beginning of the Civil War, *Godey's Lady's Book* encouraged generous contributions from its readers to preserve Mount Vernon and the memory of Washington.[31] In New England, the urge toward consecration of nationally historic space included the erection of an obelisk at Concord, marking this signal military engagement of the American Revolution. Such occasions of national commemoration generally demanded public oratory, as with President Lincoln's famous address at Gettysburg, and historian Robert A. Gross provides an incisive exegesis of the hymn that Emerson wrote for the dedication of the Concord monument in 1836. Today, says Gross, we remember the poem "for its opening lines about the 'rude bridge,' 'the embattled farmers,' and the 'shot heard round the world.' But the succeeding stanzas express a mood of meditation, not military bombast. The sounds of battle are long gone, the combatants in their graves."[32] And "the rude bridge" of battle in the first stanza has become "the ruined bridge" that time and the river have swept to sea. In the final two stanzas of the hymn, Emerson turned to invoke the present moment of commemoration.

> On this green bank, by this soft stream,
> We set to-day a votive stone;
> That memory may their deed redeem,
> When, like our sires, our sons are gone.
>
> Spirit, that made those heroes dare
> To die, or leave their children free,
> Bid Time and Nature gently spare
> The shaft we raise to them and thee.[33]

Emerson's turn to the present moment was the same turn toward meditation on the human condition invited by the landscape of the rural cemetery. Would redemptive memory secure the promise of heroic deeds as successive generations passed away? Rather than answer the question, Emerson maintained a silent equipoise of nature and culture in rhythmic cadences that carefully balanced the fixed obelisk of human deeds (which the influence of the "Spirit" might—or might not—"gently spare") and the inexorable flow of time.

Emily Dickinson was among the meditative tourists who traveled to these memorial sites. In 1846, while in Boston visiting her aunt, Lavinia Norcross, Dickinson toured Mount Auburn Cemetery. "It seems as if Nature had formed the spot with a distinct idea in view of its being a resting place for her children," she explained to her friend Abiah Root, "where wearied & disappointed they might stretch themselves beneath the spreading cypress & close their eyes 'calmly as to a nights repose or flowers at set of sun.'"[34] Although in the next chapter I want to reexamine this comment and its quotation of the poet Fitz-Greene Halleck, Dickinson's youthful impressions of Mount Auburn, taken at their face value, accurately mirrored the purposes and architecture of the antebellum cemetery. A decade later, Emily and Lavinia Dickinson visited Mount Vernon with their father while he was a member of Congress. She reported to Elizabeth Holland how "hand in hand we stole along up a tangled pathway till we reached the tomb of General George Washington, how we paused beside it, and no one spoke a word, then hand in hand, walked on again, not less wise or sad for that marble story."[35] The landscaped illusion of a natural scene and the neoclassical marble tomb alike encouraged silence, as the dead slept and the living contemplated.

MEMORY AS NOSTALGIA

In a rapidly changing society, memories are commonly tinged with nostalgia. Both the scope of change in nineteenth-century New England and a powerful sense of what was being lost in the process came together in the preaching and essays of one of Amherst College's most famous nineteenth-century alumni, Henry Ward Beecher. In an 1853 magazine essay, "New England Graveyards," Beecher fastened on mobility as the principal engine of change, since "young men, as soon as they attain their majority, push off to the West or South, or to the nearest manufacturing village or railroad depot." With this migration, New England's "old towns have grown rusty," while the manufacturing towns of the river valleys "whirl like a top with enterprise."[36] As the literary historian Nina Baym has explained in relation to Thoreau's *Walden*, although much of New England's population remained directly engaged in agriculture at midcentury, "Yankee farmers were in full-scale flight from New England, moving through New York State to the midwest's more fertile, flatter lands." Consequently, the countryside was fast becoming a "ruined landscape," a panorama of "partly cleared, derelict fields with stumps still standing, of abandoned or indebted farms, of roadsides lined with Irish immigrant shanties."[37] The future lay in commerce and manufacturing. In Beecher's pithy summary, "the loom is too strong for the plow."[38]

Beecher's response to this economic transformation is telling in its presumption that the earlier New England was irretrievable as a social reality and had become an object of nostalgic memory. Since many men now "distinguished in public life" had been reared on these homesteads, Beecher advised that they should return "during the summer vacations" and collect "the memorials of past days" that would furnish a history of past customs and passing generations. "Why should not all the old mansions and farm-houses be secured by daguerreotype, before they crumble?" In Beecher's telling, the old farms, now outside the currents of modern commerce, were not unlike the domestic sphere of women: they communicated distinctive virtues. When traveling through "the rocky parts of New England," the sight of carefully cleared fields revealed "a *moral* beauty" of indomitable perseverance.[39]

Having set the scene by describing the transition to a mobile, commercial society, Beecher focused his essay on a contrast between the old New England graveyards and "the noble cemeteries which within a few years have begun to spring up near the larger towns and cities." It was painful, Beecher lamented, to walk through the desolate graveyards of many New England towns and see memorials given over to the elements: "the fences are dilapidated, the head-stones broken, or swayed half over, the intervals choked up with briers." Beecher attributed this sad state of affairs to an ironic, unintended conspiracy between New England's traditional theology and its modern utilitarian acumen. Although "nowhere on earth is death more solemn than in New England," nonetheless, its citizens gave little thought to anything not connected in some way with practical utility, and "the only places in thrifty New England where weeds are allowed to grow unmolested are graveyards." Beecher wondered, hyperbolically, "if it were dreamed that the beautifying of the grave would even be noticed by those whose bodies sleep there," would not New Englanders lavish loving care "upon the inclosing soil?" But deeply ingrained theological habits of mind had made "a thorough separation between the living and the dead," and this theological outlook had the practical consequence of encouraging neglect of graves, since it was assumed that "the dead are utterly gone. God has them in another world. Their state is fixed and inalterable." It was, Beecher observed, a shame and a disgrace that "one of the finest orchards in Sherburne, Mass., is that which flourishes upon the old town graveyard," and "under the roots of these profitable trees" rested the remains of a succession of former pastors and a president of Harvard College. Beecher concluded that any thoughtful person would "shrink from burial" after seeing such neglect. And no friend would choose to "wade through matted grass and tangled weeds" in order to visit a grave and read the "decaying name" on a weathered stone. Instead, reluctant visitors would surely "hasten away, dreading the cheerless day that shall bring their bodies, too," to a place where they would be utterly forgotten.[40]

By contrast, Beecher affirmed that he loved to wander through Brooklyn's Greenwood and other suburban cemeteries and contemplate one of them as "a resting-place for his body when life is done." These modern, naturally landscaped cemeteries brought to mind such "cheering" and "refining" associations that they "tempt us frequently thither" and "our children are pleased" to come along. When visitors could associate scriptural truths with natural objects, "in flowers, in forests, in sunlight, and at twilight, always, everywhere, and in every thing," then "death begins to be more easily thought of." The tacit theology of the landscaped cemetery, with its shade trees, birds, perennial flowers, and unobstructed vistas "converted death into a joy" and "cheer[ed] us onward toward it, as if it were, as it is, our home and glory." Beecher's practical pastoral advice, therefore, was that the old graveyard (and perhaps also the old theology) should be remodeled along the lines suggested by the suburban cemetery. "The ladies of any parish have but to determine that the resting-places of their ancestors shall bud and blossom as the rose, and it will be done," Beecher predicted, with the grass mowed monthly and "the drooping headstones of the ancient dead" set erect with their "effaced letters" carefully re-incised.[41]

Did Beecher mean to imply that changes in theology and in cemetery design might somehow avert the forgetful disrepair into which the old graveyards—and therefore the remembrance of earlier generations— had fallen? Looking back through his essay "New England Graveyards," it seems filled with ambivalence. Nature in the form of briars and tangled weeds represented human forgetfulness, but in the guise of flowers "renewed every spring," nature was the portal "everywhere and in every thing" through which humans passed toward "our home and glory." Social mobility and industrial development had led New England to ignore its ancestral legacy, but Beecher also hoped that social progress could effect a repair of memory. Although working on a larger social template, Beecher shared Dickinson's intensely personal worries about forgetfulness on the part of those like John Graves, who "roved" rather than stayed.

MEMORY AS MOURNING

The rural cemetery movement, by encouraging mourners to visit the graves of their loved ones, represented only one element in the elaborate rituals of mourning cultivated in Victorian America. From the 1830s forward, a vast literature of consolation and advice about mourning accompanied developments in the landscape architecture of cemeteries. This literature not only sought to provide solace in loss but also proposed that, because Christianity was a religion of the heart, those who mourned were "performing an act of Christian piety." The simultaneous assertion of both the interiority of pious grief and the social etiquette surrounding the demeanor and attire of bereavement aroused "deep middle-class concerns about the hypocrisy of genteel bereavement." The tension between interiority and anxiety about appearances elevated solitude into "a crucial element of sentimental mourning because 'those who grieve unseen are sincere.'" The literary historian Karen Halttunen concludes her astute analysis of nineteenth-century bereavement and its stress on solitary grieving by proposing that mourning became "too sacred to be witnessed" outside a closely knit circle of empathetic confidants. Hence, "rings, pictures, and locks of hair were cherished in the sentimental cult of mourning because they could be handled and wept over in domestic privacy," in the same way that Dickinson privately treasured her "box of phantoms."[42]

The death of children became perhaps the most important and poignant intersection between broader cultural change and the domestic experience of loss and grief, evoking extensive writing, including poetry, by women. Elizabeth Petrino has pointed out that American women poets of the nineteenth century focused particularly on "the exemplary and pious character of the dying child," who taught "a lesson in holy living to its parents." Evangelical testimony to adults together

with unshakable faith in an afterlife became hallmarks of "the spiritu-
ally prescient child."[43] In the summer of 1836, the Methodist evangeli-
cal leader Phoebe Palmer meditated in her diary on the sudden death of
her newborn daughter, who "through a distressing casualty" had "sud-
denly been translated from earth to heaven." Palmer took solace from
her sense that during her daughter's brief life she "had seemed so akin
to heaven's inhabitants," and "the vail separating the two worlds was so
slight" that even in death she "appeared scarcely separated from me."
In this way, Palmer reasoned, "God takes our treasures to heaven, that
our hearts may be there also."[44] Barton Levi St. Armand has interpreted
the consolatory piety centered on the death of a child as part of a broader
movement away from New England's earlier "Calvinistic emphasis on
infant damnation" and original sin toward a view of the child's death as
the paradigm of purity and innocent suffering. St. Armand illustrates
his point with Emily Dickinson's efforts to console Susan Gilbert Dick-
inson following the sudden death of eight-year-old Gilbert in October
1883, when "Dickinson declared, 'I see him in the Star, and meet his
sweet velocity in everything that flies,' while she affirmed, 'now my
ascended Playmate must instruct *me*.' And she prayerfully added: 'Show
us, prattling Preceptor, but the way to thee!'"[45]

The communicative closeness of the dead child, in however many
ways this might have been understood, reflected two trajectories in
nineteenth-century religious culture. In one, assurances about the
heavenly destiny of the child signaled a shift of attention from those
who had died to those who grieved. The second, not incompatible with
the first, stressed continuing communication with the spiritual world,
affirming the hope of personal immortality for the dead and, equally,
for those who grieved. The first trajectory was decisively enunciated
in "Hebrew Dirge," by Lydia Huntley Sigourney, well known for her
poems on infant deaths. The poet's voice began by portraying an
infant being wrapped "in the shroud's embracing fold." She sighed in
lamentation.

> *Not for the babe that slept,*
> *But for the mother at its side,*
> *Whose soul in anguish wept.*

Throughout, Sigourney focused on those left behind: not the young woman whose "angel-wing is spread" but "the lover pale and lone," not the pious matron in her grave but the child left to "roam without a guide."

> *Why shall we weakly mourn for those*
> *Who dwell in perfect rest?*
> *Bound for a few sad, fleet years*
> *A thorn-clad path to tread,*
> *Oh! For the living spare those tears*
> *Ye lavish on the dead.*[46]

Dickinson pursued this same motif of tranquil rest for the dead and consolation for the living in a letter to Austin, informing him of the deaths, barely two weeks apart, of Cyrus Kingman's two young daughters: "the grass is not growing green above the grave of Martha, before little Ellen is laid close beside. I dont know but they are the happier, and we who longer stay the more to be sorrowed for."[47] When Loring Norcross died in January 1863, Dickinson incorporated a poem into the letter she wrote her cousins Louise and Frances Norcross. "Let Emily sing for you because she cannot pray," she explained.[48] Beginning with the conventional distinction made by Sigourney and others, "It is not dying hurts us so – / 'Tis living hurts us more," Dickinson portrayed the difference between the two hurts as the instinctual pattern of birds' migration. The "custom" of some birds "soon as frosts are due" was quickly to adopt (or, in a significant variant reading, accept) a more comfortable southern latitude. Others lingered in the North past the frost and into winter's snow.

> *We are the birds that stay*
> *The shiverers round farmers' doors.*
> *For whose reluctant crumb –*
> *We stipulate – till pitying snows*
> *Persuade our feathers Home.*
>
> (F528)

Dickinson's representations of time and season are a central focus of chapter 5, but at this point I would note that "the birds that stay" seemed willing to endure significant hardship and suffering in their northern climate until finally the snow was moved to pity and persuaded them to take flight toward "Home." The rural cemetery movement had apparently prompted more enthusiasm for the afterlife in Beecher than in Dickinson.

As I indicated, consolation directed toward those who remained to grieve in this world was frequently accompanied by longing for continued communication with the spiritual world that would attenuate the finality of separation. When Phoebe Palmer spoke of the "slight" veil that "scarcely separated" mortal life from a life beyond, her images resonated with a frequently voiced set of religious concerns about personal immortality, the continuity between this world and the other world, and even the possibility of establishing communication with the spirits of the dead. Various ways of thinking about the pervasive presence of a universal spirit and of individual spirits influenced rituals of mourning throughout transatlantic religious and literary culture and resonated with the diverse spiritualist movements that became ubiquitous from the 1840s onward. In the United States, such literary figures as Catharine Beecher, Harriet Beecher Stowe, Thomas Wentworth Higginson, and the poet Sarah Helen Whitman experimented with spiritualist practices, such as the séance, or wrote favorable essays about such phenomena. And in England, one of Dickinson's favorite poets, Elizabeth Barrett Browning, was among those who "found in spiritualism deeply consoling evidence for the immortality of the soul." One leading figure in American spiritualism, Andrew Jackson Davis, followed the logic of close communication with departed spirits and urged mourners to "robe yourselves with garments of light to honor the spirit's birth into a higher level." According to the historian Ann Braude, "spiritualists responded to Davis's advice by wearing white at funerals and by transforming internments into events that emphasized continuity rather than the finality of death."[49]

Metaphysical theories associated with Mesmerism and spiritualism buttressed these religious longings for immortality by asserting a scientific basis for spiritual realities, grounded in a cosmic "ether" that permeated all things mental, physical, and spiritual. Electricity and magnetism provided crucial metaphors for explaining invisible but pervasive powers at work throughout the universe and intimately connected to the human mind. The most prominent spiritualist journal throughout the 1850s was named, appropriately enough, the *Spiritual Telegraph*.[50] In *The Religion of Geology* (1852), Amherst College president Edward Hitchcock indirectly contributed to this theorizing with a chapter entitled "The Telegraphic System of the Universe." Hitchcock described recent discoveries that demonstrated that "electricity has a more intimate connection with mental operations than any other physical force." Not only did "the electric movement" of the mind alter the entire bodily system but, since "electric force" seemed to "permeate all space, and all solid matter," it also appeared likely that "those great mental efforts, and those great decisions of the will, which bring along important moral effects, do also make the strongest impression upon the material universe." In a final flash of speculation, Hitchcock wondered about the farthest reach of the universal telegraph: "there may be no spot in the whole universe where the knowledge of our most secret thoughts and purposes, as well as our most trivial outward act, may not be transmitted on the lightning's wing; and it may be, that, out of this darkened world, there may not be found any spot where beings do not exist with sensibilities keen enough to learn, through electric changes, what we are doing and thinking."[51]

Dickinson referred in her poems to "mesmeric fingers" (F123) and "Blessed Ether" (F326). She probably was familiar with Hitchcock's speculation that the "astonishing transformation" from a living body to "the spiritual or resurrection body" might soon receive explanation, since scientific understandings of light, electricity, and comets made it "almost certain" that there existed, "diffused through every part of the material universe, an exceedingly subtle and active fluid, sometimes called the luminiferous ether."[52] But the governing idea of her poetry, in its religious aspect, seems not to have been direct, spiritual communication with the departed. Instead, she built her model—derived from the formal properties of a letter—on the spectral presence of the absent through the powers of memory and imagination: "a letter always feels to me like immortality." Dickinson portrayed the presence of the departed in ways that left an ambiguous choice for the reader between what might be called a *spiritualist* and an *epistolary* interpretation. An intriguing instance of this ambiguity is a poem from the summer of 1862 that began by observing that "the Soul" experienced special times "Of nearness to her sundered Things." Such experiences were not characterized by "dimness" (of the recollection? of a figure's outline?) but by "Distinctness."

> *The Shapes we buried, dwell about,*
> *Familiar, in the Rooms —*
> *Untarnished by the Sepulchre,*
> *The Mouldering Playmate comes —*
>
> *In just the Jacket that he wore —*
> *Long buttoned in the Mold*
> *Since we — old mornings, Children — played —*
> *Divided — by a world —*

In an approach with strong analogies to Dickinson's letter to John Graves, discussed earlier in this chapter, these stanzas juxtapose the simultaneous presence of vitality and decay. The playmate is at once "Untarnished" and "Mouldering," wearing an immediately recognizable jacket that is now "Long buttoned in the Mold." Ultimately, at least in my reading, Dickinson's poem provides a commentary on the powers of memory and the limits of its capacity to bridge absence. When the grave and the passage of years yield back "our pilfered Things," and "Bright Knots of Apparitions / Salute us, with their wings," the apparitions are not materializations at a séance but memory's moment of reconstructive imagination. "Divided — by a world" from those early moments of play, Dickinson sometimes recalled them into her present with a vivid distinctness, but more often dimly. In a final twist, the "special times" convey such vibrancy that life seems a more enduring attribute of the memory than of the poet's present life.

As we — it were — that perished —
Themselves — had just remained till we rejoin them —
And 'twas they, and not ourself
That mourned —

(F337)

In *Epistolary Practices*, Decker remarks that Emily Dickinson identified "separation, the condition in which letters are written, as the fundamental sorrow of human life." For this reason, "a principle of deferral" drove her writing, and, as in this poem, both the living and the dead await a reunion that is perpetually postponed. The formal properties of the familiar letter, as a literary genre, called attention to these inevitable separations and longings, leading Decker to conclude that, for Dickinson, "language arises in bereavement."[53]

When the Civil War came, it confronted the religiosity of genteel private bereavement and the landscaped continuity of nature and spirit with unprecedented battlefield carnage and public trauma. Emerson had cautiously affirmed redemptive memory at the Concord monument, Beecher had hoped that the inviting landscape of the suburban cemetery would sustain living memories of the dead, and spiritualism had found consolation in a thin veil of separation from the other world. But none had anticipated the violent anonymity of the Civil War battlefield, with mass graves in long trenches, half-buried remains, evidence of identity placed in bottles next to bodies, or identification written on clothing by the soldiers themselves.[54] The war exerted fragmenting pressure on every aspect of Christianity in the United States, ranging from sectional divisions of the Protestant denominations to moral and theological conflicts over slavery. Consequently, the religious language seeking to comprehend the destructive conflict and its meaning took many different forms. Not surprisingly, the most publicly visible religious rhetoric appeared in sermons, poems, and political orations occasioned by the battles, legislation, and deaths of the war years. The title Harry S. Stout chose for his historical study of religion during the war, *Upon the Altar of the Nation*, is virtually a collective quotation of Civil War rhetoric, both North and South. The language of sacrifice and martyrdom constantly reappeared in the oratory of the day, as the devastating loss of life mounted over the course of the war: "the loss of the martyrs whose lives have been sacrificed," or "fallen as a noble martyr upon the altar of his country," or "a bleeding sacrifice upon the altar of its country's independence."[55] Such language sought meaning for individual deaths in the larger cause or principle in defense of which a life was lost.

Dickinson was silent on such matters. Instead, she focused on the experiences of shock and grief endured by those left behind. When Frazar Stearns, the son of Amherst's president, was killed in North Carolina in 1862, the compulsively repeated words "Frazer [sic] is killed" became for her "words of lead—that dropped so deep, they keep weighing."[56] Dickinson's poetic productivity reached its height during the Civil War, and the grief provoked by weighty "words of lead" reverberated through many of her poems, even though she rarely made explicit reference to the war and did not circulate those poems in which such direct references were made.[57]

> *I measure every Grief I meet*
> *With narrow, probing, eyes –*
> *I wonder if It weighs like Mine –*
> *Or has an Easier size –*
>
> (F550)

When Dickinson did write of the war, the links that she habitually fashioned between memory and immortality heightened awareness of the pain that surrounded an anonymous death and a body irretrievably lost. In a poem from the spring of 1863 that her early editors entitled "The Battle-Field," even natural beauty offered no consolation as, indistinguishable from one another, snowflakes, stars, and petals fell. In fact, the very naturalness of their evanescent passing made them a chilling allegory for the soldiers' deaths.

> *They dropped like Flakes –*
> *They dropped like stars –*

Like Petals from a Rose —
When suddenly across the June
A wind with fingers — goes —

They perished in the seamless Grass —
No eye could find the place —
But God can summon every face
On his Repealless — List.

(F545)

Lost to human sight in "the seamless Grass," the faces of the dead were known only to God, and ministerial rhetoric of personal sacrifice for an eternal cause has been replaced by an eternal "List" of divine decree.[58] Later that year, Dickinson portrayed the same devastating detachment in a messenger, perhaps death personified, delivering notice of a soldier killed: "It's Coming — the postponeless Creature — / It gains the Block — and now — it gains the Door" (F556). A "Simple Salute" elicited from the family "Certain Recognition," and one more house, bereaved, was dressed in crepe and "Icicle."

As a poet, Dickinson dealt especially with prolonged emotions such as grief or remorse that, by lasting, lastingly altered the person. Remorse, she wrote in 1863, was the "cureless" disease that not even God could heal, "For 'tis His institution — and / The Adequate of Hell" (F781). In the 1860s Americans had tragic opportunity to experience such enduring sorrows, and shortly after the war ended, Elizabeth Stuart Phelps dramatized the relations among grief, faith, and consolation in her popular novel *The Gates Ajar* (1868). Phelps came from a family of prominent Congregationalist ministers and was the granddaughter of Moses Stuart of Andover Theological Seminary, one of the most distinguished American biblical scholars of the century. She set her novel in a New England village where Mary Cabot has just buried her brother Roy, killed in battle. Although Mary will eventually find consolation through the ministrations of her mother's youngest sister, Winifred Forceythe, and Winifred's small daughter, Faith, the opening pages of the novel portray Mary virtually immobilized by the shock of her beloved brother's death. As the story begins, Mary has come across an old diary and, finding some empty pages, begins writing her thoughts: "The house feels like a prison, I walk up and down and wonder that I ever called it home." Grief has altered the appearance of the world: "Something is the matter with sunsets; they come and go, and I do not notice them. Something ails the voices of the children, snowballing down the street; all the music has gone out of them, and they hurt me like knives." A "great, rough man" had delivered the telegram with the news "shot dead," and Mary feels "shut up and walled in, in Hell." Days later, she remains captive to a "bare, blank sense of physical repulsion" that has not left her since "they first brought him home."[59]

In a famous, richly textured poem written in the autumn following the death of Frazar Stearns, Dickinson attempted her own portrait of the emotions Phelps would depict in the opening scenes of *The Gates Ajar*.

> *After great pain, a formal feeling comes —*
> *The Nerves sit ceremonious, like Tombs —*
> *The stiff Heart questions 'was it He, that bore,'*
> *And 'Yesterday, or Centuries before'?*
>
> *The Feet, mechanical, go round —*
> *A Wooden way*
> *Of Ground, or Air, or Ought —*
> *Regardless grown,*
> *A Quartz contentment, like a stone —*
>
> *This is the Hour of Lead —*
> *Remembered, if outlived,*
> *As Freezing persons, recollect the Snow —*
> *First — Chill — then Stupor — then the letting go —*
>
> (F372)

Anguish had almost entirely disoriented nerves, thoughts, and body in time and space. Did the suffering—a crucifixion?—happen yesterday or centuries ago? Circling heedlessly, the sufferer is unaware whether she treads on ground or air. These apparent movements, mental and physical, are detached from desire and will, which have become immobilized in the crystalline symmetry of quartz; they are formal, ceremonious, stiff, mechanical, wooden. If the sufferer lives to remember the experience, it will be the memory of freezing, immobilized in the equally crystalline symmetry of snow.

Dickinson was amazingly productive during the years of the Civil War, when she composed more than half of her extant poems. I have already identified several prominent themes in that flood of poetry during the war: the pain of loss, desire for the absent, memory, and the hope of reunion. Dickinson's artistic campaign to achieve the coherence of these various themes implied that suffering could become a state of poetic creativity, a state both painful and productive, perhaps productive because painful. "It almost appears," Denis Donoghue has suggested, "that Emily Dickinson welcomed pain and loss for the intensity they provoked; or, if that is excessive, that she was extraordinarily resourceful in finding power where common eyes see only pain."[60] Separation, memory, and irrecoverable or unattainable objects of desire became the experiential basis of the self, the price of resistant independence, and a precondition for powerful poetry.

MEMORY AS CREATIVITY

One legacy of Puritanism in particular exerted a kind of subterranean power in the literature of nineteenth-century New England: the notion that the act of writing included—and in many cases was even constituted by—the self-interrogation of the writer. Emily Dickinson had learned this lesson well. "My Soul – accused Me – and I quailed," she wrote in 1863; "tongues of Diamond" could not deliver a sharper denunciation. By comparison to an accusatory soul, all other accusations were easily absorbed, but ultimately it was the diamond-tongued soul who proved the truer friend.

Her favor — is the best Disdain
Toward Artifice of Time — or Men —
But her Disdain — 'twere lighter bear
A finger of Enamelled Fire —

(F793)

This legacy of writing as self-interrogation added another important theme to Dickinson's poetry during the war years: her maturation and growing sense of independence as a writer.[61] This existential and literary independence, as her correspondence with Higginson indicated, was hard won. After the war, Dickinson deployed the imagery of a battlefield to depict the interior struggle of a soul "fighting for his Life."

The Ordnance of Vitality
Is frugal of it's Ball.

It aims once — kills once — conquers once —
There is no second War
In that Campaign inscrutable
Of the Interior.

(F1230)

This chapter has focused on the ways in which the formal properties of the familiar letter conjoined intimacy, separation, and desire, and this conjunction prompted Emily Dickinson to treasure memories of intimate companionship, take a certain pleasure from the pain of separation, and employ images of heaven to characterize her anticipation of reunion. "To disappear enhances," Dickinson wrote, and "The Man who runs away" was gilded or tinctured with "Immortality" (F1239). In this scheme, memory, by fixing or stabilizing a past moment and abstracting it from the temporal flow, became an earthly analogue to eternity. But the two poems cited above are important reminders that memory is not only the recollection of those who are absent, lost, or departed but also the connective tissue of the self. The "Campaign inscrutable," whatever else it involved, involved arriving at a sense of personal identity. And the imagery of both poems—"A finger of Enamelled Fire"—made it clear that the self-appraisal of a life in time entailed some pain.

Henry Ward Beecher's description of building a house had developed the notion that the house expressed the owner's vision of how he "should like to live." In a poem Dickinson composed in 1863 and revised in 1865, her two most productive years as a poet, the building of a house became a process of self-construction.

> The Props assist the House
> Until the House is built
> And then the Props withdraw
> And adequate, erect,
> The House support itself
> And cease to recollect
> The Augur and the Carpenter —
> Just such a retrospect
> Hath the perfected Life —
> A Past of Plank and Nail
> And slowness — then the scaffolds drop
> Affirming it a Soul —
>
> (F729, 1865 version)

In this poem, the carpenter's tools perhaps suggested the literary craftsmanship admired by Higginson, but they seem primarily to represent the pain of augur and nail that a soul endured in achieving its independence. Even if "a Soul" ceased to remember the painstaking construction, a life required "Just such a retrospect" of plank and nail, even if these were no longer directly visible in "the perfected Life."

This "retrospect," the accumulated life of the writer, remained in evidence not only in the constructed self but in the poems that self constructed. Shifting images from house to fire, Dickinson evocatively depicted the passage from life into art as the ashes that remained from a "Departed Creature."

Ashes denote that Fire was —
Revere the Grayest Pile
For the Departed Creature's sake
That hovered there awhile —

Fire exists the first in light
And then consolidates
Only the Chemist can disclose
Into what Carbonates —

(F1097)

When Dickinson filled her memory box with mementos of departed persons, these became not simply evidence from the past but even revivified memory; a faded letter withdrawn from her "box of phantoms," she remarked, "always feels to me like immortality," exhibiting "a spectral power in thought that walks alone." The gray pile of ash, however, was not the memento of another but the residue of the writer. It was the reader of the poem who must engage in the imaginative act of memory that detected in the residue of words the life from which they had originated. As Helen Vendler has proposed, Dickinson's reader "had to become a forensic Chemist, who, studying the residue of a fire, can perform the tests determining what materials are present in the ashes, and then deduce, from these, the nature of the original substance that would have produced these particular 'Carbonates.'"[62]

Advocacy of cremation would not occur in New England for another decade, during the mid-1870s, but this identification of the writer's literary "remains" with the writer's enduring identity closely connected creativity and literary immortality. Perhaps Dickinson gestured obliquely toward the cremation of Percy Bysshe Shelley in 1822, after his death in a shipwreck off the coast of Italy.[63] More centrally, reverence toward the ashes suggested that the work of art "consolidates" the essence of the writer. Thomas Wentworth Higginson's 1862 advice to young writers had portrayed the perfected piece of literature in just this way, as an "attar of roses" both abstracting and intensifying the fragrance of the living rose. When Emily Dickinson took up this same metaphor, she fastened attention on the process of producing this condensed, intensified essence by the pressure of screws. The essence, she implied, was exuded after torturous compression, applied perhaps to the dead woman as well as to the rose.

> *Essential Oils are wrung —*
> *The Attar from the Rose*
> *Is not expressed by Suns — alone —*
> *It is the gift of Screws —*
> *The General Rose decay —*
> *While this — in Lady's Drawer*
> *Make Summer, when the Lady lie*
> *In Spiceless Sepulchre.*
>
> (F772)

In Dickinson's meditation, the fragrance of rose oil in the chest of drawers owned by a now deceased woman located the essence in the attar rather than in the decayed rose or the "Spiceless" tomb. Circulating her poems, Dickinson had placed the essence of herself in the memory boxes of her friends and family.

5

THE CADENCES OF TIME

The constant, conscious effort to demarcate time is a perennial human labor. For millennia, societies have marked the temporal cycles of nature on which water, shelter, and food production depend. Demarcation has also labored against tedium, attempting to shape the miscellaneous, undifferentiated flow of everyday life as it slips past and is lost to memory. And humans have demarcated time because they feared those moments when it demarcated itself, by natural disaster, violence, illness, and death. Such dramatic cases of temporal rupture are incised all the more deeply in memory by their seemingly random placement amid the continuous occurrences of life. As part of this work of demarcation, humans have established celebrations, created calendars, and built monuments to organize planting and harvest, tenure in political office, commercial contracts, and the passage from one generation to the next. Theories and myths have interpreted the meaning of these human activities by placing them within comprehensive accounts of time as a whole. The ritual calendar of Christianity, symbolically organized around birth, death, and resurrection, redeemed time as well as the person. The Christian Bible, beginning with Genesis and ending with Revelation, implied that it held the entirety of universal history within its covers. Christian doctrines of heaven, hell, and eternity—no matter how variously interpreted—directed human life toward a single, encompassing goal that transcended the temporal flow.

The pragmatist philosopher John Dewey, in *Art as Experience* (1934), argued that demarcating time was not only a ceaseless labor of human societies but also the defining task of art. In contrast to the inchoate or dispersed experience of daily life, Dewey pointed out that "we have *an* experience when the material experienced runs its course to fulfillment." In such cases, experience became "so rounded out that its close is a consummation and not a cessation." By this "individualizing quality," *an* experience was demarcated from other experiences without being cut off from "the general stream of experience." In Dewey's view, the process of creating and enjoying art epitomized the general social process of shaping a distinctive event. Making a work of art was "the clarified and intensified development of traits that belong to every normally complete experience."[1] Robert Pogue Harrison has traced these human activities of boundary marking, including art, back to the fact that humans, while dwelling in space, "dwell first and foremost within the limits of our mortality." Humans, that is to say, recognize their finitude: "death claims our awareness before it claims our lives." Awareness of limitation, epitomized in the limit of death, is "*generative* of the boundaries—spatial and otherwise—of the worlds where history, in its temporal unfolding, takes place. When we build something in nature, be it a dwelling, a monument, or even a fire, we create the rudiments of a world and thereby give a sign of our mortal sojourn on the earth."[2] The human proclivity to mark the boundaries of time, to mold "*an* experience" in Dewey's terms, thus exposes a fundamental interconnection between human mortality and human creativity, between death and art.[3]

This interconnection struck Emily Dickinson with full force. "The notion of time seems always to have haunted Dickinson," observes Cynthia Griffin Wolff, "and she almost never remarked time's passage without a tremor of fear."[4] The crucial phrase in Wolff's remark is "time's passage." Dickinson did not puzzle over the abstract notion of time but over the personal experience of time's extent, its contours, and its boundaries. Her "tremor" at time's passage occurred because, in the act of celebrating human participation in nature, the fear arose that humans likewise participated in the transience of all living things. But even while she trembled at the transience of human lives, Dickinson was also disquieted by the typical theological responses that shaped human experience of time around reassurances of ultimate fulfillment, in which the immortality of the soul grounded personal identity in the order of creation.

Dickinson's art refused both univocally naturalistic and supernaturalistic interpretations of the boundary marked by human mortality. Instead, her writing maintained a tension between the alternatives Dewey posed as "cessation" or "consummation." This tension, resisting any clear decision in favor of one alternative or the other, opened an artistic space in which Dickinson experimented with traditional theological terms, such as heaven, the soul, and resurrection, in order to create an alternative vocabulary for interpreting the experience of time's passage. As Helen Vendler has put it, Dickinson "invents ways to plot temporality."[5] In one undated poem, Dickinson retrospectively appraised events that, in some unstated yet fearsome way, had demarcated the course of a life.

> *My life closed twice before it's close*
> *It yet remains to see*
> *If Immortality unveil*
> *A third event to me*
>
> *So huge, so hopeless to conceive*
> *As these that twice befell.*
> *Parting is all we know of heaven,*
> *And all we need of hell.*
>
> (F1773)

In this poem, two closures have already occurred, and it remains to be seen whether death will mark the passage to a "third event" or simply cessation. In advance of that event, the idea of immortality can only be a verbal placeholder for the unknowable. It is remarkable how completely this poem maintains a perspective from within the flow of time. Looking toward the past, two decisive departures stand, a death, perhaps, a failed love affair. These experiences had been impossible to comprehend, and, looking forward, any third is equally "hopeless to conceive." From within time, looking in either direction, the only thing perceived is a painful and apparently permanent "Parting." What we know of heaven and of hell is identical: an absence.

A further feature of this poem is Dickinson's emphasis on the speaker's awareness of her own death. This awareness struck Dickinson as a distinctively human sensibility, and in a poem of 1859 she imagined a list divided into three categories.

> *Some things that fly there be —*
> *Birds — Hours — the Bumblebee —*
> *Of these no Elegy.*
>
> *Some things that stay there be —*
> *Grief — Hills — eternity —*
> *Nor this behooveth me.*
>
> *There are that resting, rise.*
> *Can I expound the skies?*
> *How still the Riddle lies!*
>
> (F68)

Dickinson began filling in her first two categories, things that fly and things that stay, and it would seem that both categories could be expanded almost indefinitely. Kites fly; imagination has its flights; and, as Dickinson explained in another poem, chimneys, like hills, "never stir at all" (F578). The third category, however, seemed to have at most a single entry. Do the dead rise? "How still the Riddle lies!" As an adolescent she had reflected, after the death of her friend Sophia Holland, "I cannot imagine with the farthest stretch of my imagination my own death scene—It does not seem to me that I shall ever close my eyes in death."[6] Yet "the Riddle" of the boundary marked by death kept recurring, and the question she posed in this poem may also be posing a challenge to her own poetic powers: "Can I expound the skies?" In several of her most famous verses the poetic voice spoke from the moment of death or just beyond it, portraying precisely the scene Dickinson had once declared she could not imagine "with the farthest stretch of my imagination."

As a problem of art, Dickinson thus concerned herself with experiences of the boundaries of time. With respect to the *boundaries* of time, she composed an experience within the flow of time, such as the opening of a letter or the flight of a bird, and events that signaled the disruption of the flow by, for instance, the end of a friendship or the death of a friend. With respect to the *experiences* of those boundaries, Dickinson was drawn especially to what I would call emotions of duration: desire for an unattainable lover, remorse for an irrevocable act of betrayal, or suffering long endured in silence. This could be termed the representation of *affective time*, the way time's passage was experienced. As she explained in a poem sent to Susan Dickinson,

> Two Lengths has every Day —
> It's absolute extent
> And Area superior
> By Hope or Horror lent —
>
> (F1354)

A devoted gardener as well as poet, Dickinson favored metaphors that arose from the cycles of nature for delineating these experiences of temporal duration and its boundaries: the daily transit of the sun, the moon crossing the night sky, the arrival of spring's first robin, or a lingering flower in late autumn. Since adolescence, the "ceaseless flight of the seasons" had fascinated her.[7] In her hands, these natural cycles could represent the span of a single lifetime, the rise and fall of nations and empires, or the course of universal time. But even as she composed experiences of bounded time, she retained the theological vocabulary of transcendent fulfillment beyond time and the immortal soul that somehow traversed the boundary of death. These two points of accent in her poetry generated dramatic tension by juxtaposing immortality and the transience of life, leaving the reader with a riddle or conundrum.

This chapter proposes that Dickinson's poetic experiments with the juxtaposition of transience and immortality resonated with widespread religious questions in American Christianity about the immortality of the soul and, more generally, about the nature of religious language. The chapter opens with the relationship between the natural cadences of time and religious interpretations of human mortality and immortality, a relationship that worried nineteenth-century religious thinkers in no small measure because of the century's advancing scientific knowledge of geological time and natural history, preeminently in the work of Charles Darwin. I then offer a reading of one of Dickinson's most famous poems, "Safe in their Alabaster Chambers," in order to interpret the significance for her poetry of these wider religious issues of time and finitude. Dickinson's use of theological ideas in this poem related to a larger debate about the nature of religious language, specifically, the language of transcendence. Indeed, the common modern meaning of the term transcendence, referring to God's distance and independence from the created world in contrast to divine immanence within the world, seems to have emerged in the early decades of the nineteenth century.[8] The chapter (and the book) concludes by appraising Dickinson's place in that wider debate.

WITHIN THE CYCLES OF NATURE

When Dewey described alternative closures of experience as "consummation" and "cessation," he indirectly raised one of the organizing theological questions of the nineteenth century. In the passage of time, were individual humans and humanity as a whole proceeding toward consummation or cessation? Of course, meditation on human mortality was by no means emerging in the nineteenth century as a new issue for Christian reflection; it had held a prominent place in Christian spirituality since antiquity. In the various traditional interpretations, facing up to human mortality was actually a double confrontation. It was the prospect of dying, of course. But behind the fact of death was the source of death, explained in Genesis 3:1–24 as a story of satanic deception and violation of divine command: "Ye shall not eat of it, neither shall ye touch it, lest ye die" (Gen. 3:3, KJV). Death was the consequence of sin. God drove Adam and Eve east out of Eden, and extended their punishment across creation: "cursed is the ground for thy sake" (3:17). Under the sway of this classic narrative, early modern theories of earth history had assumed not only that natural history must be virtually coterminous with human history but also that natural history was subsumed under the moral history of the human race. Although the classical Christian view of the cosmos had long accommodated patterns of cyclical change, it had constrained those cycles within a temporally limited cosmos directed by an underlying providential pattern. When the seventeenth-century archbishop of Armagh, James Ussher, calculated that creation occurred in 4004 B.C., his date became famous because of its inclusion in the marginal notes of some editions of the King James Bible, but its general point about the temporal boundaries of the universe was a commonplace.[9]

Older patterns of devotion, operating within this moral cosmos, had directed attention toward the absolute power of God, who redeemed souls ineradicably tainted by sin. In this earlier narrative, humans—from birth to death—ventured on a dangerous passage through the self-destructive allure of this world toward an ultimate destination that lay beyond life and time. As the title of a famous sermon series by Jonathan Edwards made clear, the governing vector of universal history was "the history of the work of redemption," extending from the human fall to the end of the world. Furthermore, Edwards and his contemporaries argued, the entire physical universe was "designed" by God to be "a resemblance and shadow" of the spiritual world of human redemption. In a notebook entitled "Images of Divine Things," which Edwards began in the late 1720s, he compiled instances from study of the Bible and from observation of nature in which natural objects were emblems, types, or figures of spiritual things. Thus, according to Edwards, Paul's argument from the sowing of seed to the resurrection of the dead (1 Cor. 15:35–44) demonstrated that God had designed natural cycles of growth to convey spiritual meanings. And, Edwards continued, Christians learned from observing the natural order that "the whole material universe is preserved by gravity, or attraction, or the mutual tendency of all bodies to each other. One part of the universe is hereby made beneficial to another. The beauty, harmony and order, regular progress, life and motion, and in short, all the well-being of the whole frame, depends on it." This gravitational "type" was "the representation or shadow" of the central, substantive truth of "the spiritual world": that divine love bound it together in coherent harmony. Nature was thus *intrinsically* symbolic, and Edwards concluded "the works of God are but a kind of voice or language of God, to instruct intelligent beings in things pertaining to himself."[10] Redemption from sin was the axis of time, and the natural world was the "language" through which God adumbrated the scriptural narrative of redemption.

This broad narrative, including its reading of nature as a coherent system of spiritual emblems, by no means disappeared during the nineteenth century. With regard to original sin, the fear remained among evangelical Protestants that a loved one might have died without experiencing salvation, a fear regularly invoked not only in sermons but also in popular fiction such as *The Gates Ajar*.[11] And "natural theology" expounded by William Paley and others, even though its presuppositions differed from those of Jonathan Edwards, continued to promulgate evidences of divine design in the structures and processes of physical nature. But, as I have already illustrated from the writings of Henry Ward Beecher, Phoebe Palmer, and the spiritualist movement, in the nineteenth century a new emphasis on reassurance suffused the traditional theological vocabulary of sin, death, and the afterlife. If anything, nineteenth-century Protestants typically thought that traditional New England theology, with its fear-inspiring stress on perdition, had confronted the fact of mortality altogether too directly. Popular theology and piety of the nineteenth century preferred, instead, to stress continuity: the immortality of the soul, the pervasive presence of spiritual energies throughout the material universe, and the thin veil "separating the two worlds." These repeated affirmations of the unending endurance of the human spirit suggest that, alongside sin, nineteenth-century popular piety perceived and was responding to another, quite different threat to the immortal soul: transience.

Starkly posed, the question of transience was this: what exempted humans from the death that awaited all other living species? The question had one of its sources in the expanding scientific knowledge of the geological history of the earth. During the eighteenth century, naturalists had examined fossils in sedimentary rock strata and come to the conclusion that species now extinct had lived in an immeasurably distant past, long before the beginning of human history. Early nineteenth-century geology focused on observation and practical utility and tended to avoid theoretical arguments, especially on the issue of the origin of humankind. But, according to historian Martin Rudwick, when geologists expanded the time scale of earth history, the "religious problem was now that of finding some human meaning in those vast spans of prehuman history." In the early 1830s, the British geologist Charles Lyell synthesized advancing studies of the fossil record and the processes of formation and erosion of soil and rock in order to expound a cyclical view of earth history that accounted for the emergence and extinction of entire species over the course of geological epochs. By midcentury, routine geological practice had largely assimilated "Lyell's explanatory use of unquantified but virtually limitless time."[12] A devout Unitarian, Lyell anguished over the growing evidence of species development and, especially, the place of the human species in that process. As the literary historian Christopher Lane concludes regarding Lyell's research, "if uniform changes were visible everywhere, including in the extinction of species, what—other than biblical insistence—made us exempt from the transmutations affecting almost everything else on earth?"[13]

In the 1840s and 1850s, influential voices in American science, letters, and theology sought to turn the cycles of nature toward reassurance of humanity's distinctive destiny in the history of the universe. The historian James R. Moore has identified these transitional decades, when the boundaries between academic disciplines remained quite fluid, as an "interval between the emergence of a conceptually and methodologically integrated geological profession and the onset of the professionalization of Old Testament scholarship" that stretched from "Charles Lyell's 1832 maxim, 'The physical part of Geological inquiry ought to be conducted as if the Scriptures were not in existence,' to Benjamin Jowett's 1860 motto, 'Interpret the Scriptures like any other book.'" During this "interval" in the professionalization of the academic disciplines, several of Lyell's American contemporaries worked to harmonize Genesis and geology, including Benjamin Silliman (1779–1864) at Yale and Edward Hitchcock at Amherst.[14] Among these harmonizers, Hitchcock's books and public lectures drew spiritually uplifting lessons, by proposing analogies between scriptural teaching and the current research in geology and earth history.

In *The Religion of Geology* (1852), Hitchcock stressed nineteenth-century scientific understanding of the immense age of the earth and the evidence that "numerous races of animals and plants must have occupied the globe previous to those which now inhabit it, and have successively passed away, as catastrophes occurred, or the climate became unfit for their residence." He estimated that "not less than thirty thousand species have already been dug out of the rocks; and excepting a few hundred species, mostly of sea shells, occurring in the uppermost rocks, none of them correspond to those now living on the globe." Since a "whole series of rocks, six miles in thickness," preserved vast numbers of fossilized animals and it was only when geologists probed "the very highest stratum, the mere superficial coat of alluvium, that we find the remains of man," Hitchcock attempted to work out a consistent relationship between these findings of modern geology and the interpretation of Genesis, in which death entered the world through the disobedience in Eden of Adam and Eve. Long epochs of species extinction, he concluded, indicated the foreordination and foreknowledge of God: this "condition of the world resulted from the divine determination, upon a prospective view of man's transgression."[15]

This encompassing theistic perspective provided Hitchcock with the framework for symbolic readings of the immediately observable cycles of seasonal change. In a sermon series, *Religious Lectures on Peculiar Phenomena in the Four Seasons* (1850), Hitchcock proceeded from "The Resurrections of Spring" to "The Coronation of Winter," in order to demonstrate that "every natural change is as really the work of God, as if the eye of sense could see his hand turning round the wheels of nature." In each sermon, he argued that evidence from "natural changes" and principles from natural science provided illustrations and analogies that clarified and adumbrated "scriptural doctrine." For example, Hitchcock advanced evidence that a form of "attenuated matter" called "luminiferous ether" acted as the agent for transmitting energy throughout the material universe, and, without wishing to leap to unjustified assertions, Hitchcock reasoned that this universal ether shared many characteristics with what one might presume about "the spiritual or resurrection body." Both ether and the spiritual body "would be of such a nature as to be unaffected by mechanical or chemical action," and they might exist "with equal freedom, and without change, in the midst of the sun, or the volcano, or in the polar ice." Of such a substance, Hitchcock concluded, "the spiritual body may be composed, or of something analogous to it." And he appealed to his "Christian friends" to consider the many forms of beauty encountered in daily life as so many "resurrections of spring," which should serve as "symbolizations of that nobler resurrection, when forms a thousand times dearer shall start into life from a deeper winter, and put on a verdure that will never decay, and a glory that will never fade."[16] The cycles of nature here symbolized a resurrected "spiritual body" that had passed beyond those very cycles, into a life destined to endure without end.

Within this evidential framework, not only spring but also autumn afforded Hitchcock emblems of eternal life. Beginning with a brief scientific description of the natural process of "decay and death" in plants and animals, Hitchcock lamented a powerful human tendency "to forget this great law of decay and mortality" and thereby avoid personal religious preparation for death. To combat this human avoidance of unpleasant inevitabilities, the wisdom of providence had, every autumn, "placed all along our path, mementos of our approaching decay and dissolution." Hitchcock then joined his meditations on autumn to his earlier consideration of spring and, thinking of the perennial regeneration of plants, asked rhetorically, "has life really all gone? No: it has only withdrawn to the citadel, and there concentrated its powers to resist the assaults of frost, and prepare for new developments, when the sun shall return from southern skies, and a more genial temperature shall revisit these northern climes. It is only a change of state, and not the extinction of life."[17] The eminent midcentury geologist attempted to harmonize his understanding of the natural sciences with classic natural emblems of the resurrection. In so doing, he kept abreast of recent research in geology and paleontology, but he adapted these scientific findings to an eighteenth-century model of "evidences" from natural history that supported the authoritative teachings of scripture by turning cycles of natural change into moral symbols prefiguring the destiny of the soul. Hitchcock's overall interpretation thus accommodated ideas of natural change and species development but did so on the basis of a divine "hand turning round the wheels of nature," a mechanism far different from the argument for species development on the principle of natural selection that Charles Darwin was then preparing for publication, *On the Origin of Species* (1859).

Hitchcock's contemporary, the journalist and poet William Cullen Bryant, also employed the cadences of natural change to interpret human destiny, but in a contrasting way. In his best-known poem, "Thanatopsis," Bryant urged the reader preoccupied by thoughts of death to "Go forth, under the open sky, and list / To Nature's teachings." These teachings were somber. The earth was "one mighty sepulchre," inexorably receiving all the human race into itself, where "surrendering up / Thine individual being, shalt thou go / To mix forever with the elements." In his concluding ethical reflection, Bryant enjoined the reader moving toward "that mysterious realm" to do so with a self-controlled serenity.

> By an unfaltering trust, approach thy grave,
> Like one who wraps the drapery of his couch
> About him, and lies down to pleasant dreams.[18]

Emily Dickinson had encountered this counsel of serenity in a poem by Fitz-Greene Halleck, which she quoted to Abiah Root in 1846, as part of her description of Mount Auburn Cemetery.[19] A Connecticut native, Halleck spent four decades in New York City, where he was one of the "Knickerbocker Group" of writers along with Bryant, James Fenimore Cooper, and Washington Irving. Dickinson quoted Halleck's "Marco Bozzaris," a poem honoring a Greek patriot who died leading a victorious battle against Turkish rule in 1821.

> His few surviving comrades saw
> His smile when rang their loud hurrah,

And the red field was won;
Then saw in death his eyelids close
Calmly, as to a night's repose,
Like flowers at set of sun.[20]

Although the youthful Dickinson made reference only to the two con-
cluding lines of Halleck's poem, the larger context of equanimity in
death on a battlefield well conveyed the general tone of composure when
confronting one's death that was a characteristic theme in Bryant's
poetry. In "To a Waterfowl," for instance, a solitary observer watches
the dark silhouette of a waterfowl making its "solitary way" across the
sky at sunset. "A Power," the observer reflects, was guiding the instinc-
tive flight of the bird, "Lone wandering, but not lost," as it disappeared
from sight: "the abyss of heaven / Hath swallowed up thy form." Once
again, Bryant concluded with a consolatory "lesson," received from his
meditation on the natural cycle of the waterfowl's migratory flight.

He who, from zone to zone,
Guides through the boundless sky thy certain flight,
In the long way that I must tread alone,
Will lead my steps aright.[21]

In both poems, Bryant portrayed a natural scene of striking
austerity—"the still lapse of ages" and "the cold, thin atmosphere"—
where the speaker engaged in formal rhetorical address rather than
conversational interaction and where the quality of personal com-
portment was a dignified yet solitary melancholy. Unlike Hitchcock's
emphasis on Christian doctrines of the soul and resurrection, Bryant's
"recurrent but inconsistently treated theme" was "a nihilistic view of
death subversive of the values" of his antebellum audience.[22] Although
Bryant shared Hitchcock's penchant for religious and moral didacti-
cism, he set aside affirming analogies between life's natural cadences
and resurrection of "the spiritual body," and instead traced an indi-
vidual's lifelong flight toward "the abyss of heaven."

Hitchcock died in 1864, and after the Civil War, efforts such as his
to buttress scriptural authority through evidence and analogies drawn

from natural history rapidly lost their hold among faculty and students of New England colleges. Interest in the question of immortality, however, continued unabated in the region's colleges and congregations. Newer approaches to the topic attempted a limited rapprochement with evolutionary theory by stressing development and change, that is, the moral and spiritual progress of humanity propelled by the purposes of a God immanent in nature and history. In this vein Emily Dickinson's contemporary, the Congregationalist minister Theodore T. Munger (1830–1910), published in 1883 a highly successful collection of sermons, *The Freedom of Faith.* "The question most eagerly urged to-day is that of immortality," Munger asserted, and he devoted fully a third of the volume to exploring the relation of the concept of immortality to modern scientific theory, natural history, biblical studies, and theology.[23] By this time in his career, Munger had become a leading figure in the movement known as Progressive Orthodoxy, which had its intellectual roots in American Romanticism and the theology of Horace Bushnell.[24] Out of this background, Munger's ideas on immortality flowed from three governing concepts. First, setting aside "a mechanical, extra-mundane conception of God," Munger presupposed "a proper conception of God as immanent in the order of nature," and he approvingly quoted Emerson's dictum, "when the master of the universe has points to carry in his government, he impresses his will in the structure of minds."[25] The second concept, derived from the thought of the German theologian Friedrich Schleiermacher (1768–1834), adumbrated Emerson's correlation between divine immanence and the structure of the human mind by stating that awareness of God was "a universal and invariable ingredient in all human consciousness."[26] As Theodore Parker had argued in 1842, "beneath all the shifting phenomena of life," every person has felt a sensation or "mysterious sentiment of something unbounded," and "this innate religious sentiment is the basis and cause of all Religion." In Parker's words, this universal human consciousness of "something without bounds, is itself a proof by implication of the existence of its object." And Parker followed this assertion with a still more emphatic statement that "a belief in this relation between the feeling in us and its object independent of us, comes unavoidably from the laws of Man's nature. There is nothing of which we can be more certain." This "intuitive perception of God" came "spontaneously" and was not the result of argumentation.[27] The third governing idea was that human cultures universally exhibited a belief in the immortality of the soul. While requiring some interpretive gymnastics in the case of Buddhism, this argument became a commonplace among nineteenth-century American students of comparative religion. Thus, when James Freeman Clarke published the second part of *Ten Great Religions* in 1883, he declared unequivocally, "of all the beliefs of man in regard to the supernatural world, the belief in a human soul as a substantial essence, capable of existing independently of the body, has prevailed most widely. It is found in all parts of the world, in all times, among all classes." This belief, Clarke proposed, had its basis in a "profound and universal fact of inward experience," namely, that "we are conscious of a thinking, feeling, and acting self, which has no bodily qualities" and which possesses "a marvelous unity, correlating and combining in a central self or ego, imagination, memory, hope and fear, love and hatred." Although "primitive man does not argue in this way," he fully shared the consciousness of "the philosopher" that this "indivisible unity" of the self "continues one and the same through all the changes of life, and therefore will continue" after the death of the physical body. "The body dissolves at death, but the self within the body is indissoluble."[28]

Munger skillfully intertwined these three ideas in his brief for personal immortality and rebuttal of natural selection. When the physical sciences proposed "that all mental and moral activities are but the operation of organized matter," then, it appeared to Munger, "anything that survives when the bond breaks that holds the whirling atoms together, is an impossibility." Adoption of such a theory, therefore, reduced the individual human personality to "a momentary lifting up of certain particles and forces from the ocean of being into which it soon falls back, like a wreath of spray snatched by the wind from the crest of a wave, drawing its energy from it, never ceasing to play into it, and finally mingling with it. The main thing is not personality but the all." Such an idea, Munger admitted, was not "wholly devoid of nobility of sentiment," but it failed to address the central issue of the soul's immortality. When it spoke of immortality, it did not mean an individually "enduring personality" but the generic continuance of human life: "men perish, but man survives; the generations pass away, but the race endures." Likewise, "the doctrine of physical evolution which holds that all forms of life are developed from preceding forms" seemed to dash the hope of immortality "by bringing all life into one category and under one law, with the apparent inference of one destiny." But, Munger responded, an immortality of impersonal life was "a matter of small concern to us," since "we want not mere continuance but some solid ground for belief in *personality* after death."[29]

Munger constructed his argument for personal immortality around the idea that the existence of a universal human sentiment implied the existence of its object. But he began his sermon "Immortality and Nature" by acknowledging that "it is a strange fact that the human mind has always held to the immortality of the soul, and yet has always doubted it; always believing but always haunted by doubt." In response to that haunting doubt, he named eight considerations, drawn from universal features of human thought and emotion, that offered "grounds for believing that the soul of man is immortal." For example, given "the longing of the soul for life, and its horror at the thought of extinction," Munger affirmed that this "inwrought desire" comported with the order of the universe: "there must be a correlation between desire and fulfillment." Similarly, Munger pointed out that in the act of thinking, the thinker was aware of embarking on an endless task, and therefore "the action of the mind in *thought* begets a sense of continuous life." Finding that "all things are linked together, and the chain stretches either way into infinity," the thinker recognized a necessity of thought to follow the infinite chain, "and the necessity indicates the fact. There can be no fit and logical end to thought till it has compassed all truth." Turning from human nature to the "divine nature," Munger concluded that if there was no immortality for humans, then there was "a failure in the higher purposes of God respecting the race; good ends are indicated but not reached." "If death ends life, what is this world but an ever-yawning grave in which the loving God buries his children with hopeless sorrow, mocking at once their love and hope, and every attribute of his own nature. Again we say, the logic of love upon the divine as upon the human side, is, there is no death. Divine as well as human love has but one symbol in language—*forever*."[30]

Dickinson shared her contemporaries' quandary over immortality, and in response to a query from Higginson in 1866, she described immortality as "the Flood subject."[31] In 1862 she had written a poem that beautifully (and wittily) narrated Munger's conundrum "that the human mind has always held to the immortality of the soul, and yet has always doubted it; always believing but always haunted by doubt." Dickinson began with a strong declarative statement.

> *This World is not conclusion.*
> *A Species stands beyond —*
> *Invisible, as Music —*
> *But positive, as Sound —*

Continuing, Dickinson observed that this world "beyond" had baffled scholars and sages with an ultimate "Riddle," even as it beckoned martyrs who were willing to undergo contempt and crucifixion "To gain it." The overall effect of the first twelve lines of the poem thus qualified its initial affirmation by presenting sages and martyrs whose thought and action struggled toward what stood "beyond" yet, despite their best efforts, remained "a Riddle, at the last." Not unlike William Cullen Bryant, Dickinson implied a certain admiration for these principled struggles with the mysterious limit of mortality. The concluding eight lines of the poem, however, changed the direction of Dickinson's critique.[32] The object of her criticism was a superficial faith that brushed aside the deeper questions pursued by sages and martyrs and seized instead on the slightest "twig of Evidence" in favor of a world "beyond," relying on a weather vane to provide directions toward heaven.

> *Much Gesture, from the Pulpit —*
> *Strong Hallelujahs roll —*
> *Narcotics cannot still the Tooth*
> *That nibbles at the soul —*

(F373)

Such trumped up confidence, Dickinson implied, was unworthy of the profound question that confronted it, and, consequently, its rolling "Hallelujahs" could not assuage a constant, underlying pain of doubt.

The pressure point for nineteenth-century faith and doubt regarding the immortality of the soul was the connection between nature and human nature. For Hitchcock, nature's cycles of dormancy and rejuvenation were earthly emblems of an eternal resurrection. For Bryant and Halleck, death's dormancy became sleep—"Calmly, as to a night's repose"—even though both men maintained an ambiguous silence about the awakening that follows natural sleep. And for Munger, God, the enduring continuity guiding natural history from within, paralleled the soul, the enduring continuity of personal identity. God "immanent in the order of nature" stirred in the human mind an intuitive "sense of continuous life." Nineteenth-century attentiveness to the transience of life intensified questions about the soul because it threatened cultural assumptions about the intrinsic unity of the cosmos and of the self. The various lines of religious thought, up to and including Romanticism, that treated nature as revelatory of the human relation to the divine had come into conflict with cyclical views of natural time in which both species and individuals were extinguished.

THE SILENCE OF THE AGES

Dickinson's own attentiveness to nature likewise probed the relations between its cycles and the boundaries of human mortality. She drew her most immediate and vivid images of temporal cycles from the cultivation of her garden, which, like all gardens (except perhaps Eden), was brought into being and maintained through time. She minutely observed the growth and withering of flowers, the seasonal migration of birds, and the changing angles of sunlight in the course of a day or the passage of a year, and these cyclical cadences became overarching metaphors that demarcated time in her poetry. House and garden became a stage on which the act of living was played out, by flowers, by birds, by humans. Faithful in cultivating daisy, rose, and narcissus and constantly anticipating the next to bloom, Dickinson was especially conscious that cyclical flourishing presaged life's decay, disruption, and dissolution. Mounds of garden loam became metaphors for tombs—"a little knoll with faces under it"—and the flight of birds was the departure of souls.[33]

> *While simple-hearted neighbors*
> *Chat of the "Early dead" –*
> *We – prone to periphrasis,*
> *Remark that Birds have fled!*
>
> (F62)

The metaphorical flight of birds in this poem is one of a number that, for the purposes of this chapter, might be referred to as Dickinson's *poems of departure*. These employed the cycles of the day and of the seasons to pose a series of questions about human mortality and immortality. In one of the poems that Dickinson enclosed in her first letter to Higginson in the spring of 1862, the passage of a day provided a metaphor of the passage of human lives. The poem opened confidently, "I'll tell you how the Sun rose," and personified a landscape of spreading sunlight: "The Steeples swam in Amethyst," and "The Hills untied their Bonnets." But sunset, personified with equal beauty, could only be known as a cluster of children dressed in fading colors—purple, yellow, gray—disappearing over a stile in the boundary fence to "the other side."

> *But how he set – I know not –*
> *There seemed a purple stile*
> *That little Yellow boys and girls*
> *Were climbing all the while –*
> *Till when they reached the other side –*
> *A Dominie in Gray –*
> *Put gently up the evening Bars –*
> *And led the flock away –*
>
> (F204)

Cynthia Wolff has aptly stated Dickinson's view that "if the seasons moved in an orderly fashion, they also moved inexorably and without regard for the individual case."[34] Thus, even though Dickinson regularly personified natural cycles in order to suggest their empathy with the human plight, in many other cases she did so in order to represent nature as emotionally detached, impassive, perhaps aware of the desires and hopes that propelled the human experience of time but completely unconcerned. An example of this "detached" natural order appeared in a letter to Susan Gilbert in October 1851, in which Dickinson wondered whether the same moon that was shining through the window on her and Lavinia would also shine on Gilbert in Baltimore. The moon, Dickinson wrote, "looks like a fairy tonight, sailing around the sky in a little silver gondola with stars for gondoliers." Attracted by the moon's serene beauty, Dickinson "asked her to let me ride a little while ago—and told her I would *get out* when she got as far as Baltimore, but she only smiled to herself and went sailing on."[35] A poem enclosed in a letter to Louise and Frances Norcross similarly depicted an observer through a windowpane who "watched the moon around the house" and recognized from its impassive independence that the moon had no "concern / For little mysteries / As puzzle us, like life and death" (F593).

In *Uncle Tom's Cabin*, Harriet Beecher Stowe employed the silence of the night sky to plot Tom's faith in a compassionate God. Early in the novel, when the slave trader Mr. Haley took Tom along with other slaves by boat to auctions along the Ohio River, the night sky was voiceless, "calm, unmoved, and glorious, shining down with her innumerable and solemn angel eyes, twinkling, beautiful, but silent. There was no speech nor language, no pitying voice or helping hand, from that distant sky." Near the end of the novel, Tom, having fallen into the cruel grip of Simon Legree, had a vision of Christ's face "bending compassionately towards him, and a voice" speaking the words of Revelation 3:21. Immediately after this vision, Tom once again "looked up to the silent, ever-living stars—types of the angelic hosts who ever look down on man." And on this occasion, "the solitude of the night rung with the triumphant words" of the hymn "Amazing Grace." Stowe quoted the stanza that envisioned heaven's eternal song of praise, noting that Tom had often sung it in earlier days, "but never with such feeling as now":

When we've been there ten thousand years,
Bright shining like the sun,
We've no less days to sing God's praise
Than when we first begun

Stowe initially left uncertain whether the hymn was angelic song or Tom's own voice, but she shifted to a psychological rendering in the next paragraph: "The psychologist tells us of a state, in which the affections and images of the mind become so dominant and overpowering, that they press into their service the outward senses, and make them give tangible shape to the inward imagining." Stowe drew the scene to a close by posing a rhetorical question to her readers: "If the poor forgotten slave believes that Jesus hath appeared and spoken to him, who shall contradict him?"[36] Unlike Jonathan Edwards, who had declared nature the language of God and, gazing on the moon, had beheld "the sweet glory of God," both Dickinson and Stowe personified natural objects precisely to underscore silence, the absence of speech. Stowe went further and represented the hymns of heaven as psychological projection.

The cadences of time thus challenged Dickinson's literary art with two questions. How would she represent human departure from life across the boundary of death? And how would she relate the cycles of natural time to the purposive desires that added "the future tense" to the human experience of temporality?[37] For eighteen months, from late 1859 to the summer of 1861, Dickinson wrestled with these questions in a poem that began "Safe in their Alabaster Chambers" (F124). In the course of revision, Dickinson crafted an enigma that imagined different relationships between cycle and cessation. She was thinking her way through perennial questions not simply about death but about the frame of reference in which humans come to terms with death's finality. Eschewing Munger's bland affirmation of "a sense of continuous life," her austere verse, in the earliest extant transcription (late 1859), began by meditating on an ornate tomb.

Safe in their Alabaster Chambers —
Untouched by morning

And untouched by noon —
Sleep the meek members of the Resurrection —
Rafter of satin,
And Roof of stone.[38]

The dead were smoothly sealed in a timeless sleep, "untouched" by the passage of days. But deciding on the stanza to follow this one became a puzzle. Dickinson's first effort contrasted the timelessness of death with an ephemeral morning on whose breezes a bee "Babbles" and "the Sweet Birds [sing] in ignorant cadence," oblivious, in their brief moment of joy, to the "sagacity" about life's impermanence that slept nearby in "Alabaster Chambers." As Helen Vendler observes, "'Sagacity' perishes, but nature's laughing ignorance, perpetually resurrected, lasts forever."[39] Dickinson sent the poem to her sister-in-law and confidant Susan Gilbert Dickinson. But Susan apparently objected to the second stanza, and Dickinson tried another approach. This time, the second stanza contrasted death's eternity not simply with life passing like a summer day but instead with the sweeping circuits of nature and the eclipse of nations.[40] Both versions of the second stanza contrasted the smoothly sealed tombs with a world "above" them. But in this second version, the world of time and change moves at a dramatically different cadence, and laughing breezes, babbling bees, and piping birds have been replaced by "Soundless" geometry: crescents, arcs, rows, dots, and discs.

Grand go the Years — in the Crescent — above them —
Worlds scoop their Arcs —
And Firmaments — row —
Diadems — drop — and Doges — surrender —
Soundless as dots — on a Disc of Snow.

Susan would not relent easily. "I am not suited dear Emily with the second verse," she wrote. "It is remarkable as the chain lightening that blinds us hot nights in the Southern sky but it does not go with the ghostly shimmer of the first verse as well as the other one—It just occurs to me that the first verse is complete in itself . . . and can't be coupled—Strange things always go alone. . . . You never made a peer for that verse, and I *guess* you[r] kingdom does'nt hold one—I always go to the fire and get warm after thinking of it, but I never *can* again."

But Emily Dickinson remained challenged by the singular stanza she had created. It held death's meaning within sealed, cool architecture—"Rafter of satin / And Roof of stone"—and she sought the analogy or the contrast that would relate it, in fruitful honesty, to the passages of life. She tried a third version, and sent it to Sue with a query: "Is this frostier?" Dickinson had shifted perspectives, away not only from the light breezes of an ephemeral summer but also from the cosmic horizon of "Arcs" and "Firmaments." She now focused her attention on reconsidering the "Alabaster Chambers" themselves. Whereas the first two options for a second stanza had contrasted the temporal world with tombs "untouched by noon," these last two revisions obliquely reintroduced time and change into the crypt itself.

> *Springs – shake the Sills –*
> *But – the Echoes – stiffen –*
> *Hoar – is the Window – and numb – the door –*
> *Tribes of Eclipse – in Tents of Marble –*
> *Staples of Ages – have buckled – there –*

In this third experiment, the first stanza's architectural images remain, but the smoothly sealed alabaster has been replaced by weather-worn windows and doors, stiff and frozen but not, perhaps, impassable. In another intriguing alteration, the silent repose of the dead in the first stanza has now become nomadic movement, "Tribes of Eclipse," whose crypts have been transformed to "Tents of Marble" for a journey that somehow mysteriously continues the pilgrimage begun in life and time.

Pursuing her experiments during the second half of 1861, Dickinson copied all these stanzas onto a sheet of stationery, adding yet another revisionary stanza.

> *Springs – shake the seals –*
> *But the silence – stiffens –*
> *Frosts unhook – in the Northern Zones –*

Icicles — crawl from polar Caverns —
Midnight in Marble —
Refutes — the Suns —

In this version, the cycles of nature contest one another for possession of the tombs. Spring's warmth having shaken "the seals" of the chambers, frost and icicles from "polar Caverns" return to stiffen them into wintry silence. Midnight supplants noon and "Refutes — the Suns." Although winter and midnight clearly held sway, the poet gave no indication that their contest with spring and sunlight had ended. Written relatively early in her career as a poet, Dickinson seems to have taken some sense of accomplishment from "Safe in their Alabaster Chambers." She included it among the first set of poems sent to Higginson for his appraisal. But experiments with language that demarcated human mortality persisted as a lifelong task of her poetry.

THE LANGUAGE OF TRANSCENDENCE

Sharon Cameron, in her study of Thoreau, *Writing Nature*, has proposed that by the middle decades of the nineteenth century American writers chafed under the constraining assumptions of the language they had inherited: "Thus Thoreau explicitly proposes the necessity of discovering a language to describe natural phenomena, much as Dickinson will propose the invention of a vocabulary to describe interior experience."[41] In the literary culture of nineteenth-century New England, both nature and interiority were, as I have observed in previous chapters, tightly connected to religion and to each other. The search for new vocabularies of nature and of interiority was thus also an inquiry into the language of religion. The longer English-speaking theological tradition, exemplified in this book in the writings of Jonathan Edwards, had sought to establish analogies through these three vocabularies that linked self, nature, and cosmos in a coherent system. The diverse interpretations of immortality advanced by Edward Hitchcock, William Cullen Bryant, and Theodore Munger suggest the pressures that were working to fragment this analogical system over the course of the nineteenth century. When Thoreau or Dickinson proposed "the necessity of discovering a language" to describe natural phenomena or interior experience, their literary projects entailed disentangling nature and interiority from inherited patterns and, at least implicitly, assembling a new pattern of relations among self, nature, and ultimate environment. For this reason, Dickinson's poetic strategies for relating these three vocabularies illustrate and illuminate larger charges in the surrounding religious culture.

From midcentury onward, controversies swirled throughout American Protestantism regarding the nature of religious language and, in particular, the source and authority of theological ideas.[42] If the source was the Bible, then theology consisted of the systematic ordering and harmonization of truths abstracted from an authoritative text. But if, as we saw in the writings of Theodore Parker, theological ideas had their source in a universal human intuition or "mysterious sentiment of something unbounded," then the articulation of that sentiment would take many different conceptual forms, both personal and cultural, over the course of time. Ministerial and lay writers advocating this latter perspective, especially, felt the necessity for "discovering a language" and the "invention of a vocabulary" that would connect religion to contemporary ideas of nature and the self. Perhaps I should say, more precisely, they sought to reinvent an inherited vocabulary in order to make those connections. Given their emphasis on the historical contingency of language and concepts, these writers particularly sought to articulate the relation between what was transient in religion and what was permanent. "A few years ago, and we were not; a few years hence, and our bodies shall not be," Parker remarked. "We have wandered on the shore, and gathered here a bright pebble, and there a shining shell," he continued, "but the ocean of Truth, boundless and unfathomed, lies before us, and all unknown." Parker interpreted these sensations of transience and limit as humanity's recognition of absolute dependence on "a Power beyond us, sublime and mysterious, which we cannot measure, nor even comprehend." This intuitive perception gave rise to theological concepts, but any "conception of God, as men express it in their language, is always imperfect; sometimes self-contradictory and impossible."[43]

Horace Bushnell pressed this line of reasoning yet further by arguing that "dogmatical propositions, such as are commonly woven into creeds and catechisms of doctrine, have not the certainty they are commonly supposed to have." Such intellectual formulations, Bushnell declared, "give us only the seeing of the authors, at the precise stand-point occupied by them, at the time, and they are true only as seen from that point—not even there, save in a proximate sense." Hence religious inquirers would be well advised to understand that "the scriptures of God, in providing a clothing for religious truth, have little to do with mere dialectics, much to do with the freer creations of poetry."[44] Later in the century, Theodore Munger identified this connection to literature as the principal hope for revitalization of theological language that was rapidly narrowing into irrelevance. "The present restlessness in the world of theological thought is due largely to the fact that the teachings of literature have prevailed over the teachings of the systems of theology," and this had occurred, Munger said, because literary works covered "the breadth of human life," while theological tracts "travel a dull round in a small world of their own creation; they no longer interest men. The protest is hardly stronger in literature than in the pulpit."[45]

A growing number of thinkers also argued that the narrowed or limited meanings of theological terms resulted, in part, from the different social contexts in which they were put to use. As denominations proliferated during the century, specific doctrines became markers of individual denominational identities, and by accentuating a certain theological idea, a denomination attributed intellectual connotations and ethical implications that the same concept did not receive in other denominational systems of thought. Meanwhile, scholars in the rapidly expanding cohort of theological seminaries were producing academic theological writing that contrasted with the theology of the pulpit. In response, virtually every nineteenth-century writer I have mentioned in this book—Beecher, Palmer, Emerson, Phelps, Bushnell—took a swipe at sectarian doctrine and abstract theological reasoning. They would have agreed with the sentiments of Emily Dickinson when she remarked in 1859 on a sermon by Amherst philosopher Julius H. Seelye: "Mr S. preached in our church last Sabbath upon 'predestination,' but I do not respect 'doctrines,' and did not listen to him, so I can neither praise, nor blame."[46] To interpret conflicting uses of theological language, the Andover Seminary professor Edwards A. Park, a scholar with close associations at Amherst College, made a controversial but influential distinction between "the theology of the intellect and that of the feelings." Speaking to a convention of Congregational ministers in 1850, Park pointed out that the "theology of the intellect" was suited "not for eloquent appeals but for calm controversial treatises and bodies of divinity; not so well for the hymn-book as for the catechism; not so well for the liturgy as for the creed." By contrast, the "theology of the feelings" drew out the affective power of Christian teaching "without necessarily pausing to draw fine distinctions or to harmonize it with other truths." It was "framed for enkindling the imagination and thereby inflaming the heart" in hymns, preaching, and liturgy. For these persuasive and affective purposes, it therefore employed statements that, in the starker light cast by progress in the theological sciences, would be found "antiquated."[47]

These wide-ranging questions about the adequacy of religious language to represent its object gained a special intensity the nearer they approached the concept of immortality. Here, the limited capacity of language to articulate its subject became most obvious. With respect to "the doctrine that Man lives forever," Parker again stressed conceptual variation. Although the hope of immortality arose "naturally from an eternal desire in the human heart," the specific conception of "the future life" varied widely, both among the world's religions and among individuals, depending on "the condition and character of the believer." Hence, Parker concluded, "the Sentiment and the Idea of immortality may be true, but the definite conception must be mainly subjective and therefore false." Furthermore, as statements approached the limit of language, they tended to expose the tacit presuppositions of the speaker, and Parker delivered the maxim: "the notion formed of the next world is the index of man's state in this."[48]

Whatever the general applicability of Parker's dictum, it aptly characterized the popular theology of immortality in his own era. The immanence of the divine, continuity between the natural world and the supernatural, and communication between the living and the dead figured prominently in both learned and popular theological discussion. As Theodore Munger summarized matters, "belief in *personality* after death" represented the crucial feature of representations of heaven, eternity, and the immortality of the soul from the 1840s to the end of the century. "The future world" replicated, in idealized form, the present state of affairs, and Elizabeth Stuart Phelps captured this reassuring replication nicely in *The Gates Ajar*, in an exchange between Mary and Aunt Winifred, in which Winifred assures Mary she will see her dead brother Roy "as you saw him here."

> "As I saw him here! Why, here I looked into his eyes, I saw him smile, I touched him. Why, Aunt Winifred, Roy is an angel!"
>
> She patted my hand with a little, soft, comforting laugh.
>
> "But he is not any the less Roy for that,—not any less your own real Roy, who will love you and wait for you and be very glad to see you, as he used to love and wait and be glad when you came home from a journey on a cold winter night."
>
> "And he met me at the door, and led me in where it was light and warm!" I sobbed.
>
> "So will he meet you at the door in this other home, and lead you into the light and the warmth."[49]

Parallel to this projection of earthly intimacy into a heavenly realm was the projection of ethical values into the infinite through aspirational rhetoric. Thus Octavius Brooks Frothingham, best known today for his 1876 history of the Transcendentalist movement, identified the "imperishable" part of humanity with its ideals. Human life, in Frothingham's view, did not pursue completion but sought an ideal aim: "it is the striving and endeavoring which ennobles," he wrote, and consequently "the ideal is never reached; if it were, it would not be the ideal." The aspirational elements of the religious sentiment, "trust in the perfect, adoration for the supreme, reverence for the sublime, thirst for beauty, hunger for righteousness, all belong to human nature. They are in essence, imperishable. They increase as man advances."[50]

Although the idealizations by Munger, Phelps, and Frothingham surpassed present life, they were congruent with and supportive of human sentiment, desire, and aspiration. They portrayed the self as an enduring human soul, continuously progressing toward the boundary of death and beyond, exempted from the natural cycles of extinction. For these writers, the language of transcendence was a language of consummation, grounding both the individual personality and social ideals in an eternal order.

A quite different application of the language of transcendence also circulated in nineteenth-century America. In this version, the vocabulary of transcendence emphasized not continuity and congruity but otherness. The sociologist Robert Bellah has characterized this approach to transcendence as "the insistence on a reality that forces itself upon our consciousness and refuses to be managed and mastered."[51] In the most famous nineteenth-century American example, Abraham Lincoln reacted in his second inaugural address to the use of religious justifications for sectional politics. "Both read the same Bible, and pray to the same God; and each invokes His aid against the other. It may seem strange that any men should dare to ask a just God's assistance in wringing their bread from the sweat of other men's faces; but let us judge not that we be not judged. The prayers of both could not be answered; that of neither has been answered fully. The Almighty has His own purposes."[52] In such cases, transcendence named realities that confounded—not confirmed—human sentiment, desire, and aspiration. And Bellah further elaborates that these realities, possessing their "own purposes," which force themselves into conscious awareness and refuse "to be managed," may be "encountered in the self as well as in the external world."[53] Emily Dickinson's writing depicted both sorts of unbidden intrusions, not only those that arrived in the form of an unanticipated external event but also those that welled up unexpectedly within a person's consciousness.

With respect to consciousness, for example, Dickinson participated in a literary and religious culture that was attentive to dreams, buried memories, and premonitions that intruded on conscious thought. She portrayed memory as "something like a house," with rear, front, and a garret occupied by discarded items (and mice). Somewhat more ominously, memory also had a cellar, the deepest "That ever Mason laid – / Look to it by its Fathoms / Ourselves be not pursued" (F1234). Unlike the garret (of our conscious mind?) where many long-used objects have been stored and forgotten—becoming nothing more than trash—the cellar contained memories that had their own agency and the ability, therefore, to rise from it and pursue those who might open the door and descend a few steps. With respect to unmanageable events in nature and history, Dickinson the lover of gardens recognized that over time the "otherwise reliable generosity" of nature could also be ruthless, when drought, storm, insects, and animals counteracted the best efforts of the gardener. Robert Pogue Harrison remarks that "a garden has its own developing plot, as it were," and gardens disclosed an implicit narrative of human agency not only sustained but also limited by forces beyond human control.[54]

Within the wider culture and within Dickinson's own writings, the language of transcendence thus took two forms, one organized around idealized continuities and the other organized around "a reality that forces itself upon our consciousness and refuses to be managed and mastered." These alternative rhetorical uses of transcendence confronted Dickinson not only with a series of artistic choices but also with a space for innovation. Rearranging and adapting these ideas, Dickinson invented "a vocabulary to describe interior experience," as Sharon Cameron has suggested. And Dickinson gave that vocabulary distinctive shape by relating it, on the one hand, to the limitations imposed by the natural cycles of life, and, on the other hand, to the desire for the unbounded and limitless that suffused nineteenth-century language of immortality.

TIME, MEMORY, AND TRANSCENDENCE

To interpret Dickinson's artistic strategy, I begin with Kenneth Burke's proposal that the function of the language of transcendence is "the building of a *terministic bridge* whereby one realm is *transcended* by being viewed *in terms of* a realm 'beyond' it." Such language, says Burke, "pontificates," because "a realm HERE is being talked about *in terms of* a realm ELSEWHERE—and there is a terminology designed to *bridge* [pontificate, make a bridge] these disparate realms."[55] As Burke's definition implies, the language of transcendence is imaginative in character. It posits, populates, and portrays a realm "beyond" daily life and then creates the symbolic bridges that connect that world to this. A writer who employed the language of transcendence in the way that Burke has described it confronted two artistic tasks. One involved "the building of a terministic bridge," inventing a vocabulary that both described passage through the boundary between "here" and "elsewhere" and represented the liminal state during this transit. Another required imaginative construal of "a realm elsewhere" from which to look back toward the place one now occupied, thus transforming the way "here" was perceived, both aesthetically and religiously.

In the course of this book, I have made several passing references to metaphors that represent crossing a threshold, boundary, or "terministic bridge" between two states, two "disparate realms." These include the sending of a letter, the transition from one season to the next, the flight of a migratory bird, falling asleep, or hitching a ride with the moon from Amherst to Baltimore. Many of the century's religious thinkers, ranging from Edward Hitchcock to Theodore Munger, employed these tropes to signify a process successfully completed. Others, including Dickinson and William Cullen Bryant, tended to leave the completion of this transition ambiguous. Would the letter receive a response; would the bird return; would the sleeper awaken? Another commonplace boundary metaphor deserves further attention: the door. Elizabeth Stuart Phelps had, of course, made the door a comforting passage into the familiar. In *The Gates Ajar*, Winifred assured Mary that Roy would "meet you at the door in this other home, and lead you into the light and the warmth." Emily Dickinson's doors were more formidable. In "Safe in their Alabaster Chambers," it was midnight and the doors were frozen shut: "Hoar – is the Window – and numb – the door."

Perhaps because she had chosen to pursue the writer's vocation in domestic solitude, the house became an omnipresent and multivalent metaphor in Dickinson's poetic repertoire. Throughout her letters and poetry—selectively illustrated in the preceding chapters— houses, their furnishings, and their surrounding gardens represented spaces of intimate companionship, the mind and its memories, the tomb, or an anticipated "heavenly" reunion with the absent and the lost. Not surprisingly, then, the door frequently became Dickinson's "terministic bridge" at the boundary between two different spaces or two different times. Since the door presupposed an "inside" and an "outside," it created the distinction between a mundane world and "a realm elsewhere." It represented the point of access to intimate companionship or the passageway back into memory, as well as the portal of death. By focusing attention on a passageway of entrance and exit, metaphorical doors composed "*an* experience" in John Dewey's definition of art, a composition demarcated from other experiences without being cut off from "the general stream of experience."

As points of access to intimate companionship, the first thing to notice about Dickinson's doors is whether they placed the reader outside or inside the parlor of friendship and familiar welcome. A lost traveler, for instance, suddenly notices "A Door just opened on a street" and glimpses within both warmth and company. But "The Door as instant shut," and the traveler finds herself "Lost doubly," without directions and also without welcome, "by contrast – most – / Informing – Misery" (F914). Dickinson also portrayed the boundary of a closing door by imagining those who gathered on its other side, within the house. In one of her most famous poems, "The Soul selects her own Society" and then "shuts the door," unmoved by pausing chariots or emperors kneeling on her doormat (F409). In yet another poem, written in 1861, the poet placed herself alongside those beseeching entry, portraying a visitor who was even more persistent than Jesus in knocking at a closed door (cf. Rev. 3:21). In Dickinson's version, Jesus finally wearies at the lack of response to his knock and turns away from the door, but the woman remains, "Patient – opon the steps – *until* then – / Heart! I am knocking – low at thee" (F263). In these poems and many others, access and intimacy were desired but withheld. These doors did not open into the welcoming parlor of Henry Ward Beecher's ideal house or of Elizabeth Stuart Phelps's imagined heaven. Neither emperors nor messiahs enjoyed privileged access. As in Dickinson's letters to Elizabeth Holland and Susan Gilbert Dickinson, intimate companionship is compared to heaven in part because it is ardently desired but seldom opened to the seeker.

But what if there were no door at all? Having once entered the house, or the crypt, or subjective interiority, one would be left with no route of progress or escape.

> Doom is the House without the Door —
> 'Tis entered from the Sun —
> And then the Ladder's thrown away,
> Because Escape — is done —
>
> 'Tis varied by the Dream
> Of what they do outside —
> Where Squirrels play — and Berries dye —
> And Hemlocks — bow — to God —
>
> (F710)

The poem's two stanzas depict worlds sealed off from one another. The absence of a door (or even a ladder) in the house of "Doom" meant that the transcendent is set apart not by a *boundary* through which one must pass but by a *limit* that cannot be traversed.[56] If the frame of reference for interpreting this poem were death and immortality, then it bears comparison to the "Alabaster Chambers" that were sealed off from the laughing breezes, babbling bees, and piping birds of mortal time. Alternatively, if the interpretive framework were subjective interiority, then the comparison would to be to remorse, which was "the adequate of hell" because the irrevocability of a deeply regretted deed prevented movement beyond or past it. The poem portrays eternal entrapment in "A Presence of Departed Acts" (F781). In such poems of doom, the imaginatively transcendent "realm elsewhere" turns out to be the mundane world of laughing breezes and the freedom to enjoy it unburdened by remorse, or bereavement, or the lasting pain of regret. Hence the only possible passageway from the house of doom is a dream "Of what they do outside." And it is only "outside" in the world of time and nature that divinity might be recognized: "And Hemlocks — bow — to God."

Dickinson's doors frequently opened onto the passage of time. In her imagination, cemeteries became villages of strangers where, to inform the living, each house had the occupant's name and age written on the door. Since the time of its earliest pioneers, this village—this cemetery—had gradually grown in size, with new homes being built daily. Pausing before a tombstone, however, the visitor recognized that she knew few of the residents.

> *The owner of this House*
> *A Stranger He must be —*
> *Eternity's Acquaintances*
> *Are mostly so — to me —*
> (F1069)

In another approach to a door in time, the visitor feared she would encounter a stranger when returning to the house that, long ago, had been home:

> *I — Years — had been — from Home —*
> *And now — before the Door —*
> *I dared not open — lest a face*
> *I never saw before*
>
> *Stare vacant into mine —*
> *And ask my Business there —*
> *My Business — just a Life I left —*
> *Was such — still dwelling there?*

Attempting to calm her nerves, the visitor to her former home "laughed a Wooden Laugh / That I — could fear a Door." But, as she lifted her hand with "trembling care" toward the latch, fear proved victorious:

> *I moved my Fingers off, as cautiously as Glass —*
> *And held my Ears — and like a Thief*
> *Stole — gasping — from the House.*
> (F440, 1862 version)

In her remarkable letter to John L. Graves, Dickinson had filled both the past and a future "heaven" with close friends, and the letter's evocation of death's poignancy had depended on the familiar and the familial. But in these poems, the return to the past was a return to strangers and to "a Life I left," while an inevitable future would incorporate us all into a village of strangers. In Dickinson's letters and poems, meditation on death had this curious effect of bending time back on itself, such that crossing the enigmatic boundary of death, she imagined encountering departed strangers, friends, and events from her own past that had "got to heaven first" and awaited her there.

In several of her most famous poems, Dickinson similarly manipulated the experience of time by standing in the middle of the "terministic bridge," as it were, and speaking from the liminal state of a person in transit from life into death. In the middle decades of the nineteenth century, the posthumous voice Dickinson invented for poems such as "I heard a fly buzz when I died" (F591) no doubt resonated with the communications from the dead that were central to the ideas and practices of spiritualism. More important, this liminal voice enabled Dickinson to invent "ways to plot temporality," as Helen Vendler has put it, not only the relation between natural cycles and human affective time but also the relation between temporality and eternity. In one familiar example, death appeared as a courtly gentleman, whose carriage slowly traveled through the village over the course of a day.

> Because I could not stop for Death –
> He Kindly stopped for me –
> The Carriage held but just Ourselves –
> And Immortality.

The carriage passed schoolchildren at recess, passed fields of grain, and then unexpectedly passed the setting sun. "Or rather – He passed Us." Although the day had continued to move toward sunset, the carriage had "paused before a House that seemed / A Swelling of the Ground," and the passenger grew chill in her gossamer gown.

> Since then — 'tis Centuries — and yet
> Feels shorter than the Day
> I first surmised the Horses' Heads
> Were toward Eternity —
>
> (F479)

The passenger does not seem to have passed beyond time into eternity but instead speaks from a place in which both time and space continue but have lost their familiar structure. The carriage passes not only the local schoolyard but also passes beyond the horizon, somehow rolling by the sun as it sets; in traversing the horizon it has also stopped at a mounded grave. A day passes, centuries pass, but the affective sensation of their lengths is jumbled. Unlike the Apostle Paul who declared that "now we see through a glass darkly; but then face to face: now I know in part; but then shall I know even as also I am known" (1 Cor. 13:12, KJV), Dickinson's deceased passenger does not know, but only "surmised," that "the Horses' Heads / Were toward Eternity."

In another poem of time continuing in disrupted form after death, two persons who have devoted their lives to ideals discover they have been laid in adjoining rooms of a crypt. A dialogue ensues.

> I died for Beauty — but was scarce
> Adjusted in the Tomb
> When One who died for Truth, was lain
> In an adjoining Room —
>
> He questioned softly "Why I failed"?
> "For Beauty," I replied —
> "And I — for Truth — Themselves are One —
> We Bretheren, are," He said —
>
> And so, as Kinsmen, met a Night —
> We talked between the Rooms —
> Until the Moss had reached our lips —
> And covered up — our names —
>
> (F448)

Like "Alabaster Chambers," these rooms were occupied in night, but, instead of sleep, Dickinson chose to portray conversation. The night's dialogue began quickly when the two were "scarce / Adjusted in the Tomb." But it then slowed, drawing out across decades, a fact that the reader learns through Dickinson's surprising transformation of the two "Kinsmen" into their respective tombstones, on which the slowly encroaching moss silenced the words of their epitaphs and obscured their names. More radically than Henry Ward Beecher's lamentation over the decay of old New England graveyards, Dickinson depicted the slow dissolution of personal identity and defining ideals, as the two kinsmen were lost to living memory.

Nineteenth-century efforts to buttress the permanence of the self and of human social ideals employed various combinations of scriptural authority, scientific analogy, and theological argument to narrow the distance or emphasize the continuity between the temporal world and the eternal. The immortal soul—aligned not with the changing physical world but with the divine principle that guided those changes— became the indispensable idea in all of these arguments, ranging from the Methodist holiness of Phoebe Palmer to Theodore Munger's affirmation of a God immanent in the operations of nature. Against this religious backdrop, Dickinson is striking in her unflinching representation of the self embedded in the cycles of nature and the enigmatic silence—even indifference—of nature regarding human desires and ideals. She had inherited the vocation of solitude from Edwards and Emerson, but she displayed a remarkably disciplined bravery by maintaining that vocation in a silent universe. "It is, after all," Robert Ferguson remarks, "harder to stand alone if the cosmos does not care about you."[57]

Where, then, did Dickinson's writing address the second aspect of Kenneth Burke's definition of the language of transcendence? Did she construe "a realm elsewhere" from which to look back toward the mundane world, thus transforming the way "here" was perceived, both aesthetically and morally? My own view is that Dickinson employed the vocabulary of "the future life"—immortality, eternity, heaven, and resurrection—in order to dramatize the capacity of imaginative perception to transform our experience of this mundane world, making "here" seem like "a realm elsewhere." She reinvented theological language, as Barton Levi St. Armand has said, to "italicize" features of experience that might otherwise escape our attention.

One final poem illustrates her art of "italicizing" features of experience in order to create "*an* experience" of enriched and extended wholeness. Dickinson's early editors had entitled the poem "Indian Summer," and its reflections on the sudden arrival of beautiful, summerlike days in a New England autumn were a commentary on the interaction between the seasonal and the ritual cadences of time. In the poem, Dickinson explored how memory added new, supplementary details that reorganized or even reversed our perception of the present situation. The imaginative work accomplished by the poem is perhaps most easily recognized by contrasting it with the impression that a walk through the forest in Indian summer had made on Ralph Waldo Emerson. In his second series of essays, Emerson opened the essay "Nature" with a long paragraph on the incomparable days in which "a perpetual morning" cast light through the woods. "The incommunicable trees begin to persuade us to live with them," Emerson declared, "and quit our life of solemn trifles. Here no history, or church, or state, is interpolated on the divine sky and the immortal year. How easily we might walk onward into the opening landscape, absorbed by new pictures, and by thoughts fast succeeding each other, until by degrees the recollection of home was crowded out of the mind, all memory obliterated by the tyranny of the present, and we were led in triumph by nature."[58]

Dickinson chose to write not of the immediate experience of natural beauty in autumn. Instead, she emphasized that memory performed synthetic work, encompassing past and present and teaching something about both that would have been impossible if either were considered singly. Her poem arose from the experience of holding together in memory two superficially similar days, one in June, the other in October. Memory was by no means "obliterated" by the "tyranny of the present" but achieved its reflective power by recognizing what might be learned from the comparison of two experiences separated in time.

These are the days when Birds come back —
A very few — a Bird or two —
To take a backward look.

These are the days when skies resume
The old — old sophistries of June —
A blue and gold mistake.

Oh fraud that cannot cheat the Bee.
Almost thy plausibility
Induces my belief,

Till ranks of seeds their witness bear —
And softly thro' the altered air
Hurries a timid leaf.

Oh sacrament of summer days,
Oh Last Communion in the Haze —
Permit a child to join —

Thy sacred emblems to partake —
Thy consecrated bread to take
And thine immortal wine!

(F122)

Bees recognized the "fraud" of these misleadingly balmy days, and
the few birds present were similarly undeceived. They had paused
for "a backward look" at the season now ended before fleeing toward
warmer climes. Dickinson further considered, however, that the
"fraud" of Indian summer was itself replicating the "sophistries of
June." Rather than Emerson's "immortal year," Dickinson portrayed
the seasonal cadences as a finite cycle, which through repetition
offered an illusory sense of permanence. Nor did she agree with Emer-
son that history, church, and state had interposed themselves between

humanity and an "eternal sky." She would, instead, have concurred with Robert Pogue Harrison's judgment that "when we build something in nature, be it a dwelling, a monument, or even a fire, we create the rudiments of a world and thereby give a sign of our mortal sojourn on earth." She therefore linked June and October by means of Christianity's quintessential act of memory, the Lord's Supper. "Remembrance" became whatever there might be of immortality in a world in which even the natural order presented only the illusion of permanence.

NOTES

CHAPTER 1

1. The publishing history of Emily Dickinson's poetry is described in Franklin, "Introduction," *Poems of Emily Dickinson*, 1:1–47.
2. Dickinson, *Letters of Emily Dickinson*, 2:327. She left ambiguous whether the "anthems" came from the church or from birds and insects in the lawn and trees surrounding her.
3. Ibid., 1:111, 217, 235, 312; Nettleton, *Village Hymns for Social Worship*; Habegger, *My Wars Are Laid Away in Books*, 29–30.
4. Bartlett and Warner, *Hymns of the Church Militant*; Welter, "Feminization of American Religion," 162; McLoughlin, *American Evangelicals*, 28.
5. Vendler, *Dickinson*, 4–5; St. Armand, *Emily Dickinson and Her Culture*, 159; Barrett, *To Fight Aloud*, 45; Miller, *Reading in Time*, 37, 45, 49; and Marini, "Hymnody and History," for an overview of evangelical hymns and hymnals of the era.
6. McKelvy, *English Cult of Literature*, 14–15.
7. Howe, *Political Culture of the American Whigs*, 3, 12–13, 16–18, 21, 29–31, 33.
8. James, *Varieties of Religious Experience*, 141.
9. Dickinson, *Letters of Emily Dickinson*, 2:329.
10. Alter, *Pen of Iron*, 4, 180.
11. James, *Varieties of Religious Experience*, 31.
12. See Faust, *Ideology of Slavery*; Noll, *Civil War as a Theological Crisis*.
13. Masur, "'Age of the First Person Singular'"; Carroll, *Spiritualism in Antebellum America*.
14. Lewis, *American Adam*, 1–2.
15. Albanese, *Republic of Mind and Spirit*, 496, 515.
16. All citations of Dickinson's poems come from Franklin's edition and are identified in the body of the text by the poem number Franklin assigned, for example, F1263.
17. Donoghue, *Emily Dickinson*, 17.
18. Bercovitch, *Puritan Origins of the American Self*, 136.
19. Representative texts by these scholars include Miller, *Errand into the Wilderness*; Heimert, *Religion and the American Mind*; Lewis, *American Adam*; Mead, *Lively Experiment*; Handy, *Christian America*; Ahlstrom, *Religious History of the American People*; Marty, *Righteous Empire*.
20. Ahlstrom, *Religious History of the American People*, 899.

21. Miller, *Errand into the Wilderness*, 184–203. More recent monographs have tended to substitute Lincoln for Emerson; see Noll, *America's God*, and Howe, *Making the American Self*.

22. Edwards, *Works of Jonathan Edwards*, 8:541.

23. Niebuhr, "Idea of Covenant," 127.

24. Ibid., 130, 135.

25. Representative scholarship would include Butler, *Awash in a Sea of Faith*, on the diminished explanatory power of Puritanism; Albanese, *Republic of Mind and Spirit*, on religious eclecticism; and Gregerson and Juster, *Empires of God*, on the transnational circulation of peoples and ideas.

26. Bender, "Strategies of Narrative Synthesis," 152.

27. See Johnson's introduction to *Letters of Emily Dickinson*, xx.

28. Wolosky's *Emily Dickinson: A Voice of War* was the notable first step in this reassessment of the relation between Dickinson's poetry and the Civil War. More recent interpretations of Dickinson's poetry in its Civil War context include Barrett, *To Fight Aloud*, 130–86; Miller, *Reading in Time*, 147–75; and Barrett and Miller, *"Words for the Hour,"* 351–61.

29. Geertz, *Interpretation of Cultures*, 87–125.

30. Lakoff and Johnson, *Metaphors We Live By*, 10.

31. Howe, *Making the American Self*, 63, 66, 91.

32. Looby, "Constitution of Nature," 253, 256.

33. Hecker, *Questions of the Soul*, 55, 293.

34. Bushnell, *Views of Christian Nurture*, 21–22.

35. Hutchison, *Religious Pluralism in America*, 19, 24.

36. Handy, *Christian America*, 25–43, 52; Marty, *Righteous Empire*, 5–33, 46–56.

37. Hitchcock, *Inseparable Trio*, 5–6, 8–9.

38. Bushnell, *Barbarism the First Danger*, 4–5, 32.

39. Barnes, *Home Missions*, 8, 21–34, 40–41.

40. Dickinson, *Letters of Emily Dickinson*, 1:49.

41. Anderson, *Powers of Distance*, 4, 6–7.

42. Ginzburg, *Wooden Eyes*, 7, 12, 16.

43. Vendler, *Dickinson*, 87.

44. Child, *Progress of Religious Ideas*, 1:vii–ix.

45. Hobsbawm, *Age of Revolution*, 217.

46. See Stout and Brekus, "New England Congregation," for the history of Center Church, New Haven, from the seventeenth century to the twentieth as an illustration of evolving understandings of membership in a congregation, church discipline, and denominational identity.

47. Colton, *Old Meeting House*, 164–68.

48. Dickinson, *Letters of Emily Dickinson*, 1:27.

49. Ibid., 1:30–31, 38.

50. Ibid., 1:27–28, 30–31, 60, 67, 98, 100; Habegger, *My Wars Are Laid Away in Books*, 80, points out that Dickinson's mother, Emily Norcross Dickinson, had joined Amherst's First Church in 1831.

51. Stevenson, *Scholarly Means to Evangelical Ends*, 36, 41–43, 57.

52. Dickinson, *Letters of Emily Dickinson*, 1:27–28.

53. Hadot, *Philosophy as a Way of Life*, 81–83, 85–86; and see Corrigan, *Business of the Heart*, for the religious discipline of the emotions in nineteenth-century revivalism.

54. Dickinson, *Letters of Emily Dickinson*, 1:28, 32, 38.

CHAPTER 2

1. Sewall, *Life of Emily Dickinson*, 154, 156, 288, 448, 463; see Lundin, *Emily Dickinson and the Art of Belief*, 188–93, for a vivid description of Dickinson's seclusion.

2. Donoghue, *Emily Dickinson*, 9.

3. Sewall, *Life of Emily Dickinson*, 240; Farr, *Passion of Emily Dickinson*, 30, and generally, 30–42.

4. See Barbour, *Value of Solitude*, for the relation of solitude to literature, especially autobiography; Schmidt, *Restless Souls*, 63–100, for its place in the history of American spirituality; and Slauter, "Being Alone in the Age of the Social Contract," for the relation of solitude to the public sphere.

5. Bunyan, *Pilgrim's Progress*, 8–10.

6. Thoreau, *Walden*, 392.

7. Among the many books that address the connections among writing, solitude, and nature, see especially Albanese, *Nature Religion in America*; Cameron, *Writing Nature*; Cherry, *Nature and Religious Imagination*; Gatta, *Making Nature Sacred*; Lane, *Landscapes of the Sacred*.

8. Smith, "Concept of Conversion."

9. Edwards, *Works of Jonathan Edwards*, 16:792–93.

10. Ibid., 16:793, 780.

11. Cherry, *Nature and Religious Imagination*, 16, 23–24.

12. Edwards, *Works of Jonathan Edwards*, 16:793–94.

13. Ibid., 16:794.

14. Cf. Chidester and Linenthal's introduction to *American Sacred Space*, 1–13.

15. See Sibbes, "The Art of Self-Humbling," in *Complete Works*, 6:44–58, for a classic exposition by a leading Puritan preacher of the early seventeenth century.

16. Edwards, *Works of Jonathan Edwards*, 16:796.

17. Hambrick-Stowe, *Practice of Piety*, 162; Taylor, *Rule and Exercises of Holy Living*, 225; Edwards, *Works of Jonathan Edwards*, 16:757.

18. Edwards, *Works of Jonathan Edwards*, 16:795.

19. Ibid., 16:798.

20. Ibid., 16:794.

21. Brekus, *Sarah Osborn's World*, 4, 15–32.

22. Wheatley, *Life and Letters of Mrs. Phoebe Palmer*, 28, 252–57, 507.

23. Dickinson, *Letters of Emily Dickinson*, 2:408.

24. Sewall, *Life of Emily Dickinson*, 220.

25. Montaigne, *Complete Essays of Montaigne*, 175–76.

26. Livingston, *Philosophic Solitude*, 3, lines 11–18; see also Elliott, *Revolutionary Writers*, 26, 48, 177–78.

27. Livingston, *Philosophic Solitude*, 6–8, lines 89–130; 18–23, lines 380–537; 24–28, lines 548–665.

28. Ibid., 11, lines 201–4.
29. Ibid., 16, lines 344–47.
30. Slauter, "Being Alone in the Age of the Social Contract," 35, 37; Elliott, *Revolutionary Writers*, 17, 26, 48–49, 131–32, 145 (quotation).
31. Brown, *Rhapsodist and Other Uncollected Writings*, 5–8, 13–15.
32. Mitchell, *Reveries of a Bachelor*, v–vii, 16, 29, 53–54, 99–145.
33. Turner, "Solitude," 122.
34. Emerson, *Letters of Ralph Waldo Emerson*, 2:237–38.
35. Emerson, *Early Lectures*, 3:86, 95–96, 100.
36. Ibid., 3:85–89, 102; see Howe, *Making the American Self*, 107.
37. Emerson, *Essays and Lectures*, 412.
38. Thoreau, *Walden*, 329–30.
39. Emerson, *Heart of Emerson's Journals*, 55.
40. Thoreau, *Walden*, 334.
41. Emerson, *Essays and Lectures*, 7–9.
42. Emerson, *Early Lectures*, 3:88–89, 97–99.
43. Emerson, *Heart of Emerson's Journals*, 40.
44. Emerson, *Journals and Miscellaneous Notebooks*, 5:189.
45. Ibid., 7:392.
46. Emerson, *Essays and Lectures*, 471.
47. Fuller, *Summer on the Lakes*, 27, 40.
48. Ibid., 20, 33, 72.
49. Douglass, *Autobiographies*, 1.
50. Emerson, *Essays and Lectures*, 142.
51. Douglass, *Autobiographies*, 57, 59, 95.
52. Dickinson, *Letters of Emily Dickinson*, 2:327–28.
53. Bianchi, *Life and Letters of Emily Dickinson*, from unnumbered preliminary pages printed in italics; in Bianchi's text, Dickinson's spelling, capitalization, and punctuation were edited, and I cite the poem from the Franklin edition.
54. Bianchi, *Life and Letters of Emily Dickinson*, 105; again, I quote the poem from Franklin's edition.
55. Certeau, *Mystic Fable*, 1–3.

CHAPTER 3

1. Dickinson, *Letters of Emily Dickinson*, 2:415; Farr, *Gardens of Emily Dickinson*, 2, 6, 31.
2. Dickinson, *Letters of Emily Dickinson*, 2:411.
3. Lundin, *Emily Dickinson and the Art of Belief*, 128.
4. For the relation of social class to Whig politics in the Dickinson household, see Howe, *Political Culture of the American Whigs*; Erkkila, "Emily Dickinson and Class."
5. For examples, see especially Hambrick-Stowe, *Early New England Meditative Poetry*, and for "Huswifery," 132. This literal and metaphorical identification of solitude with the house was not, of course, restricted to seventeenth-century New England or to the Puritans. See, for example, the counsel of Thomas More that for spiritual exercises one should "choose some secret solitary place in his own house," as discussed in Greenblatt, *Renaissance Self-Fashioning*, 45–46, 75.
6. Walker, *Creeds and Platforms of Congregationalism*, 207.
7. Bain, *Whitman's and Dickinson's Contemporaries*, 9–11.

8. Sellers, *Market Revolution*, 226;
Nylander, *Our Own Snug Fireside*,
74–102, 143–62; McDannell,
Christian Home in Victorian America, 7–9.

9. Hambrick-Stowe, *Early New
England Meditative Poetry*, 132.

10. Dickinson, *Letters of Emily Dickinson*, 2:315.

11. Brown, *Domestic Individualism*,
45–53; Merish, "Sentimental
Consumption," 3.

12. Dickinson, *Letters of Emily Dickinson*, 2:345.

13. Shamir, *Inexpressible Privacy*, 2–8,
13, 22, 39, 95; St. Armand, *Emily
Dickinson and Her Culture*, 20;
Rose, "Religious Individualism";
McDannell, *Christian Home in Victorian America*, 20–51 (quotation
from Andrew Jackson Downing
on 23).

14. Hawthorne, *Novels*, 355.

15. Channing, *Works of William E.
Channing*, 14–15, 20.

16. Ibid., 14–16, 19.

17. Ibid., 23–24.

18. Davidson, *Revolution and the Word*,
72; Brodhead, *Cultures of Letters*,
54.

19. Sewall, *Life of Emily Dickinson*,
353, 683–88; Dickinson, *Letters
of Emily Dickinson*, 1:85, 102, 165.
For example, the younger Dickinsons read Longfellow's *Kavanagh*
soon after its publication in 1849
and circulated it among their
friends.

20. Certeau, *Practice of Everyday Life*,
xiv–xv, 16–18, 32, 34–39.

21. Beecher, *Star Papers*, 285.

22. Ibid., 286, 288–90; see also
Howe, *Making the American Self*,
136–37.

23. Beecher, *Star Papers*, 291–92, 300.

24. Long, "Consecrated Respectability"; Ward, "Madame Guyon and
Experiential Theology"; Wheatley,
*Life and Letters of Mrs. Phoebe
Palmer*, 252, 256–57.

25. Wheatley, *Life and Letters of
Mrs. Phoebe Palmer*, 252.

26. Hedrick, *Harriet Beecher Stowe*, 77.

27. Ibid., 76–77, 82.

28. Dickinson, *Letters of Emily Dickinson*, 1:116; Ackmann, "Biographical Studies of Dickinson," 19–20.

29. Wheatley, *Life and Letters of
Mrs. Phoebe Palmer*, 614.

30. Brekus, *Strangers and Pilgrims*,
267–306 (quotation from Nettleton on 276).

31. Wheatley, *Life and Letters of
Mrs. Phoebe Palmer*, 28, 598–99,
606–7; see Kelley, *Private Woman,
Public Stage*, for women's ambivalence about publication; and
Reynolds, *Mightier Than the Sword*,
for the commercial success and
theatrical productions of *Uncle
Tom's Cabin*.

32. Hedrick, *Harriet Beecher Stowe*, 77,
79.

33. See Dickinson, *Letters of Emily
Dickinson*, 1:75–76, 91, for Dickinson's theatrically composed
Valentines.

34. Ibid., 2:327, 333, 367.

35. Ibid., 1:194.

36. Ibid., 1:150–51.

37. Ibid., 2:348–49.

38. Merish, "Sentimental Consumption," 8; Bennett, "'Descent of the
Angel.'"

39. Piatt, "Giving Back the Flower,"
in Hollander, *American Poetry*,
2:349–50. Piatt was born in
Kentucky to a wealthy slaveholding family, and early in the
Civil War moved to Washington

with her husband, who worked for the Department of the Treasury; for Piatt's wartime poetry, see Barrett, *To Fight Aloud*, 197–225.

40. Dickinson, *Letters of Emily Dickinson*, 1:143, 161.

41. Gilbert, "Wayward Nun Beneath the Hill," 22.

42. Longfellow, *Kavanagh*, 3, 7.

43. Ibid., 68–69, 89–93, 96–97, 104.

44. Ibid., 39, 71, 82–85.

45. Ibid., 168–69.

46. Jackson, *Dickinson's Misery*, 210, 212.

47. Brodhead, *Cultures of Letters*, 6–9, 86; for the complexities of this authorial decision, see 66, 85.

48. Buell, *New England Literary Culture*, 62.

49. Emerson, *Essays and Lectures*, 1169–73.

50. Higginson, *Magnificent Activist*, 528–42.

51. Dickinson, *Letters of Emily Dickinson*, 1:255–56, 260; LaPorte and Rudy, "Editorial Introduction."

52. Dickinson, *Letters of Emily Dickinson*, 1:27.

53. Vendler, *Dickinson*, 103.

54. Dickinson, *Letters of Emily Dickinson*, 403–15.

55. Ibid., 1:14, 45, 48, 282, 2:409. Habegger, *My Wars Are Laid Away in Books*, 376, 416–27, surveys the various candidates whom biographers have nominated for "master," including his own argument for the Reverend Charles Wadsworth.

56. Longfellow, *Kavanagh*, 142–43; Margolis, *Public Life of Privacy*, 68–69.

57. Dickinson, *Letters of Emily Dickinson*, 2:412.

58. Vendler, *Dickinson*, 260.

59. Dickinson, *Letters of Emily Dickinson*, 1:140, 181.

60. Ibid., 2:411–12.

61. Quoted in Baker, *Emerson Among the Eccentrics*, 283–84.

62. Dickinson, *Letters of Emily Dickinson*, 2:412, 413; see also Miller, *Reading in Time*, 3, 194.

63. Brooks, *Enigmas of Identity*, 150, 166–67.

64. Dickinson, *Letters of Emily Dickinson*, 2:413.

CHAPTER 4

1. Dickinson, *Letters of Emily Dickinson*, 2:338.

2. Messmer, *Vice for Voices*, 27–48.

3. Dickinson, *Letters of Emily Dickinson*, 1:152.

4. Decker, *Epistolary Practices*, 22, 47.

5. Habegger, *My Wars Are Laid Away in Books*, 257.

6. Dickinson, *Letters of Emily Dickinson*, 2:338.

7. Ibid., 1:161.

8. Ibid., 1:293.

9. Ibid., 1:309; for another instance of the imaginary letter, see 1:81.

10. Ibid., 1:310; for another instance of Dickinson dreaming of the Hollands, see 2:319. The image of the bird that will return with new melodies was a variant of a poem (F4) that Dickinson had sent to Susan Gilbert; see ibid., 1:306.

11. Ibid., 2:329.

12. Ibid., 1:229.

13. Ibid., 2:327–28.

14. Ibid., 1:242.

15. Certeau, *Practice of Everyday Life*, 86–88.

16. Decker, *Epistolary Practices*, 22–23.

17. St. Armand, *Emily Dickinson and Her Culture*, 73–74. For the idea that Dickinson "italicized" everyday objects and events into symbols, see also Weisbuch, *Emily Dickinson's Poetry*, 1–2.

18. Bachelard, *Poetics of Space*, 8–9.

19. Dickinson, *Letters of Emily Dickinson*, 1:156; for the parable of the prodigal son, see Luke 15:11–32.

20. Dickinson, *Letters of Emily Dickinson*, 2:315; for other references to Dickinson and Susan Gilbert sitting together on the stone doorstep, see ibid., 1:194, 209.

21. Ibid., 2:330, 337, 375.

22. Ibid., 2:460. Donnelly, "Power to Die," 137, notes that Dickinson reused the aphorism "a letter always feels to me like immortality" thirteen years later, in a letter following her mother's death.

23. Thoreau, *Walden*, 404.

24. Bachelard, *Poetics of Space*, 88.

25. Dickinson, *Letters of Emily Dickinson*, 2:354, 357; Farr, *Gardens of Emily Dickinson*, 209–13.

26. Halttunen, *Confidence Men and Painted Women*, 127; Laderman, *Sacred Remains*, 39–50; Sears, *Sacred Places*, 99–116; Wills, *Lincoln at Gettysburg*, 63–89.

27. Braude, *Radical Spirits*, 53.

28. Quoted in Sears, *Sacred Places*, 103.

29. Laderman, *Sacred Remains*, 55.

30. Schwartz, *George Washington*, 174–77.

31. *Godey's Lady's Book*, January–June 1860, 80–81, 274.

32. Gross, "Celestial Village," 273.

33. Emerson, *Collected Poems and Translations*, 125.

34. Dickinson, *Letters of Emily Dickinson*, 1:36.

35. Ibid., 2:319.

36. Beecher, *Star Papers*, 121.

37. Baym, "English Nature, New York Nature," 170–71, 182–83.

38. Beecher, *Star Papers*, 121.

39. Ibid., 122.

40. Ibid., 123–24, 126.

41. Ibid., 125–27.

42. Halttunen, *Confidence Men and Painted Women*, 127–29, 133, 136.

43. Petrino, *Emily Dickinson and Her Contemporaries*, 56–57.

44. Wheatley, *Life and Letters of Mrs. Phoebe Palmer*, 30, 32.

45. St. Armand, *Emily Dickinson and Her Culture*, 46–47.

46. Quoted in Bain, *Whitman's and Dickinson's Contemporaries*, 4–5.

47. Dickinson, *Letters of Emily Dickinson*, 1:157.

48. Ibid., 2:421.

49. Braude, *Radical Spirits*, 54, 66, 73 (quotation from Davis on 54); Hedrick, *Harriet Beecher Stowe*, 346, 391; Owen, *Darkened Room*, 20–21; Reynolds, *Mightier Than the Sword*, 19–24, 186–88.

50. Carroll, *Spiritualism in Antebellum America*, 68–69, 121–22; Albanese, *Republic of Mind and Spirit*, 303, 307.

51. Hitchcock, *Religion of Geology*, 422–23.

52. Hitchcock, *Peculiar Phenomena in the Four Seasons*, 27–28.

53. Decker, *Epistolary Practices*, 144–45; see also 169 for Decker's emphasis on the term *bereavement*.

54. I gesture inadequately toward a vast, erudite body of scholarship; see especially Faust, *This Republic of Suffering*; Laderman, *Sacred Remains*, 89–154; Stout, *Upon the Altar of the Nation*.

55. Stout, *Upon the Altar of the Nation*, 134, 200, 228.

56. Dickinson, *Letters of Emily Dickinson*, 2:399.

57. Miller, *Reading in Time*, 11, 147, 175.

58. See Barrett, *To Fight Aloud*, 144–46, for an alternative reading of this poem.

59. Phelps, *Three Spiritualist Novels*, 3–5, 7.

60. Donoghue, *Emily Dickinson*, 28.

61. Habegger, *My Wars Are Laid Away in Books*, 468; Vendler, *Poets Thinking*, 64–71.

62. Vendler, *Dickinson*, 400, 402–3.

63. Prothero, *Purified by Fire*, 9, 17–18.

CHAPTER 5

1. Dewey, *Art as Experience*, 35, 46.

2. Harrison, *Dominion of the Dead*, 19.

3. Fuss, *Dying Modern*, and Steiner, *Grammars of Creation*, elaborate the connections among death, creation, and literature.

4. Wolff, *Emily Dickinson*, 82–83.

5. Vendler, *Poets Thinking*, 64.

6. Dickinson, *Letters of Emily Dickinson*, 1:32.

7. Ibid., 1:37.

8. Placher, *Domestication of Transcendence*, 6.

9. Rudwick, "Shape and Meaning of Earth History," 300, 302.

10. Edwards, *Works of Jonathan Edwards*, 11:53, 62, 67, 74, 81.

11. Phelps, *Three Spiritualist Novels*, 9–14.

12. Rudwick, "Shape and Meaning of Earth History," 300, 302–3, 307–11, 316.

13. Lane, *Age of Doubt*, 43–47, 49.

14. Moore, "Geologists and Interpreters of Genesis," 336–38.

15. Hitchcock, *Religion of Geology*, 55, 71, 73, 111.

16. Hitchcock, *Peculiar Phenomena in the Four Seasons*, 110, 9–20, 27–29, 48–49.

17. Ibid., 83–86, 95.

18. Bryant, *Poems*, 32–35.

19. Dickinson, *Letters of Emily Dickinson*, 1:36.

20. Halleck, *Poetical Works*, 21.

21. Bryant, *Poems*, 41–42.

22. Buell, *New England Literary Culture*, 108–9.

23. Munger, *Freedom of Faith*, 217–18.

24. Dorrien, *Making of American Liberal Theology*, 293–304; see Kuklick, *Churchmen and Philosophers*, 216–29, for Munger's theology and his role in the movement of Progressive Orthodoxy.

25. Munger, *Freedom of Faith*, 242, 326.

26. Gerrish, *Prince of the Church*, 53–54.

27. Parker, *Matters Pertaining to Religion*, 17, 20, 22–23, 28.

28. Clarke, *Ten Great Religions*, 162–65.

29. Munger, *Freedom of Faith*, 219–20, 223, 225.

30. Ibid., 237, 241–43, 248, 251–52.

31. Dickinson, *Letters of Emily Dickinson*, 2:454.

32. Vendler, *Dickinson*, 173, notes that the initial group of twelve lines was published separately in 1896 and was only rejoined to the final eight lines in Thomas Johnson's 1955 edition of the poems.

33. Dickinson, *Letters of Emily Dickinson*, 2:357.

34. Wolff, *Emily Dickinson*, 82–83.

35. Dickinson, *Letters of Emily Dickinson*, 1:143.

36. Stowe, *Three Novels*, 152, 456–57.
37. Steiner, *Grammars of Creation*, 7.
38. The following quotations from Dickinson and her sister-in-law, Susan Gilbert Dickinson, come from Franklin's edition, *Poems of Emily Dickinson*, 1:159–64. For an extended discussion of the features of the Amherst landscape that might have contributed to the poem's imagery, see Mitchell, *Emily Dickinson*, 258–99.
39. Vendler, *Dickinson*, 39.
40. A version published in the *Springfield Daily Republican* on March 1, 1862, had the second stanza "Light laughs the breeze"; the version Dickinson sent to T. W. Higginson had the second stanza "Grand go the Years."
41. Cameron, *Writing Nature*, 64.
42. See Gilpin, *Preface to Theology*, 42–80, for the relationship of theological language to the culture of Protestantism, 1830–80.
43. Parker, *Matters Pertaining to Religion*, 16, 24, 27.
44. Bushnell, *God in Christ*, 76–77, 79–80.

45. Munger, *Freedom of Faith*, 30–31.
46. Dickinson, *Letters of Emily Dickinson*, 2:346.
47. Park, "Theology of the Intellect," 535–39; Habegger, *My Wars Are Laid Away in Books*, 311.
48. Parker, *Matters Pertaining to Religion*, 111.
49. Phelps, *Three Spiritualist Novels*, 31–32.
50. Frothingham, *Spirit of the New Faith*, 67, 83.
51. Bellah, "Transcendence in Contemporary Piety," 897.
52. Lincoln, *Portable Abraham Lincoln*, 321.
53. Bellah, "Transcendence in Contemporary Piety," 898.
54. Harrison, *Gardens*, 7, 27–28.
55. Burke, "I, Eye, Ay—Emerson's Early Essay 'Nature,'" 151.
56. See Dalferth, "Idea of Transcendence," 158–59, for the distinction between boundary and limit in the language of transcendence.
57. Ferguson, *Alone in America*, 7.
58. Emerson, *Essays and Lectures*, 541–42.

WORKS CITED

Ackmann, Martha. "Biographical Studies of Dickinson." In *The Emily Dickinson Handbook*, ed. Gudrun Grabher, Roland Hagenbuchle, and Cristanne Miller, 11–23. Amherst: University of Massachusetts Press, 1998.

Ahlstrom, Sydney E. *A Religious History of the American People*. New Haven: Yale University Press, 1972.

Albanese, Catherine L. *Nature Religion in America: From the Algonkian Indians to the New Age*. Chicago: University of Chicago Press, 1990.

———. *A Republic of Mind and Spirit: A Cultural History of American Metaphysical Religion*. New Haven: Yale University Press, 2007.

Alter, Robert. *Pen of Iron: American Prose and the King James Bible*. Princeton: Princeton University Press, 2010.

Anderson, Amanda. *The Powers of Distance: Cosmopolitanism and the Cultivation of Detachment*. Princeton: Princeton University Press, 2001.

Bachelard, Gaston. *The Poetics of Space*. Translated by Maria Jolas. Boston: Beacon Press, 1994.

Bain, Robert, ed. *Whitman's and Dickinson's Contemporaries: An Anthology of Their Verse*. Carbondale: Southern Illinois University Press, 1996.

Baker, Carlos. *Emerson Among the Eccentrics: A Group Portrait*. New York: Viking, 1996.

Barbour, John D. *The Value of Solitude: The Ethics and Spirituality of Aloneness in Autobiography*. Charlottesville: University of Virginia Press, 2004.

Barnes, Albert. *Home Missions: A Sermon in Behalf of the American Home Missionary Society*. New York: American Home Missionary Society, 1849.

Barrett, Faith. *To Fight Aloud Is Very Brave: American Poetry and the Civil War*. Amherst: University of Massachusetts Press, 2012.

Barrett, Faith, and Cristanne Miller, eds. *"Words for the Hour": A New Anthology of American Civil War Poetry*. Amherst: University of Massachusetts Press, 2005.

Bartlett, Anna Warner, and Susan Warner. *Hymns of the Church Militant*. New York: R. Carter and Brothers, 1858.

Baym, Nina. "English Nature, New York Nature, and *Walden*'s New

England Nature." In *Transient and Permanent: The Transcendentalist Movement and Its Contexts*, ed. Charles Capper and Conrad Edick Wright, 148–89. Boston: Massachusetts Historical Society, 1999.

Beecher, Henry Ward. *Star Papers: Or, Experiences of Art and Nature*. New York: J. C. Derby, 1855.

Bellah, Robert N. "Transcendence in Contemporary Piety." In *The Religious Situation: 1969*, ed. Donald N. Cutler, 896–909. Boston: Beacon Press, 1969.

Bender, Thomas. "Strategies of Narrative Synthesis in American History." *American Historical Review* 107 (2002): 129–53.

Bennett, Paula. "'The Descent of the Angel': Interrogating Domestic Ideology in American Women's Poetry, 1858–1890." *American Literary History* 7 (1995): 591–610.

Bercovitch, Sacvan. *The Puritan Origins of the American Self*. New Haven: Yale University Press, 1975.

Bianchi, Martha Dickinson. *The Life and Letters of Emily Dickinson*. Boston: Houghton Mifflin, 1924.

Braude, Ann. *Radical Spirits: Spiritualism and Women's Rights in Nineteenth-Century America*. 2nd ed. Bloomington: Indiana University Press, 2001.

Brekus, Catherine A. *Sarah Osborn's World: The Rise of Evangelical Christianity in Early America*. New Haven: Yale University Press, 2013.

———. *Strangers and Pilgrims: Female Preaching in America, 1740–1845*. Chapel Hill: University of North Carolina Press, 1998.

Brodhead, Richard H. *Cultures of Letters: Scenes of Reading and Writing in Nineteenth-Century America*. Chicago: University of Chicago Press, 1993.

Brooks, Peter. *Enigmas of Identity*. Princeton: Princeton University Press, 2011.

Brown, Charles Brockden. *The Rhapsodist and Other Uncollected Writings*. Edited by Harry R. Warfel. New York: Scholars' Facsimiles and Reprints, 1943.

Brown, Gillian. *Domestic Individualism: Imagining Self in Nineteenth-Century America*. Berkeley: University of California Press, 1990.

Bryant, William Cullen. *Poems*. Philadelphia: Carey and Hart, 1848.

Buell, Lawrence. *New England Literary Culture: From Revolution Through Renaissance*. Cambridge: Cambridge University Press, 1986.

Bunyan, John. *The Pilgrim's Progress from This World to That Which Is to Come*. Edited by Roger Sharrock. 2nd ed. Oxford: Clarendon Press, 1960.

Burke, Kenneth. "I, Eye, Ay—Emerson's Early Essay 'Nature': Thoughts on the Machinery of Transcendence." In *Emerson's Nature: Origin, Growth, Meaning*, ed. Merton M. Sealts and Alfred R. Ferguson, 150–63. 2nd ed.

Carbondale: Southern Illinois University Press, 1979.

Bushnell, Horace. *Barbarism the First Danger*. New York: American Home Missionary Society, 1847.

———. *A Discourse of the Moral Tendencies and Results of Human History*. New York: M. Y. Beach, 1843.

———. *God in Christ*. Hartford, Conn.: Brown and Parsons, 1849.

———. *Views of Christian Nurture, and of Subjects Adjacent Thereto*. Hartford, Conn.: Edwin Hunt, 1847.

Butler, Jon. *Awash in a Sea of Faith: Christianizing the American People*. Cambridge: Harvard University Press, 1990.

Cameron, Sharon. *Writing Nature: Henry Thoreau's Journal*. New York: Oxford University Press, 1985.

Carroll, Bret E. *Spiritualism in Antebellum America*. Bloomington: Indiana University Press, 1997.

Certeau, Michel de. *The Mystic Fable*. Translated by Michael B. Smith. Chicago: University of Chicago Press, 1992.

———. *The Practice of Everyday Life*. Translated by Steven Randall. Berkeley: University of California Press, 1984.

Channing, William Ellery. *The Works of William E. Channing*. Boston: American Unitarian Association, 1891.

Cherry, Conrad. *Nature and Religious Imagination: From Edwards to Bushnell*. Philadelphia: Fortress Press, 1980.

Chidester, David, and Edward T. Linenthal, eds. *American Sacred Space*. Bloomington: Indiana University Press, 1995.

Child, Lydia Maria. *The Progress of Religious Ideas, Through Successive Ages*. 3 vols. New York: Charles S. Francis, 1869.

Clarke, James Freeman. *Ten Great Religions, Part II: A Comparison of All Religions*. Boston: Houghton, Mifflin, 1883.

Colton, Aaron Merrick. *The Old Meeting House and Vacation Papers*. New York: Worthington, 1890.

Corrigan, John. *Business of the Heart: Religion and Emotion in Nineteenth-Century America*. Berkeley: University of California Press, 2002.

Dalferth, Ingolf U. "The Idea of Transcendence." In *The Axial Age and Its Consequences*, ed. Robert N. Bellah and Hans Joas, 146–88. Cambridge: Belknap Press of Harvard University Press, 2012.

Davidson, Cathy N. *Revolution and the Word: The Rise of the Novel in America*. New York: Oxford University Press, 1986.

Decker, William Merrill. *Epistolary Practices: Letter Writing in America Before Telecommunications*. Chapel Hill: University of North Carolina Press, 1998.

Dewey, John. *Art as Experience*. New York: Minton, Balch, 1934.

Dickinson, Emily. *The Letters of Emily Dickinson*. Edited by Thomas H. Johnson, with Theodora Ward. 3 vols. Cambridge: Belknap Press of Harvard University Press, 1958.

———. *Poems: Including Variant Readings Critically Compared with All Known Manuscripts*. Edited by Thomas H. Johnson. 3 vols. Cambridge: Belknap Press of Harvard University Press, 1955.

———. *The Poems of Emily Dickinson: Variorum Edition*. Edited by R. W. Franklin. 3 vols. Cambridge: Belknap Press of Harvard University Press, 1998.

Donnelly, Daria. "The Power to Die: Emily Dickinson's Letters of Consolation." In *Epistolary Selves: Letters and Letter-Writers, 1600–1945*, ed. Rebecca Earle, 134–51. Aldershot, UK: Ashgate, 1999.

Donoghue, Denis. *Emily Dickinson*. Minneapolis: University of Minnesota Press, 1969.

Dorrien, Gary. *The Making of American Liberal Theology: Imagining Progressive Religion, 1805–1900*. Louisville: Westminster John Knox Press, 2001.

Douglass, Frederick. *Autobiographies*. New York: Literary Classics of the United States, 1994.

Edwards, Jonathan. *The Works of Jonathan Edwards*, vol. 8, *Ethical Writings*. Edited by Paul Ramsey. New Haven: Yale University Press, 1989.

———. *The Works of Jonathan Edwards*, vol. 11, *Typological Writings*. Edited by Wallace E. Anderson, Mason I. Lowance, and David Watters. New Haven: Yale University Press, 1993.

———. *The Works of Jonathan Edwards*, vol. 16, *Letters and Personal Writings*. Edited by George S. Claghorn. New Haven: Yale University Press, 1998.

Elliott, Emory. *Revolutionary Writers: Literature and Authority in the New Republic, 1725–1810*. New York: Oxford University Press, 1982.

Emerson, Ralph Waldo. *Collected Poems and Translations*. New York: Literary Classics of the United States, 1994.

———. *The Early Lectures of Ralph Waldo Emerson*. Vol. 3. Edited by Robert E. Spiller and Wallace E. Williams. Cambridge: Harvard University Press, 1972.

———. *Essays and Lectures*. New York: Literary Classics of the United States, 1983.

———. *The Heart of Emerson's Journals*. Edited by Bliss Perry. Boston: Houghton Mifflin, 1926.

———. *The Journals and Miscellaneous Notebooks of Ralph Waldo Emerson*. Edited by William H. Gilman et al. 16 vols. Cambridge: Harvard University Press, 1960–82.

———. *The Letters of Ralph Waldo Emerson*. Vol. 2. Edited by Ralph L. Rusk. New York: Columbia University Press, 1939.

Erkkila, Betsy. "Emily Dickinson and Class." *American Literary History* 4 (1992): 1–27.

Farr, Judith. *The Passion of Emily Dickinson*. Cambridge: Harvard University Press, 1992.

Farr, Judith, with Louise Carter. *The Gardens of Emily*

Dickinson. Cambridge: Harvard University Press, 2004.

Faust, Drew Gilpin, ed. *The Ideology of Slavery: Proslavery Thought in the Antebellum South, 1830–1860.* Baton Rouge: Louisiana State University Press, 1981.

———. *This Republic of Suffering: Death and the American Civil War.* New York: Knopf, 2008.

Ferguson, Robert A. *Alone in America: The Stories That Matter.* Cambridge: Harvard University Press, 2013.

Frothingham, Octavius Brooks. *The Spirit of the New Faith: A Series of Sermons.* New York: Putnam, 1877.

Fuller, Margaret. *Summer on the Lakes, in 1843.* Edited by Susan Belasco Smith. Urbana: University of Illinois Press, 1991.

Fuss, Diana. *Dying Modern: A Meditation on Elegy.* Durham: Duke University Press, 2013.

Gatta, John. *Making Nature Sacred: Literature, Religion, and Environment in America from the Puritans to the Present.* New York: Oxford University Press, 2004.

Geertz, Clifford. *The Interpretation of Cultures: Selected Essays.* New York: Basic Books, 1973.

Gerrish, Brian A. *A Prince of the Church: Schleiermacher and the Beginnings of Modern Theology.* Philadelphia: Fortress Press, 1984.

Gilbert, Sandra M. "The Wayward Nun Beneath the Hill: Emily Dickinson and the Mysteries of Womanhood." In *Emily Dickinson: A Collection of Critical Essays,* ed. Judith Farr, 20–39. Upper Saddle River, N.J.: Prentice Hall, 1996.

Gilpin, W. Clark. *A Preface to Theology.* Chicago: University of Chicago Press, 1996.

Ginzburg, Carlo. *Wooden Eyes: Nine Reflections on Distance.* Translated by Martin Ryle and Kate Soper. New York: Columbia University Press, 2001.

Godey's Lady's Book and Magazine, January–June 1860. Philadelphia: Louis A. Godey, 1860.

Greenblatt, Stephen. *Renaissance Self-Fashioning: From More to Shakespeare.* Chicago: University of Chicago Press, 1980.

Gregerson, Linda, and Susan Juster, eds. *Empires of God: Religious Encounters in the Early Modern Atlantic.* Philadelphia: University of Pennsylvania Press, 2011.

Gross, Robert A. "The Celestial Village: Transcendentalism and Tourism in Concord." In *Transient and Permanent: The Transcendentalist Movement and Its Contexts,* ed. Charles Capper and Conrad Edick Wright, 251–81. Boston: Massachusetts Historical Society, 1999.

Habegger, Alfred. *My Wars Are Laid Away in Books: The Life of Emily Dickinson.* New York: Random House, 2001.

Hadot, Pierre. *Philosophy as a Way of Life: Spiritual Exercises from Socrates to Foucault.* Edited by Arnold I. Davidson.

Translated by Michael Chase. Oxford: Blackwell, 1995.

Halleck, Fitz-Greene. *The Poetical Works of Fitz-Greene Halleck*. New York: Appleton, 1847.

Halttunen, Karen. *Confidence Men and Painted Women: A Study of Middle-Class Culture in America, 1830–1870*. New Haven: Yale University Press, 1982.

Hambrick-Stowe, Charles E., ed. *Early New England Meditative Poetry: Anne Bradstreet and Edward Taylor*. New York: Paulist Press, 1988.

———. *The Practice of Piety: Puritan Devotional Disciplines in Seventeenth-Century New England*. Chapel Hill: University of North Carolina Press, 1982.

Handy, Robert T. *A Christian America: Protestant Hopes and Historical Realities*. New York: Oxford University Press, 1971.

Harrison, Robert Pogue. *The Dominion of the Dead*. Chicago: University of Chicago Press, 2003.

———. *Gardens: An Essay on the Human Condition*. Chicago: University of Chicago Press, 2008.

Hawthorne, Nathaniel. *Novels*. New York: Literary Classics of the United States, 1983.

Hecker, Isaac T. *Questions of the Soul*. 5th ed. New York: Appleton, 1864.

Hedrick, Joan D. *Harriet Beecher Stowe: A Life*. New York: Oxford University Press, 1994.

Heimert, Alan. *Religion and the American Mind: From the Great Awakening to the Revolution*. Cambridge: Harvard University Press, 1966.

Higginson, Thomas Wentworth. *The Magnificent Activist: The Writings of Thomas Wentworth Higginson (1823–1911)*. Edited by Howard N. Meyer. Cambridge, Mass.: Da Capo Press, 2000.

Hitchcock, Edward. *The Inseparable Trio*. Boston: Dutton and Wentworth, 1850.

———. *The Religion of Geology and Its Connected Sciences*. Boston: Phillips, Sampson, 1852.

———. *Religious Lectures on Peculiar Phenomena in the Four Seasons*. Amherst: J. S. and C. Adams, 1850.

Hobsbawm, E. J. *The Age of Revolution, 1789–1848*. Cleveland: World Publishing, 1962.

Hollander, John, ed. *American Poetry: The Nineteenth Century*. 2 vols. New York: Literary Classics of the United States, 1993.

Howe, Daniel Walker. *Making the American Self: Jonathan Edwards to Abraham Lincoln*. Cambridge: Harvard University Press, 1997.

———. *The Political Culture of the American Whigs*. Chicago: University of Chicago Press, 1979.

Hutchison, William R. *Religious Pluralism in America: The Contentious History of a Founding Ideal*. New Haven: Yale University Press, 2003.

Jackson, Virginia. *Dickinson's Misery: A Theory of Lyric Reading*. Princeton: Princeton University Press, 2005.

James, William. *The Varieties of Religious Experience: A Study in Human Nature*. New York: Longmans, Green, 1902.

Kelley, Mary. *Private Woman, Public Stage: Literary Domesticity in Nineteenth-Century America*. New York: Oxford University Press, 1984.

Kuklick, Bruce. *Churchmen and Philosophers: From Jonathan Edwards to John Dewey*. New Haven: Yale University Press, 1985.

Laderman, Gary. *The Sacred Remains: American Attitudes Toward Death, 1799–1883*. New Haven: Yale University Press, 1996.

Lakoff, George, and Mark Johnson. *Metaphors We Live By*. Chicago: University of Chicago Press, 1980.

Lane, Belden C. *Landscapes of the Sacred: Geography and Narrative in American Spirituality*. Exp. ed. Baltimore: Johns Hopkins University Press, 2001.

Lane, Christopher. *The Age of Doubt: Tracing the Roots of Our Religious Uncertainty*. New Haven: Yale University Press, 2011.

Laporte, Charles, and Jason R. Rudy. "Editorial Introduction: Spasmodic Poetry and Poetics." *Victorian Poetry* 42 (2004): 421–27.

Lewis, R. W. B. *The American Adam: Innocence, Tragedy, and Tradition in the Nineteenth Century*. Chicago: University of Chicago Press, 1955.

Lincoln, Abraham. *The Portable Abraham Lincoln*. Edited by Andrew Delbanco. New York: Viking, 1992.

Livingston, William. *Philosophic Solitude: Or the Choice of a Rural Life; A Poem*. Trenton: Isaac Collins, 1782.

Long, Kathryn T. "Consecrated Respectability: Phoebe Palmer and the Refinement of American Methodism." In *Methodism and the Shaping of American Culture*, ed. Nathan O. Hatch and John H. Wigger, 281–307. Nashville: Kingswood, 2001.

Longfellow, Henry Wadsworth. *Kavanagh: A Tale*. 1849. Boston: Ticknor, Reed, and Fields, 1851.

Looby, Christopher. "The Constitution of Nature: Taxonomy as Politics in Jefferson, Peale, and Bartram." *Early American Literature* 22 (1987): 252–73.

Lundin, Roger. *Emily Dickinson and the Art of Belief*. 2nd ed. Grand Rapids: Eerdmans, 2004.

Margolis, Stacey. *The Public Life of Privacy in Nineteenth-Century American Literature*. Durham: Duke University Press, 2005.

Marini, Stephen A. "Hymnody and History: Early American Evangelical Hymns as Sacred Music." In *Music in American Religious Experience*, ed. Philip V. Bohlman, Edith L. Blumhofer, and Maria M. Chow, 123–54. New York: Oxford University Press, 2006.

Marty, Martin E. *Righteous Empire: The Protestant Experience in America*. New York: Harper, 1970.

Masur, Louis P. "'Age of the First Person Singular': The Vocabulary of the Self in New England, 1780–1850."

Journal of American Studies 25 (1991): 189–211.

McDannell, Colleen. *The Christian Home in Victorian America, 1840–1900*. Bloomington: Indiana University Press, 1986.

McKelvy, William R. *The English Cult of Literature: Devoted Readers, 1774–1880*. Charlottesville: University of Virginia Press, 2007.

McLoughlin, William G., ed. *The American Evangelicals, 1800–1900*. New York: Harper, 1968.

Mead, Sidney E. *The Lively Experiment: The Shaping of Christianity in America*. New York: Harper and Row, 1963.

Merish, Lori. "Sentimental Consumption: Harriet Beecher Stowe and the Aesthetics of Middle-Class Ownership." *American Literary History* 8 (1996): 1–33.

Messmer, Marietta. *A Vice for Voices: Reading Emily Dickinson's Correspondence*. Amherst: University of Massachusetts Press, 2001.

Miller, Cristanne. *Reading in Time: Emily Dickinson in the Nineteenth Century*. Amherst: University of Massachusetts Press, 2012.

Miller, Perry. *Errand into the Wilderness*. Cambridge: Harvard University Press, 1956.

Mitchell, Domhnall. *Emily Dickinson: Monarch of Perception*. Amherst: University of Amherst Press, 2000.

Mitchell, Donald Grant. *Reveries of a Bachelor: Or, A Book of the Heart*. New York: Baker and Scribner, 1851.

Montaigne, Michel de. *The Complete Essays of Montaigne*. Translated by Donald M. Frame. Stanford: Stanford University Press, 1965.

Moore, James R. "Geologists and Interpreters of Genesis in the Nineteenth Century." In *God and Nature: Historical Essays on the Encounter Between Christianity and Science*, ed. David C. Lindberg and Ronald L. Numbers, 322–50. Berkeley: University of California Press, 1986.

Munger, Theodore T. *The Freedom of Faith*. Boston: Houghton, Mifflin, 1883.

Nettleton, Asahel. *Village Hymns for Social Worship*. Hartford, Conn.: Goodwin, 1824.

Niebuhr, H. Richard. "The Idea of Covenant and American Democracy." *Church History* 23 (1954): 126–35.

Noll, Mark A. *America's God: From Jonathan Edwards to Abraham Lincoln*. New York: Oxford University Press, 2002.

———. *The Civil War as a Theological Crisis*. Chapel Hill: University of North Carolina Press, 2006.

Nylander, Jane C. *Our Own Snug Fireside: Images of the New England Home, 1760–1860*. New Haven: Yale University Press, 1994.

Owen, Alex. *The Darkened Room: Women, Power, and Spiritualism in Late Victorian England*. Chicago: University of Chicago Press, 1989.

Park, Edwards A. "The Theology of the Intellect and That of the Feelings." *Bibliotheca Sacra* and *Theological Review* 7 (1850): 533–69.

Parker, Theodore. *A Discourse of Matters Pertaining to Religion*. 3rd ed. Boston: Charles C. Little and James Brown, 1847.

Petrino, Elizabeth A. *Emily Dickinson and Her Contemporaries: Women's Verse in America, 1820–1885*. Hanover: University Press of New England, 1998.

Phelps, Elizabeth Stuart. *Three Spiritualist Novels*. Edited by Nina Baym. Urbana: University of Illinois Press, 2000.

Placher, William C. *The Domestication of Transcendence: How Modern Thinking About God Went Wrong*. Louisville: Westminster John Knox Press, 1996.

Prothero, Stephen. *Purified by Fire: A History of Cremation in America*. Berkeley: University of California Press, 2001.

Reynolds, David S. *Mightier Than the Sword: Uncle Tom's Cabin and the Battle for America*. New York: W. W. Norton, 2011.

Rose, Anne C. "Religious Individualism in Nineteenth-Century American Families." In *Perspectives on American Religion and Culture*, ed. Peter W. Williams, 319–30. Oxford: Blackwell, 1999.

Rudwick, Martin J. S. "The Shape and Meaning of Earth History." In *God and Nature: Historical Essays on the Encounter Between Christianity and Science*, ed. David C. Lindberg and Ronald L. Numbers, 296–321. Berkeley:

University of California Press, 1986.

Schmidt, Leigh Eric. *Restless Souls: The Making of American Spirituality from Emerson to Oprah*. San Francisco: HarperSanFrancisco, 2005.

Schwartz, Barry. *George Washington: The Making of an American Symbol*. New York: Free Press, 1987.

Sears, John F. *Sacred Places: American Tourist Attractions in the Nineteenth Century*. Amherst: University of Massachusetts Press, 1989.

Sellers, Charles. *The Market Revolution: Jacksonian America, 1815–1846*. New York: Oxford University Press, 1991.

Sewall, Richard B. *The Life of Emily Dickinson*. Cambridge: Harvard University Press, 1994.

Shamir, Milette. *Inexpressible Privacy: The Interior Life of Antebellum American Literature*. Philadelphia: University of Pennsylvania Press, 2006.

Sibbes, Richard. *The Complete Works of Richard Sibbes*. Edited by Alexander Balloch Grosart. 6 vols. Edinburgh: James Nichol, 1862–67.

Slauter, Eric. "Being Alone in the Age of the Social Contract." *William and Mary Quarterly*, 3rd ser., 42 (2005): 31–66.

Smith, John E. "The Concept of Conversion." *Mid-Stream* 8 (1969): 12–23.

St. Armand, Barton Levi. *Emily Dickinson and Her Culture: The Soul's Society*. Cambridge: Cambridge University Press, 1984.

Steiner, George. *Grammars of Creation*. New Haven: Yale University Press, 2001.

Stevenson, Louise L. *Scholarly Means to Evangelical Ends: The New Haven Scholars and the Transformation of Higher Learning in America, 1830–1890*. Baltimore: Johns Hopkins University Press, 1986.

Stout, Harry S. *Upon the Altar of the Nation: A Moral History of the Civil War*. New York: Viking, 2006.

Stout, Harry S., and Catherine Brekus. "A New England Congregation: Center Church, New Haven, 1638–1989." In *American Congregations*, ed. James P. Wind and James S. Lewis, 2 vols., 1:14–102. Chicago: University of Chicago Press, 1994.

Stowe, Harriet Beecher. *Three Novels: Uncle Tom's Cabin, The Minister's Wooing, Oldtown Folks*. New York: Literary Classics of the United States, 1982.

Taylor, Jeremy. *The Rule and Exercises of Holy Living*. London: W. Pickering, 1852.

Thoreau, Henry David. *A Week on the Concord and Merrimack Rivers, Walden; or, Life in the Woods, The Maine Woods, Cape Cod*. New York: Literary Classics of the United States, 1985.

Turner, J. S. "Solitude." *Godey's Lady's Book and Magazine*, July–December 1860, 122.

Vendler, Helen. *Dickinson: Selected Poems and Commentaries*. Cambridge: Harvard University Press, 2010.

———. *Poets Thinking: Pope, Whitman, Dickinson, Yeats*. Cambridge: Harvard University Press, 2004.

Walker, Williston, ed. *The Creeds and Platforms of Congregationalism*. 1893. Reprint, Philadelphia: Pilgrim Press, 1960.

Ward, Patricia A. "Madame Guyon and Experiential Theology in America." *Church History* 67 (1998): 484–98.

Weisbuch, Robert. *Emily Dickinson's Poetry*. Chicago: University of Chicago Press, 1975.

Welter, Barbara. "The Feminization of American Religion: 1800–1860." In *Religion in American History: A Reader*, ed. Jon Butler and Harry S. Stout, 158–78. New York: Oxford University Press, 1998.

Wheatley, Richard. *The Life and Letters of Mrs. Phoebe Palmer*. New York: W. C. Palmer, 1876.

Wills, Garry. *Lincoln at Gettysburg: The Words That Remade America*. New York: Simon and Schuster, 1992.

Wolff, Cynthia Griffin. *Emily Dickinson*. New York: Knopf, 1986.

Wolosky, Shira. *Emily Dickinson: A Voice of War*. New Haven: Yale University Press, 1984.

INDEX

sermons. *See* preaching
Sewall, Richard, 32, 43
Shakespeare, William, 64, 72
Sigourney, Lydia Huntley, 66–68,
123–24
Slauter, Eric, 45
Smith, Alexander, 90
solitude as a religious practice, 6, 8–9,
32–34, 122
in domestic spaces, 26, 43–48,
65–66
in nature, 8–9, 35, 38–40, 43–48,
54–60
as practiced by Dickinson, 9, 17, 26,
31–32, 34, 58–65, 80–86, 96–98
and the writer's vocation, 8–9, 17,
48–54, 96–102
See also Edwards, Jonathan, Emer-
son, Ralph Waldo, nature
Spasmodic School of poetry, 90
spiritualism, 112, 125–28
Springfield Daily Republican, 64, 103
St. Armand, Barton Levi, 3, 110, 123,
174
Stearns, Frazar, 129, 131
Stout, Harry S., 128–29
Stowe, Harriet Beecher, 68–69, 78, 79,
94, 125, 156–57

Taylor, Edward, 66, 68
theological language, 9, 17
during Civil War, 128–30

Dickinson's adaptation of, 8, 105–8,
110–11, 173–76
of transcendence, 160, 164–66,
173–74
See also heaven, immortality,
transience
theological seminaries and divinity
schools, 11, 20, 106, 130, 163
Thoreau, Henry David, 8–9, 33, 50–51,
63, 74, 114, 119
Todd, Mabel Loomis, 31
transience, 9, 99, 139–42, 145, 153–54.
See also theological language
Turner, J. A., 47–48

Upham, Thomas C., 76

Vendler, Helen, 3, 22, 96, 135, 139, 158

Ward, Theodora, 13
Warner, Susan, 3, 79, 92
Whig political culture, 4–5
Whitman, Walt, 2, 13
Wolff, Cynthia Griffin, 138–39, 155–56
writing and authorship, 4, 89–90
Dickinson's views on, 89–93,
95–102
as spiritual discipline, 25–28,
36–43, 132–33
of women, 3, 79
See also Emerson, Ralph Waldo, and
Higginson, Thomas Wentworth

INDEX OF POEMS

RELIGION AROUND